Conversations with Christopher Isherwood

Literary Conversations Series

Peggy Whitman Prenshaw
General Editor

Photo credit: © 2001 Nancy Crampton

Conversations
with Christopher Isherwood

Edited by
James J. Berg and Chris Freeman

University Press of Mississippi
Jackson

www.upress.state.ms.us

Copyright © 2001 by University Press of Mississippi
Manufactured in the United States of America

09   08   07   06   05   04   03   02   01   4   3   2   1
∞

Library of Congress Cataloging-in-Publication Data

Conversations with Christopher Isherwood / edited by James J. Berg and Chris Freeman.
     p.   cm. — (Literary conversations series)
   Includes index.
   ISBN 1-57806-407-4 (alk. paper) — ISBN 1-57806-408-2 (pbk. : alk. paper)
   1. Isherwood, Christopher, 1904–   —Interviews.   2. Authors, English—20th
century—Interviews.   I. Berg, James J.   II. Freeman, Chris, 1965–   .   III. Series.
PR6017.S5 Z627   2001
823'.912 dc–21
[B]   2001026735

British Library Cataloging-in-Publication Data available

Works by Christopher Isherwood

All the Conspirators. London: Cape, 1928. Norfolk, Connecticut: New Directions, 1958, 1979.

Intimate Journals. Charles Baudelaire. Translated by Isherwood. Introduction by T. S. Eliot. London: Blackamore Press; New York: Random House, 1930. Boston: Beacon Press, 1957.

The Memorial: Portrait of a Family. London: Hogarth Press, 1932. Norfolk, Connecticut: New Directions, 1946.

Mr Norris Changes Trains. London: Hogarth Press, 1935. (*The Last of Mr. Norris*. New York: Morrow, 1935.)

Sally Bowles. London: Hogarth Press, 1937.

Lions and Shadows: An Education in the Twenties. London: Hogarth Press, 1938. Norfolk, Connecticut: New Directions, 1947.

Plays and Other Dramatic Writings 1928–1938. With W. H. Auden. Edward Mendelson, editor. Princeton: Princeton University Press, 1988. Includes *The Dog beneath the Skin*, *The Ascent of F6*, and *On the Frontier*.

Journey to a War. With W. H. Auden. London: Faber and Faber, and New York: Random House, 1939.

Goodbye to Berlin. London: Hogarth Press, and New York: Random House, 1939.

Bhagavad Gita. With Swami Prabhavananda, trans. Hollywood: Marcel Rodd, 1944. New York: Harper, 1951.

Vedanta for the Western World. Editor. Hollywood: Marcel Rodd, 1945.

The Berlin Stories. New York: New Directions, 1945, 1954.

Prater Violet. New York: Random House, 1945. London: Methuen, 1946.

The Condor and the Cows: A South American Travel Diary. New York: Random House, 1949.

Vedanta for Modern Man. Editor. New York: Harper, 1951.

How to Know God: The Yoga Aphorisms of Patanjali. With Swami Prabhavananda, translator. New York: Harper, 1953. Hollywood: Vedanta Press, 1981.

The World in the Evening. New York: Random House, 1954.

Great English Short Stories. Editor. New York: Dell, 1957.

Down There on a Visit. New York: Simon and Schuster, 1962.

An Approach to Vedanta. Hollywood: Vedanta Press, 1963.

A Single Man. New York: Simon and Schuster, 1964.

Ramakrishna and His Disciples. New York: Simon and Schuster, 1965. Second edition, Hollywood: Vedanta Press, 1980.

Exhumations: Stories, Articles, Verses. New York: Simon and Schuster, 1966.

A Meeting by the River. New York: Simon and Schuster, 1967.

Kathleen and Frank. New York: Simon and Schuster, 1971, 1972.

Frankenstein: The True Story. With Don Bachardy. New York: Avon, 1973.

Christopher and His Kind, 1929–1939. New York: Farrar, Straus & Giroux, 1976. London: Methuen, 1977.

My Guru and His Disciple. New York: Farrar, Straus & Giroux, 1980.

People One Ought to Know. London: Macmillan, and New York: Doubleday, 1982.

October. Drawings by Don Bachardy. London: Methuen, 1983.

The Wishing Tree: Christopher Isherwood on Mystical Religion. Robert Adjemian, ed. San Francisco: Harper & Row, 1987.

Where Joy Resides: A Christopher Isherwood Reader. Don Bachardy and James P. White, eds. New York: Farrar, Straus & Giroux, 1989.

The Mortmere Stories. With Edward Upward. London: Enitharmon Press, 1994.

Diaries: Volume One, 1939–1960. Katherine Bucknell, ed. London: Methuen, 1996. New York: HarperCollins, 1997.

Jacob's Hands. With Aldous Huxley. London: Bloomsbury, and New York: St. Martin's Press, 1998.

Lost Years: A Memoir, 1945–1951. Katherine Bucknell, ed. London: Chatto and Windus, and New York: HarperCollins, 2000.

Contents

Introduction

"To Christopher, Berlin meant boys," Isherwood reveals, slightly tongue-in-cheek, in his autobiography *Christopher and His Kind* (1976). To readers, most often, Christopher Isherwood means Berlin, though of course Isherwood was much more than that. Throughout his career, he was a keen observer, always seemingly in the right place at the right time, and he published works in seven decades of the twentieth century. In Berlin in the 1930s and again in Los Angeles in the 1960s and '70s, Isherwood reflected on his life and his world—using his memory and his voluminous diaries—and wrote perceptive commentary on contemporary European and American history and culture. In *Christopher and His Kind,* Isherwood candidly re-told the period of his life covered in his early memoir, *Lions and Shadows* (1938), and in *The Berlin Stories* (1945) from the perspective of the 1970s, attempting to write the better truth allowed by a freer society and more open publishing industry. As he told Winston Leyland in a 1973 interview for *Gay Sunshine,* "Christopher is the narrator, so he mustn't stand out too prominently. To have made him homosexual, in those days, would have been to feature him as someone eccentric. I would have made a star out of a supporting actor."

In interviews, Isherwood is the star, and he is free to be as eccentric, as outspoken, and as forthcoming as he wants to be. In the conversations collected here, his candor and outspokenness vary depending on who is interviewing him and in what context. Regarding Isherwood's responses to particular questions or topics, much depends on the interviewer. The friendly exchange with Tony Russo, for the magazine *Christopher Street* in the 1970s, illustrates Isherwood's increased availability to and ease with the gay press during this period of his life.

Isherwood's comment to Mark Thompson, a former editor of the *Advocate,* in a 1984 joint interview with Don Bachardy (not reprinted here) sheds light on the quality and depth of all of the interviews included in this volume, and on his attitude toward talking about deeply personal matters: "I do think one has to be reticent. . . . You probably realize that we've been completely frank with you because we were being asked serious questions."[1]

A majority of these interviews are from the 1970s, a period of increased recognition for Isherwood. Several factors contributed to his fame in the 1970s, including the emergence of the gay liberation movement, Isherwood's own coming out in *Kathleen and Frank* (1971), his subsequent retelling of the Berlin years in *Christopher and His Kind,* and the success of the movie musical *Cabaret* (1972). Naturally, many interviews in this collection are occasioned by the publication of particular books, so the material covered will sometimes overlap.

The interviews are presented here in the order in which they were conducted, between 1946 and 1985. They originally appeared in a variety of publications, including newspapers, such as the *Los Angeles Times,* gay publications such as the *Advocate,* and academic journals such as *Twentieth Century Literature* and the *Journal of Narrative Technique.* In addition, two interviews have not been published previously: Len Webster's 1971 interview and Studs Terkel's 1977 radio conversation. The interviews address a wide range of issues, and several common themes run through them, including the importance of diary-keeping to Isherwood's life and work; the interplay between fiction and autobiography; the role of religion, particularly Vedanta; Isherwood's circle of friends, including W. H. Auden, Aldous Huxley, and E. M. Forster; and several important places in Isherwood's life: Berlin, England, and California.

The best of these interviews are substantive, smart, and insightful, allowing Isherwood to discuss his approach to writing both fiction and nonfiction. As he tells Stanley Poss, "More and more, writing is appearing to me as a kind of self-analysis, a finding-out something about myself and about the past, and about what life is like, as far as I'm concerned: who I am; who these people are; what it's all about." This emphasis on self-discovery comes as no surprise from a writer who mined his own diaries and experiences for inspiration. "I do try to convey . . . the inwardness of experience," Isherwood explains to George Wickes; "that's what the books are really about, and the experience of meeting certain kinds of people, the experience of the encounter, that's very important to me."

On the other hand, Isherwood's work in Hollywood—using a visual medium to tell stories—emphasized the outward experience. Isherwood points out to Charles Higham in "Isherwood on Hollywood," "you must remember that all my novels, or almost all, have been written post-screenwriting, as it were." The effect of Isherwood's writing for the screen on his narrative technique and style is a heightened understanding of surfaces and gestures. Screenwriting, Isherwood explained, is "very good in the first place for most writers to be forced to visualize: you have to learn to stop relying on the word and thinking in terms of possible silent sequences or sequences where the dialogue plays against the image." Yet Isherwood accepted the secondary position of the writer in filmmaking: "The person who matters in a film . . . is the director. . . . In the last resort, it should be the director who decides what he's going to use and what he's not going to use." Isherwood's position in Hollywood was similar to his position in the Berlin stories—that of a participant but not the main focus of the action.

When he turns to writing his own family history, in *Kathleen and Frank* and his later memoirs, Isherwood takes on the roles of director and editor himself. For example, Isherwood uses film terminology to explain the technique of *Kathleen and Frank* to Robert Wennerstein in a 1971 interview (not printed here): "It flashes back and it flashes forward. So that, for example, already on page two you know that Frank is going to be killed in the War, long before they've even met. . . . So you get a double movement in this book."[2] Writing *Kathleen and Frank* allowed Isherwood to reexamine his personal history as a British expatriate. Rita Delfiner refers to the book as Isherwood's "reconciliation with his family," which corresponds to "his joy that England 'is the place that I used to want it to be.' It was 'frumpy,' but now on his frequent visits there, he sees it as 'quite the most ebullient country, I love that.'"[3]

One of the things that most alienated Isherwood from his homeland was his early rejection of Christianity and of organized religion in general. His turn to Vedanta, an ancient branch of Hindu philosophy, was one of Isherwood's most American acts. Traveling to California to consult with Gerald Heard and to meet Huxley, Isherwood was introduced to Swami Prabhavananda in 1939. As he told Webster in 1971, the meeting led to lifelong devotion to Vedanta and to his collaboration on translations of the Bhagavad Gita and other Hindu texts. Isherwood's status as a Californian is closely connected to his devotion to Swami Prabhavananda: "This business of meeting Prabhavananda had a lot to do with sort of rooting me here. . . . It seemed to me a very important reason for staying—well it still seems an important reason for staying."

Isherwood's ties to California grow throughout the 1950s and '60s as shown by his use of southern California as a setting in *The World in the Evening* (1954), *Down There on a Visit* (1962), and *A Single Man* (1964). Isherwood the writer becomes less British and more American, to the extent that Anne Taylor Fleming treats him as a Los Angeles writer in her 1972 profile. "I'll be seventy next year," he tells her. "I have spent half my life in the United States. Los Angeles is a great place for feeling at home because everybody's from someplace else." In fact, Isherwood can be credited for helping to make Los Angeles an acceptable setting for serious fiction, paving the way for John Rechy, Joan Didion, Paul Monette, and Bernard Cooper, among others. As he tells Jeffrey Bailey in 1974, "As far as I was concerned [Los Angeles] has always been the place where everything was happening. This has been the scene of my life, of everything that's meant the most to me."[4]

By the late 1960s scholars began to take Isherwood's work seriously. Carolyn Heilbrun's 1970 monograph was the first book-length study published on Isherwood. Her 1976 interview was the centerpiece of a special issue of *Twentieth Century Literature* she edited. Heilbrun is one of Isherwood's most perceptive and empathetic critics. Their conversation ranges from very frank discussions of sexuality ("I don't see, theoretically, why there shouldn't be the most powerful sort of love, like St. Francis's, applied to one-night stands, where you really love a different person each night") to his own interest in her response to *Christopher and His Kind*: "What I should be very curious to know is if you feel that this book, although nonfiction and although autobiographical, is a kind of novel. There are themes that run through it. And there's a sort of payoff. . . . It is a description of the inner drives and external forces which took me away from England. And I wonder to what extent all this will seem to form an artistic whole." With David Geherin, Isherwood defines himself as a "serious comic writer" and declares that he is "much, much more concerned with character than plot. Because a little plot goes a long way." Carola M. Kaplan was writing what was probably the first dissertation on Isherwood when she interviewed him in 1973. Their wide-ranging discussion covers several aspects of Isherwood's work, particularly *A Meeting by the River* (1967), its stage adaptation, and the influence of Vedanta on his writing and his life.

Isherwood's literary "canonization" occurred at the convention of the Modern Language Association in New York in 1975, where he gave a talk called "Homosexuality and Literature." Tony Russo met Isherwood at that event and reminds him of it on the occasion of their interview, conducted two years later. Russo mistakenly assumes that this was Isherwood's first public statement of his homosexuality, but Isherwood sets the record straight: the MLA was not "the first place where I had spoken in that way. It was more that the MLA 'came out.' What I mean by that is—and I'm not saying this arrogantly—it was a question of their introducing this subject and facing it for the first time ever, and they just brought me in as one of the people to make it happen. So, really, the big deal was not that I announced it, but that they sat still for it." The significance of this exchange points to Isherwood's centrality in the emerging field of gay and lesbian studies and to his prominence as a figure in gay liberation.

The publication of *Christopher and His Kind* brought Isherwood more attention as an out gay man, and he made himself available to the gay press as an example: "If a writer doesn't want to admit his homosexuality publicly, that's his affair," he told Winston Leyland in the journal *Gay Sunshine*. "But to refuse specifically to do so in the gay magazines, that's sheer snobbery. That means he's ashamed of his brothers and sisters." Isherwood himself was open with family and friends about his sexuality from an early age. As he tells Leyland: "About eighty percent of my friends have always been gay, and I feel curiously ill at ease when I have been away from gay people for long; it's a feeling almost like a lack of oxygen." In an interview published later in *London Magazine,* W. I. Scobie asks Isherwood, "Why is it so tricky to write an overtly homosexual novel?" The closest Isherwood came to writing such a novel is *A Single Man*, in which George is single in part because his lover, Jim, dies in a car accident before the novel takes place. Scobie's question implies the need for a romantic or domestic gay novel, one predicated on the type of situation Isherwood lived in with his partner of over thirty years, the artist Don Bachardy. However, Isherwood seemed to believe that writing about gay romance (or sex for that matter) would lead inexorably to gay politics, and he felt he could not write a book that would be seen as special pleading. As he told David Geherin earlier about Forster's *Maurice,* "It's a partisan book, it's a very slanted book. There's no question about that. It's really an absurdly militant book. But that, of course, is also its charm." Isherwood was especially fond of *Maurice* because he'd read it in manuscript in the 1930s and because Forster left him the rights to the work, which he saw into print in 1971. Nevertheless, Isherwood tells Scobie, "I don't see why one shouldn't be able to do it successfully. . . . It's certainly difficult to write a novel of that sort [e.g., *The Charioteer* or *The Front Runner*], today, without making it to some degree political. A love affair given the sanction of society is quite different from one that takes place under the conditions that homosexuals face. Even though you may not stub your toe against the prohibitions, they are there. And they make the homosexual act of love into an act of protest, a political act. When you come to write about it, you cannot escape the political climate."

The novel Isherwood did write, *A Single Man,* treats the homosexual protagonist, George, as an emblem of minorities in general. He told Leyland that it "is the best thing I've ever written. This was the only time when I succeeded, very nearly, in saying exactly what I wanted to say." In a strained conversation with Clifford Solway for the Canadian Broadcast Corporation, Isherwood defends the political philosophy behind his novel: "What I do feel about all minorities is simply this: when they are fighting for equality, which is after all what it amounts to, they are always bound to over-compensate. I mean that while one is conducting any kind of a campaign, it always goes further than one's objective, and certainly homosexuals are no exception to this rule." Solway's line of questioning demonstrates his apparently deliberate misapprehension of Isherwood's use of homosexuality in the novel.[5]

Although he never wrote about gay domesticity, Isherwood lived such a relationship for over thirty years with Don Bachardy. Isherwood's final interviews, those conducted in the 1980s, tend to include Bachardy. The last interview Isherwood gave was in 1985 to Armistead Maupin for the *Village Voice.* Maupin, who had known Isherwood and Bachardy for almost a decade, approaches the two men as partners in their lives and their work. When he asks about AIDS, Isherwood responds: "I don't feel I know nearly enough about the AIDS situation. But these younger men who find they have it—some absolutely awful pressures begin to assert themselves. They're told by their relatives that it's a sort of punishment, that it's dreadful and it's God's will and all that kind of thing. And I think they have to get very tough with themselves, and really decide which side they're on. You know, fuck God's will. God's will must be circumvented, if that's what it is."

This comment about AIDS, which is apparently the only recorded statement Isherwood ever made about the epidemic, indicates the value of author interviews. The interviews collected here supplement Isherwood's novels, autobiographies, and posthumously published diaries, all of which prove to be, as he said about *Kathleen and Frank,* "chiefly about Christopher."

The editors would like to thank Susan McLaughlin, Steven Galbraith, and Erin Paveglio at the University of Maine, as well as Jane Lindsay Miller and the staff of the Center for Teaching and Learning at the Minnesota State Colleges and Universities. At St. John's University, we received valuable assistance from the Faculty Development committee and from reference librarian Molly Ewing. Our editors, Anne Stascavage and Seetha Srinivasan, were very helpful and encouraging. Finally, we would like to thank friends and colleagues who were supportive or offered valuable assistance, including Ozzie Mayers, Will Brantley, Dan Luckenbill, Jim Marks, Patrick Merla, Tom Steele, Jane Roberts, Matthew Blaisdell, Jared Scherer, and Gary Schiff.

JJB
CF

Notes

1. Mark Thompson, "Double Reflections: Isherwood and Bachardy on Art, Love, and Faith," in *Gay Spirit: Myth and Meaning* (New York: St. Martin's Press, 1987), 36–48.

2. Robert Wennerstein, "Christopher Isherwood, Interview," *Transatlantic Review,* Vol. 42–43 (Spring/Summer 1972): 7.

3. Rita Delfiner, "The Camera Speaks," New York *Post* (17 February 1972).

4. Jeffrey Bailey, "Interview: Christopher Isherwood," *California Quarterly,* Vol. 11–12 (Winter/Spring 1977): 96.

5. Clifford Solway, "An Interview with Christopher Isherwood," *Tamarack Review* no. 39, 30 May 1965: 22–35.

Chronology

1904 Christopher William Bradshaw Isherwood is born in Cheshire, England, 26 August.

1914–18 A student at St. Edmund's School, Surrey, where he meets W. H. Auden.

1915 Father, Frank, dies at the battle of Ypres.

1919–22 A student at Repton School, where he meets Edward Upward.

1923–25 At Cambridge, Corpus Christi College, writes Mortmere fantasies with Upward; leaves in 1925 without a degree.

1928 First novel, *All the Conspirators,* published by Jonathan Cape; meets Stephen Spender through Auden.

1929 Visits Auden in Berlin; moves to Berlin in the fall, where he lives until 1933 writing and teaching English.

1930 Translates Charles Baudelaire's *Intimate Journals,* which is published by Blackamore Press (UK) and Random House (NY).

1931 Meets Jean Ross, the model for Sally Bowles, and Gerald Hamilton, the model for Arthur Norris.

1932 Second novel, *The Memorial,* published by Hogarth Press; meets E. M. Forster and Gerald Heard.

1933 Begins work with Berthold Viertel in London on the film *Little Friend.*

1935 *Mr Norris Changes Trains* published by Hogarth Press; in the United States, published as *The Last of Mr. Norris* by Morrow.

1936 Collaboration with W. H. Auden, the play *The Dog beneath the Skin,* opens in London.

1937 *The Ascent of F6,* another theater collaboration with Auden, opens; *Sally Bowles* is published by Hogarth Press.

1938   Goes to China with Auden; his first autobiography, *Lions and Shadows,* published by Hogarth; first visit to United States in July; his final play with Auden, *On the Frontier,* opens.

1939   Leaves London with Auden on 19 January, arriving in United States on 26 January; *Goodbye to Berlin* published by Hogarth (UK) and Random House (US) and *Journey to a War* published by Faber (UK) and Random House (US); moves to California in the spring and meets Swami Prabhavananda.

1940   Works for MGM on the film, *Rage in Heaven;* inherits Wyberslegh Hall, the family estate, in July, and gives it to his brother, Richard; initiated into the Vedanta Order.

1941   Goes to Haverford, Pennsylvania, to work with German refugees as a conscientious objector and pacifist.

1943   Moves into Vedanta Center in Hollywood, where he lives for six months.

1944   Writes *Jacob's Hands* as a film treatment with Aldous Huxley (published in 1998 by St. Martin's Press); translation with Swami Prabhavananda of the Bhagavad Gita is published by Marcel Rodd (reissued by Harper in 1951).

1945   New Directions publishes *The Berlin Stories* which includes *The Last of Mr. Norris* and *Goodbye to Berlin; Prater Violet* published in US by Random House (UK, 1946, Methuen); edits *Vedanta for the Western World,* which is published by Marcel Rodd.

1946   8 November becomes United States citizen.

1947   *Lions and Shadows* published in the United States by New Directions.

1949   South American travel book, *The Condor and the Cows,* published by Random House; works at MGM; meets Evelyn (Caldwell) Hooker, Igor and Vera Stravinsky.

1951   John van Druten's theatrical adaptation of *The Berlin Stories, I Am a Camera,* opens in Hartford, Connecticut, on 8 November, and moves to Broadway later that month.

1953   Meets Don Bachardy in February; publishes *How to Know God* with Swami Prabhavananda.

1954   *The World in the Evening* published by Random House.

1955   Film version of *I Am a Camera,* with Julie Harris and Laurence Harvey, premieres.

1957   Edits *Great English Short Stories,* which is published by Dell.

1959   Begins teaching at various southern California colleges, including Los Angeles State College, UC Santa Barbara, UC Riverside, and UCLA.

1960   Mother, Kathleen, dies on 15 June.

1962   *Down There on a Visit* published by Methuen (UK) and Simon and Schuster (US).

1963   *An Approach to Vedanta* published; lectures at UC Berkeley on "The Autobiography of My Books."

1964   *A Single Man* published; meets David Hockney.

1965   *Ramakrishna and His Disciples* published.

1966   *Cabaret,* the stage musical adapted by John Kander and Fred Ebb from *The Berlin Stories* and *I Am a Camera,* opens in New York; *Exhumations* published.

1967   *A Meeting by the River,* his final novel, published in April.

1970   E. M. Forster dies, leaving Isherwood the rights to *Maurice,* which is published in 1971.

1971   *Kathleen and Frank* published in United Kingdom (1972, US).

1972   *Cabaret,* Bob Fosse's film starring Liza Minnelli, Michael York, and Joel Grey, premieres; stage version of *A Meeting by the River* by Isherwood and Bachardy premieres in Los Angeles.

1973   Isherwood and Bachardy's collaboration on *Frankenstein: The True Story* broadcast on NBC and published by Avon; W. H. Auden dies; Jean Ross dies.

1975   Addresses the Modern Language Association in New York on "Homosexuality and Literature."

1976   *Christopher and His Kind* published (1977, UK); Swami Prabhavananda dies.

1979   Brother, Richard, dies.

1980   *My Guru and His Disciple* published.

1981   Diagnosed with prostate cancer.

1983   *October,* a collaboration with Bachardy, published.

1986   Isherwood dies at his home in Santa Monica on 4 January.

Conversations with Christopher Isherwood

Ado about Novel Amuses Author: *Prater Violet* Causes Flurry over Isherwood, Long in Hollywood

Philip K. Scheuer / 1946

From *Los Angeles Times,* 13 January 1946, Part 3: 1, 7. Copyright ©
Los Angeles Times. Reprinted by permission.

> *"Christopher Isherwood, where have you been?"*
> *"I've been to London to write for the screen."*
> *"Christopher Isherwood, what did you there?"*
> *"I squeaked like a mouse and brought forth a bear."*

The bear is *Prater Violet,* a short, satirical novel about movie making, and Isherwood has it by the tail. Not yet a best seller (its author modestly says it has sold 10,000 copies "and may go to 15,000"), *Prater Violet* has been called "probably the year's best novel" and has caused a flurry of excitement in Hollywood over Isherwood's presence. This amuses Isherwood, who has been present since 1939, knocking around the studios.

Not that he's easy to catch up with. I finally located him in a walk-up apartment, shared with two others over a restaurant in Santa Monica Canyon. It might have reminded him of his lodgings in London. He seemed surprised but not displeased that anyone would want to interview him, and offered me a highball. We talked.

The dominant figure in *Prater Violet* is Dr. Friedrich Bergmann, a refugee director from Vienna with a bush head, heavy glasses and "the face of Central Europe." His creator readily admitted that Bergmann is a "composite" of Berthold Viertel, well known both here and abroad as a director and the husband of writer Salka Viertel, and other iconoclasts Isherwood subsequently met in Hollywood.

In 1934 he collaborated with Viertel in London on *Little Friend,* which was to star Nova Pilbeam. It bore no resemblance to "Prater Violet," the picture described in the book; and neither did its eccentric director row with his bosses, Isherwood added hastily, the way Bergmann does.

Composed, slight in build and with a boyish smile that makes him look

1

much younger than he is (forty-one), Christopher Isherwood reflects that pe-
culiar agelessness somehow typical of the British writers of his generation.
He has much in common with Evelyn Waugh, with Aldous Huxley, a close
friend, with Graham Greene, a cousin, and even with the older Somerset
Maugham.

Isherwood has heatedly denied that he is the original, or part-original, of
Maugham's character Larry in *The Razor's Edge*. Yet it is an extraordinary
fact that, like Larry, Isherwood—and, indeed, all the brilliantly cynical men
in this group—has turned from the negative aspect of world weariness to the
positive one of spiritual contemplation.

With Isherwood as with Huxley, the answer lay in Hindu mysticism. As a
disciple of the Vedanta Society, Isherwood has translated the Bhagavad Gita
(The Song of God) with Prabhavananda, a local swami. I asked him if this
activity extended, or would extend, to his fictional writings.

"I'm certainly not aware of it if it has." He smiled. "Would you say that
becoming a Catholic—as Graham Greene did a decade ago—has affected his
mystery thrillers?

"Eastern religion teaches extreme toleration toward other religions; that
they are ALL right in some ways. It is a philosophy, really."

Rather abruptly, I'm afraid, I wondered aloud what he thought of the
world's chances for survival.

He smiled again. "I don't know—and it's nonsense for me to say—but I
have a hunch we won't blow ourselves up.

"You see, nature has certain limited qualities which are self-defeating in
both directions. Beyond a certain point it is equally hard to build OR destroy.
Take your sulfa drugs—as soon as they became effective the streptococci
promptly developed a resistance to them!

"But if I believe we'll survive, I also believe we shall never have an earthly
millennium. The same limiting factors will prevent that.

"However, that doesn't mean we won't have to try!"

Isherwood is presently writing the second of three novelettes about refugees (of which *Prater Violet* was the first). "They will cover the whole period
of immigration between Hitler and the war," he said.

Meanwhile his publishers are reissuing *The Berlin Stories*—two short tales
of pre-Hitler Germany. As for movie jobs, which he can take or leave, he
recently did some tinkering on Maugham's *Up at the Villa* for Warners.

He likes pictures, Isherwood said. "But I believe the star system upsets the balance of any story. Every picture is just a vehicle for them, and not, strictly, a story at all.

"However, the studios started it, the public demands it and there isn't anything we can do about it. It's the cult of the actors that makes movies so popular!"

He himself, I suspect, is not too unwilling a convert. When he asked if I thought Ingrid Bergman would win an award and I said yes, I did, cultist Isherwood beamed like the most orthodox fan.

A Conversation on Tape

Stanley Poss / 1960

From *London Magazine* New Series 1 (June 1961): 41–58. Reprinted by permission.

This interview with Christopher Isherwood was recorded by Stanley Poss at Mr Isherwood's home in Santa Monica, California, in the summer of 1960.

Q: I thought we might begin with the routine questions: work habits, that sort of thing. Do you write every day?

A: I try to, yes. I work in the morning rather than any other time. And I try every day simply to make the effort of writing.

Q: Whether it's fiction or whatever?

A: To write something, yes, to keep the hand flexible, as it were.

Q: How much do you get done in a day, normally?

A: Well, that varies enormously, but it would be a very, very good day if I could write 3,000 words.

Q: Revise a lot?

A: Yes.

Q: On that day?

A: No, I used to, but now my view is that one should write whole drafts, several whole drafts, each time going right through the whole thing. I used to revise with a feeling that if I didn't secure my rear I couldn't advance. I felt that I had to have chapter one absolutely perfect; but then I realized how silly that is, because you can only revise chapter one in the light of chapter thirty, or whatever it is.

Q: Do you find it easier to write dialogue than straight narrative?

A: Oh, that's a hard question. I don't feel very much difference. . . .

Q: I think critics maybe would have expected you to answer yes on that. They speak of the general sense of ease in all of your dialogue.

A: Well, like thousands of other writers, I find that the great thing with dialogue is to have, well, as a musician would say, "Give me a chord": You know, if I can once hear the kind of noise this character makes, then I can go on writing the dialogue. If I have, as it were, three or four specimen sentences that he would say and I have the sound of his or her voice in my ear, then I find it very easy.

Q: Do you write from notes? Letters? Diaries?

A: Diaries, yes. I've always kept diaries extensively, and they give me a great sense of security because I feel at least this part is factual. Having, however, built on these little islands of fact, I think one goes back and reconstructs everything and changes everything and interferes with everything. But I do find it a great reassurance—the only kind of reassurance one can have—to have had some notes of an actual experience or an actual scene or people or whatever.

Q: I wonder if you have a potential reader in mind when you're writing fiction?

A: No, I don't think so. One's friends, of course, to some extent. Yet more and more I write for myself, I think. More and more, writing is appearing to me as a kind of self-analysis, a finding-out something about myself and about the past, and about what life is like, as far as I'm concerned; who I am; who these people are; what it's all about. And this comes from a subconscious level to some extent, so that I really don't know what may spring out of the typewriter.

Q: Hemingway answered the question "How do you name your characters?" by saying "The best I can." How would you answer it?

A: Oh, well, I think a good deal about that, and I always feel that there are ideal names for them. Of course, where there's some kind of living model, then the person's actual name is taken into consideration; and names, don't you think, go in groups—and so one chooses another name out of the same group.

Q: How about someone like Mary Scriven, for example?

A: You mean, why was she named Scriven?

Q: Yes.

A: Simply because it is a fairly unusual Irish name, and I happened to know a boy at school with the name Scriven, and I liked the name, rather.

Q: Let me fire a lot of questions at you all at once. I think the answers will probably form kind of a unit. How much do you admit to modelling your characters from real people? Do all your characters have real life models? Can you say anything about the process of turning a real person into a fictional one?

A: Well, yes, I'd say that the great majority of them have real life models; I don't feel at all secure when I'm not writing out of my personal experience.

Q: Back to the diaries—

A: Yes. As for turning them into fiction, well that's pretty obvious, isn't it? The demands of the form gradually make themselves felt and you modify, simplify, exaggerate, heighten, lower various characteristics for persons.

Q: Can we talk about form? You've been praised for your handling of structural problems. Is there any general statement you could make about the organization of a novel, or take a particular novel which had, say, an organizational problem or problem of technique that gave you trouble? Could you enlarge upon meeting that problem and handling it?

A: Well, my whole life as a writer has really been teetering between trying to do two different things. One is a real constructed novel, very much with E. M. Forster as my master, or in a funny way, Ibsen. Yes, Ibsen, undoubtedly—all the excitement and fun of the awful thing that happened twenty years ago and which gradually rears its head—that fascinates me. So I'm tremendously interested in form and construction. On the other hand, in some of my books I've turned away from it. For example, in *Prater Violet,* in *Goodbye to Berlin.* In fact you might say *All the Conspirators, The Memorial,* I suppose *Mr. Norris* and *The World in the Evening* are constructed novels; and that *Goodbye to Berlin* and *Prater Violet* and the novel I'm writing now are something else again altogether; they are, as it were, portraits. I've constantly used a rather stupid and pretentious sounding phrase, "dynamic portraits," but what I mean is a portrait that grows, a little bit like the portrait of Dorian Gray grew or changed. Rather the idea, if you can imagine, of uncovering a picture, a painting of somebody and everybody looks at it and says "Yes, yes," and then you say, "No, wait a minute, you think you've looked at this picture, but you haven't. Allow me to point out certain things about it." And by successive stages, the viewer is encouraged to look deeper and deeper into the picture, until finally it looks completely different to him.

Q: Wasn't that the intent of the shuffling of the time sequence in *The Memorial?*

A: Yes, it was. I think I discuss that in *Lions and Shadows,* don't I?

Q: I thought I found a kind of contrapuntal organization (if you'll forgive such a pretentious term) in *Goodbye to Berlin.* For example, the six parts seem to me to be played off against one another. The first diary section, "Autumn 1939," could be juxtaposed, let's say, deliberately, with the last diary section '32–'33. And then, "Sally Bowles" and "On Ruegen Island" seem to me to be in a way halves, that is, kind of polarities of one another; and "The Nowaks" and "The Landauers" certainly seem to be related.

A: Well, obviously, I tried to organize these portraits. I arrange them, I relate them to each other. In the book I'm writing now the portraits are as much related to each other as I can manage. But that's only a secondary consideration, whereas in writing one of these constructed novels the structure is enormously important, as I at present feel, too important. I think it's rather strangling.

Q: I take it you would admit to the influence of the movies generally upon your work?

A: Oh certainly. You see I had my first training in writing movies before I even wrote *The Last of Mr. Norris.*

Q: What movies were those?

A: Well, it was the movie that is described in *Prater Violet,* except that it's quite a different movie. It was a movie based on an Austrian novel called *Kleine Freundin, Little Friend,* it sounds dreadful in English, certainly. It was one of these fundamentally very saccharine stories about a little girl who brings her divided parents together again. But it was all dressed up in psychoanalysis, which was a relatively new thing at that time, so it was quite an amusing picture; and the man who directed it, Berthold Viertel, is, of course, described in *Prater Violet.*

Q: He's of course written about it in, I think, *The Saturday Review.* Have you read that piece?

A: I probably did, yes—he's dead now, you know. He was a great, great friend of mine and a great instructor in many things.

Q: He worked with Brecht too, didn't he?

A: Yes. He knew Brecht quite well when Brecht lived here during the war, and in many ways the fact that I'm sitting in this room is due to the Viertels. They used to live in a house just down here at the bottom of Santa Monica Canyon, and when I came to America one of my objectives was to meet his wife, Mrs. Salka Viertel, which I then did, and we became great friends. So

I settled in the Canyon here, and on and off, with interruptions, for the last twenty years I've lived in different houses in this area, most of them visible from this window.

Q: Is this the slide area?

A: Well, strictly speaking, the slide area is around the corner there—that's where the cliff comes down.

Q: Is that where Gavin Lambert lives?

A: Oh no, you can throw a stone on Gavin's roof; he's just down there on the road below us.

Q: I understand you admired his novel *The Slide Area?*

A: Very much so. I thought it was marvellous.

Q: Did you know Brecht when he lived here?

A: Yes, indeed.

Q: I have been reading a new book on him by Esslin.

A: Yes, I knew there was a new book. Salka Viertel had a tremendous salon, all kinds of people came to the house. Thomas Mann came constantly; he lived just across on the other side of the hill, and, of course, Chaplin was there a great deal and Heinrich Mann and Schönberg and all sorts of people who were around in this area.

Q: When I asked you about the movies I was thinking of their connections with fictional structures specifically. For example, were you ever struck by the film device called montage as a fruitful thing to use in fiction: rapid juxtaposition of scenes, that sort of thing?

A: Yes, to some extent, but, more importantly, I think what the movies taught me was visualization. Of course, the art of the movie is fundamentally opposed to that of literature, because the fewer words you have in a movie, the better—let's not kid ourselves. One is always trying to tell the thing in visual terms and not yak. But you do learn a great deal, at least I did, from just seeing the people in a room and seeing them in relative positions in a room and all this kind of thing, which purely non-dramatic writers simply don't think about. They don't think in those terms.

Q: Would you agree that Dickens is one of the finest scenario writers the movies have ever had?

A: Oh well, yes, and of course he was an actor of considerable talent and obviously, in a way, a dramatist. Whether he would have liked to have written real plays or not, I don't know. But he certainly did write them, in his way.

Q: On a completely different tack, the autobiographical element and so on, would Stephen Spender be the model for Peter Wilkinson in "On Ruegen Island"?

A: No, the only description of Stephen is in *Lions and Shadows,* where he's called "Stephen Savage."

Q: I don't know who "Allen Chalmers" is. Can one know who he is?

A: Oh yes. "Allen Chalmers" is a very gifted and interesting writer who's unfortunately done very little, but I'm sure he will be heard of in a very big way soon. His name is Edward Upward. He wrote one novel years ago, called *Journey to the Border;* did you ever read that one?

Q: No, I haven't. I've only seen his name.

A: Well, it's a slightly Kafkaesque kind of novel—quite a masterpiece, both structurally and in the writing. He also wrote a couple of pieces which appeared in John Lehmann's *New Writing.* He's now working on a very ambitious novel. All these years he's been a schoolmaster in London. He's still the final judge, as far as I'm concerned, of my work; I always send everything to him.

Q: Whatever happened to the Rats Hostel–Mortmere manuscripts?

A: I think he has them. Really, the only Rats Hostel thing of any interest was the thing that he wrote called "The Railway Accident," which came out in *New Directions,* number eleven, was it?

Q: I was struck by many characters carrying over from one of your novels to the next, and that made me wonder to what degree is each novel an entirely new experiment. Does it help take the shock off the plunge into a new work to have characters—Mary Scriven, for example—carry over from one novel to the next?

A: Well, no, I don't feel that it really helps very much. But you know, if you're producing a play, let's say, and you can have one of the actors or actresses from an earlier production, then there's a nice kind of family feeling, a "How nice to be working with you again" kind of feeling.

Q: On the part of the reader, you mean, or on the part of the writer?

A: On the part of the writer.

Q: But it does give the reader that sense too; he feels he's among friends when he meets characters he's met before.

A: As a matter of fact, of course, my work is all part of an autobiography, and in every case there's a slight advance in time; the end of the work takes place a little later each time. The novel that I just finished the rough draft of ends in the early fifties.

Q: Has it a title?

A: *Down There on a Visit,* which is a reference to Huysmans's *La Bas,* because it is partly a novel about hell.

Q: Does it have an American setting?

A: Yes. But a lot of it is set in Germany (not Berlin), Greece and London. You see this novel has arisen out of another novel which I wrote just before this and which was also called *Down There on a Visit,* but which somehow didn't jell. I wrote the entire novel and then realized it wouldn't work the way it was.

Q: Had you read *The Sound and the Fury* when you wrote *The Memorial?*

A: No, to be quite frank with you I never have gotten through *The Sound and the Fury.*

Q: It's organized almost identically with your novel.

A: Oh, really; well, it's quite accidental.

Q: Cyril Connolly devoted several pages to you in *Enemies of Promise,* particularly on style and construction. He thought *The Memorial* was very well constructed but he wondered pessimistically whether even faultless construction would be enough to offset the limitations of the "impoverished realist vocabulary" that you seemed headed for at that time.

A: Well. . . .

Q: How about the later works in this connection?

A: I wouldn't say my vocabulary is so impoverished, would you? On the contrary, I've since then been accused of writing purple passages.

Q: He was concerned with your "fatal" readability, at that time.

A: I don't think one should ever apologize for readability, I must say.

Q: In your introduction to the *New Directions* edition of *All the Conspirators,* you spoke of your attempts at imitating the techniques of Joyce, Virginia Woolf, E. M. Forster: streams of consciousness, management of time, flashbacks, etc. But really you didn't wholly abandon such techniques when you came to write the novels that we now think of as distinctly your own, did you? You seem to find particularly congenial the flashback technique that Forster has used so effectively.

A: Oh yes, that's quite true.

Q: Would you say that problems of ego and the abandonment of self are the core of your work? Were you thinking along such lines before your interest in Vedanta?

A: I think I must have been to some extent because, since philosophies are made for man and not vice versa, I obviously became interested in Vedanta because it suited me, it spoke to my condition, and therefore, I suppose, I was thinking of it. But not consciously.

Q: The end of *Prater Violet* does seem to suggest the necessity of the loss of the ego, doesn't it?

A: Yes, however, it's very important for me to stress that—I have to say this very often to people—I was trying to give a picture of myself at a special moment in my life. Therefore I stressed an acute sense of despair.

Q: Walking the streets at 3 A.M. . . . .

A: Yes, after the book came out quite a lot of people said, well, this is all that his philosophy has brought him to. That is, completely schizoid, tortured by both worlds, which I don't think is true at all. But looking back on this period, I was trying to convey a sense of acute malaise, which was my condition at the time.

Q: Can you briefly distinguish for me between Vedanta and Hinduism proper?

A: Of course, Vedanta is Hindu philosophy. There are many schools of Hindu philosophy but this is the basic teaching. It's called "Vedanta" simply because it's based on the teachings of the Vedas, which are the most ancient sacred books of the Hindus. And it's a non-dualistic philosophy, that is to say it says that that which is outside is also inside.

Q: Yes, as you explained in your little booklet "What Vedanta Means to Me."

A: Yes, that's right.

Q: You spoke of your hostility to the dualism of Christianity.

A: Yes, an enormous amount of the attacks on religion are based on the assumption that religion is necessarily dualistic. And not only necessarily dualistic but unchangeably, and irrevocably, and sternly dualistic. They say, "Look: up there is the boss, the landowner, the oppressor (or whatever word they use from their own province), and we're down here. Of course we're opposed to him, of course we hate his heaven and love his hell. Who wouldn't revolt?" Now this is a completely wrong formulation, whether you're dealing with Christianity or any other religion, because the dualism always, to some extent, arises out of non-dualism. I mean it's all very nice for me to say that God is inside me, but I can't feel it. So what can I do? I look around for somebody else who seems to be more God-like than I and establish a cult of him or her; but you see this is dualism based on a fundamental non-dualism. Well, there's a lot of difference psychologically there.

Q: Stephen Monk's coming to consciousness is, if not a reflection of your preoccupation with Vedanta ideas, certainly at any rate not uncongenial to them, not hostile to them. Did you intend anything specifically religious in his progress, in his journey through the book?

A: Well, perhaps that's the whole trouble. Maybe it should have been much more or much less than it was, you know. There's something there which is, to my mind, fundamentally wrong. I don't like the character. I think that whole part should be taken out and put together again differently. But what I was trying to show, of course, was the revolt of a birthright Quaker away from that and then finally to some extent coming around to feeling that after all the Quakers have got something.

Q: Can I talk about the Vedanta and the Test that you spoke of in *Lions and Shadows*? Passing the Test was a crucial issue. Has Vedanta obviated passing the test, or is it a much more demanding test than riding the AJS motorcycle flat out while you counted to one hundred?

A: Well, whatever it's done for me personally (which is, of course, always a question the individual can't answer), obviously it obviates or does away with the necessity of a test, because a test has something to do with the ego, doesn't it? It has to do with establishing the importance of one's ego. And it has to do with will and aggression and so forth. Vedanta, or indeed, I would think, any other religious faith, has to do with quite the opposite, with the concept of mercy, with the concept of acceptance, with the concept of love rather than . . .

Q: Competiton?

A: Yes, rather than competition.

Q: A switch again. You wrote in your foreword to Gerald Hamilton's *Mr. Norris and I,* that on looking back to *The Last of Mr. Norris,* you were re-pelled by the heartlessness of the book, that it was a heartless fairy story about real people with acute miseries, suffering starvation, that the real mon-ster of the book was the young narrator who passed so gaily through it, constructing his own private fantasies. Is that still your view of *The Last of Mr. Norris,* though not *Goodbye to Berlin?*

A: Yes, it doesn't bother me terribly, but I think it is true. Perhaps, if one could rewrite things, perhaps one should heighten this a little and project it rather more, and then it would be rather charming. I mean it's just a matter of how you present it. Cyril Connolly once said to me that he did feel that a change took place in the character and that the character got slightly more mature toward the end of the book. Be that as it may, I would like to point that out. In fact in the book I'm writing now, which covers a rather large area of my life, I think perhaps this point is brought out a bit more.

Q: You thought yourself that the narrator in *Goodbye to Berlin* was an advance over the narrator in *Mr. Norris?*

A: Yes.

Q: You thought he was a little less the anonymous, blandly accepting cam-era-eye character?

A: You see, it's a terribly difficult problem. The world, with all its woes and sufferings, makes us feel that we should behave decently, as though we were in church, you know, and be sad with the sad and so forth. On the other hand, the heartless delight of the artist in any kind of experience goes con-trary to that, and there we have a situation. I wouldn't mind how heartless Chris was if this were projected a little more. I mean, why shouldn't he have a ball watching the goings-on in Germany. You know the way the young are. It's fascinating—it's a tremendous drama, and if he didn't see the excitement of it he wouldn't have written it down; and in so far as the creation of art works is desirable, it's presumably preferable that he should have written it down. So if he'd sat down mourning and weeping over the whole thing and being just too depressed for words, he would probably have left in a week and that would have been the end of it.

Q: John Wain was very impressed by Elizabeth Rydal of *The World in the Evening.*

A: Oh, really?

Q: Yes, have you read his review? Do you read critics of your work?

A: Well, I do, but I've never read that, no.

Q: Well, it's a strange review because it starts out very snidely; he quotes Bergmann in *Prater Violet* on "The English tragedy," which is, as he tells Chris, that the Englishman always marries his mother, a subject that Bergmann intends to write a novel about, to be called "The Diary of an Etonian Oedipus." Wain rather maliciously quotes that passage and says, we now have, in this novel, "The Diary of an Etonian Oedipus," and he sounds rather snide about it. Then he goes on in his review to make it quite clear that he's very impressed by the novel and that he's especially impressed by Elizabeth Rydal. I wonder if you could enlarge upon the creation of her character? That is, was there anything, let's say, of Katherine Mansfield or Virginia Woolf in your mind?

A: Yes, there undoubtedly was. That's another thing which I think is wrong with that book. She somehow or another doesn't have any real roots for me in life. That is, she seems to me a sort of literary character, and I wish I had desanctified her more. The funny thing was that everybody said it must have been very difficult to write her letters. But actually those letters were much the easiest part of the book to write. And perhaps that shows something suspicious. They just flew off the pen. I could write you a whole volume of the letters of Elizabeth Rydal.

Q: I never understood the title of *All the Conspirators.*

A: Neither has anybody else. I just thought it was a beautiful Shakespearean phrase.

Q: Does Stephen Monk derive from Christopher Garland, whom you described in *Lions and Shadows* as a "pseudo-monk," a "life-snob"?

A: Yes, I suppose he does. There's something bad, bad there, there's a bad smell that comes off him.

Q: Monk or Garland or both?

A: Both. No, the parts of that book I like are, well, the part about the Quakers, I think is good. And in fact I think maybe the description of the meeting and one or two other things are really quite good. And, of course, all that is soundly rooted in my own experience, too. I spent quite a long time with the Quakers.

Q: Was Stephen's crucial and self-precipitated accident in *The World in the Evening* a memory of the motorcycle spill you described in *Lions and Shadows* when you were lying there and looking at the truck?

A: I really don't know; I expect so, yes, it seemed right somehow.

Q: Was Stephen and Michael Drummond's climbing of that hazardous outcrop in the novel a memory of *The Ascent of F6*?

A: Oh no, no, I've been to the rock I describe and been thoroughly scared by it myself. I suffer acutely from vertigo and it really was a drastic place; not that we attempted to climb it, but we climbed around it. And it's perfectly true about the Nazi climbing it and putting up the flag; that incident was true. All that scenery is taken from places I've been to.

Q: Do you think you'll ever write another play with Auden?

A: I wish we could, but you know we always seem to be so occupied with our own things. There was a period, I still don't know whether it may not come to pass, when we thought we were going to do a musical together based on *Goodbye to Berlin*. And he was interested with Chester Kallman in doing the lyrics. I'm sorry that hasn't come off, but perhaps it will.

Q: In your collaboration with him, did it generally work out that you handled the dialogue, the prose sections, while he of course wrote the lyrics? Could you say anything about your collaboration with him on any one of the plays—*F6*, or *The Dog beneath the Skin*?

A: Well, they all varied. In the case of *The Dog beneath the Skin*, Auden had written a complete play which was called *The Search*. We then got into correspondence about it and I made suggestions and he made suggestions. I suggested several entire scenes which weren't in the other version, but then again he made counter-suggestions. We did a great deal of it by correspondence. And then finally, I was living in Copenhagen at the time, he came over and we spent a short time together and got it all done. I always thought of myself as a librettist to some extent with a composer, his verse being the music; and I would say "Now we have to have a big speech here," you know, and he would write it.

Q: It must have been a lot of fun.

A: Oh, yes, we had a wonderful time together and worked very quickly and easily and at enormous speed. *F6* especially was written very fast. By the time we got to *On the Frontier*, Auden was also more experienced at play writing. Originally, I was the expert in charge of construction; because of my connection with the movies I was supposed to know all about dramatic writing. But by this time we both, you know, just shared the whole job more or less. I think there's more of Auden's work in *On the Frontier* than any of the plays, because he not only wrote all the poetry but also a big share of the prose.

Q: Back to this idea of to what extent is the new novel an entirely new thing. Wain said in this review that I mentioned before of *The World in the Evening* that you had been marking time for fifteen years since *Prater Violet* because you didn't want to do again what you had done. Was that an accurate guess?

A: Well, that's a kind of statement that you can never make about yourself. I mean that it's not the way a writer's mind works at all. It might be perfectly true, but I rather doubt it. You see people get a wonderful view of my lack of production by blissfully ignoring two-thirds of my work. I *only* produced, I don't know, what was it—three, four books related to Vedanta in one way or another. And then, of course, there was this travel book, *The Condor and the Cows,* which I now see is one of my best books.

Q: I'd better read that one.

A: I managed to put an enormous amount of things into it that I wanted to say. But who's going to read a book about South America? It did very well in England, but . . .

Q: We're too close to the border, maybe.

A: Yes, nobody here reads about it. But I have a tremendously romantic thing about Quito. I always longed to go to Ecuador. And this is one of the great places I've wanted to see in the world. I've seen all of them now except Papeete and Lhasa, which I'll never get to go to, I guess. Papeete, of course, is almost too easy. I think a travel book is a marvelous medium for political and philosophical remarks.

Q: Which of your books satisfies you the most?

A: *Prater Violet* and the one I'm doing now. I think this new one's much better than anything else.

Q: What length is the novel you're doing now?

A: Very long. It's made up of four episodes, and they vary rather drastically in length. One of them is much longer than the others. A novelette in itself.

Q: Pritchett thought that your career represents the interaction of the reporter and the artist at its most delicate balance. Does that seem to you a fair generalization?

A: Yes, I see what he means.

Q: He spoke of the distance between the narrator and the rest of the characters. He says the characters are tragic, squalid, comical because the narrator was cut off from them, fundamentally indifferent. Is that more true for, let's say, the Chris of *Mr. Norris* than for the Chris of *Goodbye to Berlin*? Is the Chris of *Goodbye to Berlin* more able to share the life of Otto Nowak than the Chris of *Mr. Norris* able to share the life of Arthur Norris?

A: Yes, I would suppose so, yes.

Q: Gerda criticizes Elizabeth Rydal's book for its apolitical nature. It was published in 1934, that is, her novel was. One wonders in reading Stephen's defense of Elizabeth's book whether this is in a way your own statement for those who criticized your work as apolitical.

A: No, I don't think so. I simply thought that it was a facet of Gerda's character that she wouldn't approve of this kind of book and so naturally, since Stephen was Elizabeth's husband, he has to defend it. But at the end, you know, he and Charles Kennedy admit that it wasn't really very good at all.

Q: Who interests you among the younger American writers?

A: I quite liked *The Subterraneans,* and I do plan to read more Kerouac. If you call him younger, I think Ray Bradbury's *The Martian Chronicles* is one of the most extraordinary works of fantasy ever written in the English language. I very much like a couple of books by Calder Willingham, particularly one—*Geraldine Bradshaw.* I cried laughing all the way through that. I thought it was the most marvellous comic masterpiece. I hope one day that it will be famous.

Q: Have you read *Breakfast at Tiffany's*?

A: Yes. I think that Truman Capote, whom I know very well, has an enormous talent. Somehow or other (and I've said this to him constantly) I feel that he hasn't yet quite written about the things that he'd be best at writing about. I always say to him, "Why don't you be our New York Proust? Why don't you write about feuds and social goings-on in Manhattan?" because he knows this stuff inside out. You see with Truman, he's so fond of writing about the humble and the little and the insulted and injured. But I want him to write about the president of US Steel. I'm sure that he could do wonderful things on the largest scale showing the whole nature of society today.

Q: I enjoyed Colin MacInnes's *Absolute Beginners.* Have you read that?

A: No, I read, what's the one before, *City of Spades,* I liked it very much.

Q: Again this introduction to *All the Conspirators,* the angry young man business: you spoke of the pleasure in the sense of a temperamental sympathy between yourself and them, the pleasure of reading Osborne's plays.

A: I admire Osborne very much.

Q: How about Kingsley Amis?

A: I adored *That Uncertain Feeling.*

Q: More than *Lucky Jim?*

A: Well, perhaps it was simply that I read it first. But I was reading it in England on a train, and I just dropped the book and roared. The specific thing which perhaps wouldn't amuse you because it was rather a period joke, but he's having this terrible scene with a poetic dramatist, and he says, "Furthermore, you've written the worst play since *Gammer Gurton's Needle.*" God, I laughed! No—I think *Lucky Jim* is very good, too; it's one of the books that I'm going to use when I teach at Santa Barbara this fall.

Q: What are you going to teach?

A: Well, I said that I would gladly talk about American writers, but they said, oh no, you stick to English. I'm only using them as conversation pieces. We're going to have *A Taste of Honey, Look Back in Anger, Lucky Jim.* And William Golding's *Lord of the Flies.* Did you read his science fiction story? *Envoy Extraordinary.* It's a paperback with two other science fiction stories. That's quite remarkable.

Q: You spoke of the enormous impact of Forster's account of the organization of *The Counterfeiters* way back there, at least as far back as *Lions and Shadows.* Are you interested in Gide now?

A: Well, I'm interested in him as a personality, as a man, as an influence. I often look into his journals. What interested me about the idea in *The Counterfeiters* was the old thing of the relation between life and art. The thing that is half-way hatched out of life, and just starting to turn into art and the interaction between these two.

Q: Point counterpoint.

A: Yes, I actually don't like *The Counterfeiters* very much at all as a novel. It's one of the things I like least of Gide's.

Q: Point counterpoint makes me think of Huxley and the conjunction that is made between your names sometimes. Do you see your careers as in any way similar? How would you differentiate between them?

A: I think we're the most dissimilar creatures alive. I'm very fond of Huxley personally and we've been friends now for about twenty years. But Aldous, in the first place, is an intellect, and I'm a purely intuitive person.

Q: Spender in *World Within World* spoke of that aspect of you. He said that you had no opinions about anything, that you were wholly and simply interested in people. Does that still hold—did it hold then?

A: Well, I see now how right I was, in a way, but I think I said it in those days out of a kind of aggression. I don't think I meant it quite in the way I would now. Of course I have opinions, in fact very strong opinions, about a lot of quite specific things. But what I think was good, or good for me—the right way for me to do things—was that I can really only understand things through people.

Q: Would you say that that is the primary difference between yourself and Huxley?

A: Yes.

Q: You spoke of Forster earlier, and it's quite evident in *Lions and Shadows* that you thought a great deal of him at one time, that he had revolutionized the novel. Can you speak of any influence he had on your work? One of the characters in *All the Conspirators,* Victor Page, was said to be modeled on Charles Wilcox, for example.

A: Oh, really? Well, he might have been unconsciously modeled on him, that's perfectly true, because I suppose that certainly the whole thing was tremendously influenced by *Howards End,* or by all of Forster. Well, I think the great revelation about Forster (and Trilling has said all of this marvelously in his book) is that Forster is a comic writer, and that was our great slogan, Edward Upward's and mine, when we were young, that we were going to be essentially comic writers, since tragedy was no longer modern.

Q: Tune down the pitch, play down the big scenes, tea-table it.

A: Yes, but now, of course, I see that it's not by any means necessary to tune down the big scenes.

Q: Yes, the violence of the first chapter of *The World in the Evening* is not at all Forsterian.

A: For instance, Dostoevsky is essentially a comic writer. I think at least *The Brothers Karamazov* is the greatest sort of farce ever written. There's something in Dostoevsky that you find in the life of Francis of Assisi and that was very much in Ramakrishna. Farce and truth became identical in the most drastic manner in the great scenes with Zossima; and, of course, in the murder, the whole thing is this farce which is heightened to the utmost.

Q: Was moving to America a political gresture, a cutting off of national affiliation, or anything of that sort?

A: Oh no, no, really not at all. People who think I moved to America as a symbolic gesture really aren't acquainted with my movements before that. I was eternally wandering about. I didn't live in England properly after I was twenty-four. So that I spent about ten years, first in Germany, then living in all kinds of countries in Europe, then going to China, and then going to America. I really like England a great deal more now. I mean not because I don't live there now, but because since the war I think it's a marvellous place, much better in every way.

Q: Auden and Spender seem to be there more or less for good; at any rate, that's how it seems at the moment. Do you think you'll ever move back?

A: No, I very much doubt it. Auden, you know, is an American citizen and maintains a residence here. He spends every winter in New York.

Q: Has living in America changed your attitude towards your work?

A: I really don't know the answer to that. You see, you have to realize that I've never lived, since I've been grown up, in any place nearly as long as I've lived in America. I'm so completely habituated to living in America that everything else seems very remote from me. Now I don't mean by this that I don't feel foreign here, because I do. But that I like. And I think it sort of heightens one's awareness of things to feel a little bit out of it.

Q: You've read *Lolita,* of course. The travel scenes in it show a kind of awareness of the American scene that could only come from a foreigner; the writer's stance makes the familiar appear tantalizingly out of focus. It's something an American couldn't or at any rate hasn't done.

A: Yes, the travel part was marvellous. And I think I can see in a way how Nabokov managed to bring it off. Of course, I am very distressed by the terrible ugliness of the commercial things, the billboards and the spawning of that awful kind of prefabricated structure that goes up everywhere, but all my life I've had a tremendous romantic feeling about the far west, and I used to read about that and think about it and think about the deserts and the mountains years before I ever thought I would live here.

Q: Do you think that an academic job for a writer, generally speaking, can be harmful?

A: I think that that depends on the spirit in which you do it. It's exactly the same as writing for the movies. People say that if you write for the movies, you're sunk. But it entirely depends on the spirit in which you write for the movies. I don't see why a writer shouldn't have an intensely academic side to his nature and be interested in academic matters. Just look at Auden— Auden is the greatest Professor of English Literature in the world. What Auden knows is simply stunning. And he knows it in an academic way; I mean, he knows the whole theory and history and practice of prosody, for instance, and can tell the experts, can set them right on all sorts of matters. But he thrives on it; it is part of his make-up as a writer. It won't do you any harm necessarily. I ran away from it because I think I realized that it would do me harm. And my only reaction in those days was a sort of simple escape thing. But that's a criticism of me, not of the academic process. But, on the other hand, there's the utter sloppiness of that sort of pseudo-Zen approach to everything where "You just have to feel it, man."

Q: How about that in Kerouac? You said you liked *The Subterraneans.*

A: I do like him, yes, but I mean I don't think that's all there is to Kerouac. What is true is that the dry as dust academic thing on the one hand and the sloppy solarplexus thing on the other, end in both cases in utter artistic death. But the writers form a great line in between those two and some are more at one end and some are more at the other.

Q: You are a pacifist, are you not?
A: Yes.

Q: Do you feel that it is a difficult position to maintain?

A: I don't feel that it's a difficult position, as far as I'm concerned, to maintain, because I don't bother about justifying it with a tremendous lot of intellectual reasoning: I just *know* that I personally ought to do this. And I hope I will have the gumption to go on saying so under any necessary circumstances. As it happened in World War II, when the draft age was raised, I was in a very permissive area outside of Philadelphia, and they took pacifists in their stride at the draft board. I was immediately classified as a conscientious objector. I definitely said all along that I would go into the medical corps as

long as they guaranteed that under no circumstances would I have to bear
arms. At first they wouldn't guarantee, but later they did and so I said "Very
well, I will enlist." But by this time they'd lowered the military age again
and I was over-age and so the problem didn't arise.

Q: How do you feel about those who refuse to register for the draft at all,
even as conscientious objectors?

A: Well, it's a tremendously difficult question, where you individually
decide to draw the line. Take anything—take vegetarianism. Will you eat
blades of grass, they're growing too, etc., etc. Everybody finally finds out
that they have to draw the line somewhere. Now I respect thoroughly people
who refuse to register for the draft. That's a position. My particular position
is that I will go along to the utmost extent, and as long as the authorities have
set up a provision for the conscientious objectors, I feel that I should meet it
halfway by registering—you see what I mean? But I would never defend this
opinion against somebody who felt otherwise. It's a purely individual matter.

Q: Don't you think pacifism has spread enormously in recent years?

A: Oh yes. And whatever people say, in the last resort it's our only hope.
I mean, that this thing spreads to a point where it really will have some
influence on the council of nations. One may say that that's completely unre-
alistic, but after all what can you do except at least do it yourself? You can't
really do any more than that.

Q: You are no doubt aware of the kind of generalization made about the
writers of the thirties, the group with which you are identified, Auden,
Spender, and their famous sympathy with social movements. Do you feel that
your present position is a great distance removed from your position of the
thirties or not? Do you feel that Auden and Spender, for example, have moved
into positions that are not too dissimilar from your own at the moment?
Pacifism, for example. Has there been a change?

A: Well, neither Auden nor Spender are pacifists, as far as I can understand. I think that in some way in the thirties we rather failed to see that there
was going to be a clash between pacifism and our general liberalistic attitudes
in other matters. A liberal or whatever you call it, I have always remained
and certainly Spender has, and Auden has. In that way we are united still,
and there are many, many issues on which we feel the same. And, of course,
from time to time one becomes associated with people who have other views
in many areas. I belong to the American Civil Liberties Union, which con-

tains all sorts of people. But we agree on general principles, and I guess that both Auden and Spender would subscribe to that, too.

Q: Would you go along with the ACLU to the extent of defending someone who is personally most unsympathetic to you, like the infamous George Lincoln Rockwell, the American Nazi?

A: Oh yes, I think given the principles of the ACLU this action is inescapable. And indeed is very, very important, not so much for itself as to show the integrity of their other actions. Yes, I would support that. Absolutely.

Q: What are your views on literature which is "engaged" in the service of stating political or other kinds of truth?

A: I don't know that there's anything you could say for or against it as such. I see clearly now that any kind of stimulus may produce good art or good polemics, which is a form of art. So how can you say that you're against it or for it?

Q: Thank you very much.

A: Did you really get anything, do you think?

Q: I haven't any idea. What's your own feeling about it?

A: Perhaps in places.

Q: I hope I can find the places.

An Interview with
Christopher Isherwood

George Wickes / 1965

From *Shenandoah* 1965: 22–52. Reprinted by permission.

Christopher Isherwood was born in his family's ancestral manor in Cheshire in 1904. His father, a career officer, was killed in the First World War, and Isherwood, like others of his generation, grew up with a sense of inadequacy because he was too young to take part in the war. From this neurotic obsession (as he regarded it) he derived his theory of "the Test": only in war or through similarly daring exploits could one prove his courage or manhood. After boarding school Isherwood attended Cambridge for two years and medical school for two terms, in each case abandoning his studies for more diverting activities. His family background and his formative experiences provide raw material for his first two novels and for his autobiography, *Lions and Shadows,* published in 1938, when he was only thirty-three.

   Lions and Shadows ends with Isherwood's departure for Berlin in 1929. He stayed there for four years, observing the night life and Hitler's rise to power with a mixture of amusement and deep concern. These sights and events are vividly recorded in his two best-known novels, *Mr Norris Changes Trains* and *Goodbye to Berlin* (published together in this country as *The Berlin Stories*). There Isherwood perfected his distinctive technique of observing through a dispassionate narrator bearing his own name: "I am a camera with its shutter open, quite passive, recording, not thinking." Later one of Isherwood's stories was made into a highly successful play and movie, *I Am a Camera.*

   In the latter thirties Isherwood collaborated with W. H. Auden on three verse dramas which reflect the politics of that anxious time: *The Dog beneath the Skin, The Ascent of F6,* and *On the Frontier.* They also wrote *Journey to a War,* a travel diary of their visit to China during the Japanese invasion. In 1939 both Auden and Isherwood settled in this country, Isherwood in southern California. He now became deeply absorbed in Hindu religion, and for a decade or more dedicated his talents as writer, editor, and translator to publications of the Vedanta Society. In collaboration with Swami Prabhavananda he translated some of the Hindu Scriptures, notably the Bhagavad Gita.

At the same time Isherwood supported himself as a scriptwriter in Hollywood. He had always had a keen interest in the films and had worked in British studios before coming to this country. His only work of fiction of the forties, *Prater Violet,* provides an excellent description of the filmmaking world, together with an ironic comment on its tawdry values. He has since written three more novels and appears to have regained his momentum as a novelist with the last two, *Down There on a Visit* (1962) and *A Single Man* (1964).

The interview took place on a balmy day in January. Isherwood lives in a one-story house overhanging Santa Monica Canyon, with all its windows looking out at an angle toward the Pacific, about a quarter of a mile below. It is a cheerful setting, light and airy. The walls are covered with paintings and drawings, a number of them portraits by Don Bachardy, with whom Isherwood shares the house.

As I came down the steps from the street I heard typing, and as I looked into the open front door I could see Isherwood at his typewriter facing me across an old-fashioned circular dining room table. When he rose to greet me, I realized that it was his image I had seen, reflected in a wall-size mirror. The impression was rather disconcerting as he materialized opposite his double, but altogether appropriate for a writer who has so often reflected himself in his fiction.

Isherwood is a rather small man, but by no means slight. He gives the impression of great animation and vigor. He looks out under shaggy brows, and his face, weathered and lined, is that of a sixty-year-old man, but otherwise he seems eternally youthful. His look suggests a quick good nature, and his eyes though searching are kind. There are permanent twinkles in their corners, and in speaking he occasionally overflows with laughter. But this exterior may be a persona, like the Christopher Isherwood of his fiction, concealing a deeper, more solemn self. His answers are more deliberate and controlled than one would expect. He is in fact the ideal subject for an interview, giving thoughtful, carefully composed answers. He speaks in a modified English accent with a slight American overlay which comes and goes.

Isherwood offered me a beer and took a mug of coffee himself. Then he sat down on the living room floor cross-legged, Hindu-style, explaining that he had got into the habit and found that posture quite comfortable. The interview went on most of the afternoon, with occasional breaks.

Interviewer: Would you tell me first what you now are writing?

Isherwood: I am now at work on a book which I am calling *Exhumations,* because it consists of dug-up pieces of various kinds: some short stories that I have published at different times in my life, not very many; a certain amount of book reviewing; some articles that I wrote, for instance on the deaths of Klaus Mann, Virginia Woolf, and Ernst Toller; some travel pieces, just a few; and an unpublished fragment of a novel.

Interviewer: These pieces go pretty far back, I take it.

Isherwood: Oh, yes. There is a poem which was my first printed work, outside of school magazines. It came out when I was very young, I guess about nineteen or twenty.

Interviewer: Are you working on anything else?

Isherwood: Not right at the moment. But I do have another novel in mind and also another autobiographical book. When I was up at Berkeley the year before last I gave some lectures which were called "The Autobiography of My Books." This made me see the possibility of writing a slightly different kind of autobiography. In these talks I didn't say especially what the books were about, nor did you have to have read my books, but I talked about the various themes that I had dealt with in my writing, and in this way got at the material more indirectly.

Interviewer: I have heard that you are writing reminiscences of Aldous Huxley. Is this true?

Isherwood: Well, it is true that I wrote a short piece about him, reminiscences, which is going to be printed in a memorial volume very shortly in England. What pleased me was that his brother Julian liked the piece very much. It was really just a lot of things about Aldous which I found in my diary and strung together.

Interviewer: Then several years ago you spoke of doing a musical with Auden and Chester Kallman.

Isherwood: That's quite right. We had the idea of doing a musical based on *I Am a Camera.* We had some good ideas, both Wystan and Chester certainly had brilliant ideas, but somehow or other we were all so damned tired of the material—I particularly—and got the feeling that somebody else had to come along and do it. It would be better to go off and write something new.

Interviewer: Had you worked on the film version of *I Am a Camera*?

Isherwood: Not at all on the film version. What happened is quite a charming story of good will on the part of my friends. Dodie Smith, who used to live out here, said one day to John van Druten at lunch, "You know, it would be wonderful to dramatize some of Chris's Berlin stories, but it would be almost impossible to do it." John, who was also a very good friend of mine and who loved having impossible problems set before him as a writer, immediately said, "Oh, I think I could do it." He went off and I believe that very evening or anyway next day he called up Dodie and said, "Well, I've got the first half planned already." They didn't tell me at all until John had done a complete draft. Well, of course I was enchanted, as you may imagine, because it was not only a grand gesture, but John van Druten was in a very important position in the theatrical world, and it meant almost certain production of this play, and what is more that he would direct it himself. I had complete freedom to make all kinds of suggestions, and I was present at most of the rehearsals too. He was a very remarkable director, one of the best I have ever seen; he had a wonderful way of apparently not interfering at all and getting a great deal out of the actors. When it came time to do the film, both John van Druten and I were asked if we cared to work on it. But we were both busy with other things and couldn't do it.

Interviewer: It seems to me that a few years ago you also said you were working on the drama of Socrates.

Isherwood: Yes. That was a project that I had with Charles Laughton. Charles wanted to play Socrates, and we were trying to devise some kind of theatrical evening, which was not exactly a recital of passages from the *Dialogues,* and not exactly a play, but something that started off almost like a kind of lecture and turned into a drama, because of course the last act is a ready-made drama, the death of Socrates. Everybody has always used this on the stage, and it's amazingly powerful. We used to work in an appropriately Socratic setting, on the edge of a swimming pool, reading the *Dialogues* to each other and making selections of bits that might be used and trying to see how one would lead into the other. And we did have a rough idea that something could be done on the basis of an actors' group which Laughton had had some years previously, in which they discussed plays and then performed them. Perhaps a group of boys and girls on the stage could be discussing this thing and then gradually tending toward a performance. But alas, Charles got sick and died before this scheme had gone very far.

Interviewer: Let's talk a little about how you go about working. You know, these interviews make a great fetish of the kind of pencil you use and whether you wear shoes while you're writing fiction. Do you have any particular discipline?

Isherwood: Well, the chief discipline I have is the plunge into the work. If I get an idea of any kind for writing, I try to sit down at the typewriter—I always write on the typewriter—and just make a stab at it, almost with the freedom of free association on an analyst's couch, just saying: it doesn't matter what this is but just pour it out. And I find this very, very helpful. I can hardly proceed with anything until I have got something to correct, something to mold, and therefore there has to be a rough draft.

Interviewer: Does it come of itself? Henry Miller, for instance, speaks of "the dictation," and you can see in his work where he sat down to write and where he got up again.

Isherwood: Oh, well, I get up, yes, and wander about, and make phone calls, and look into books.

Interviewer: What I mean is, do you have a sense that the writing is doing itself?

Isherwood: I think everybody has a great sense that they are contacting some other part of their mind or psychological self when they are writing. There's no question about that. Now, for instance, I often feel in a sort of Platonic way that somewhere down there is the perfect book, or at any rate the perfect book according to my capacity, and the trouble is to fish it out. That I have always felt. And I feel a sort of disturbance, a sort of itch, to write about something, and then I ask this other part of myself, "Well, why do you want to write about it? Tell me, tell me what's so interesting?" For instance, some years ago—and this didn't directly come to anything—I got a tremendous feeling about the nature of a border, a frontier between two countries, in this case specifically the Mexican-American border at Nogales. I started to write around this the idea of a trip into Mexico and what it would mean. I wrote a whole novel, which was called *Down There on a Visit*. Most of this has completely disappeared. No, it hasn't disappeared, I've got it, but I didn't use it then. I kept the title, of course, and used it for a book which is quite different.

Interviewer: Do you have many such unfinished novels in your files?
Isherwood: No, nothing really of any value.

Interviewer: What I mean is, do you often make false starts of this sort?
Isherwood: Oh, yes, but I find that it's amazing how much you can use

them. Most of them have been used up. A great deal of back material was used in the second version of *Down There on a Visit,* the published version. There was a diary, for instance, I had about that Greek island which is described in the section called "Ambrose." There was a good deal of material written about the boy who is called Waldemar and his affair with the English girl. At one time I planned an entire novel about this. And then again I had material about the first episode, about Mr. Lancaster, as he is called.

Interviewer: Which dates back very far too?

Isherwood: Very far, yes.

Interviewer: I get the impression that you never throw anything away and that sooner or later you find a use for a great deal of material that you wrote a long time ago.

Isherwood: Well, there is use, you see, no question about it. Quite early in one's life one has accumulated enough material. The only thing is, will your interests change, will you perhaps not want this material any more?

Interviewer: I was interested in reading *Down There on a Visit* to see how you were able to fetch up material from a great span of time and bring it together—which leads me to ask, do you keep diaries, do you use actual diaries and letters in your novels?

Isherwood: I keep diaries rather irregularly, but I do have quite a considerable lot of diaries. I haven't got anything earlier now than 1939 because the earlier stuff, after being absorbed into various books, has disappeared, except for some very brief notes. But when I came to the United States I started to keep a diary and later I rewrote and added to it, and I have a big, big manuscript, especially good from 1939 to the end of 1944, then rather patchy, but then gathering up again. I have been bad the last few months, but I have a great deal of stuff in it. Now most of this is not the conventional day-to-day material of a diary, nor is it terribly indiscreet in any way. It's more impressions which can be easily generalized and can in fact be used under other circumstances.

Interviewer: You used such materials in *Down There on a Visit,* didn't you?

Isherwood: Oh, very much. Yes. There is a great deal in that.

Interviewer: That diary about the Munich crisis must have been written at the time.

Isherwood: That's right. That is an absolutely authentic diary—I mean the basis of it is. On the other hand, you'd be astounded at how much of this is invented. If I can only have one little fact, then I start inventing.

Interviewer: That Munich Diary is marvelous in its immediacy. You give a very vivid sense of that moment in history.

Isherwood: Well, actually, I was putting into it many other times of great anxiety, many of the post-war crises and things that other people have said to me they felt about such crises.

Interviewer: I was much struck there too by the comments that you record in the diary, comments made by E. M. Is that E. M. Forster?

Isherwood: Yes. Perhaps it was rather silly not to say E. M. Forster, but some people dislike this kind of name-dropping. And yet it's very hard, when you are dealing with this curious method of narration which is partly historical and true and partly invented, to know how to do that.

Interviewer: Forster is a writer who has meant a great deal to you, I gather.

Isherwood: Tremendous great deal. The most, I think. I don't think any other writer has really inspired me in the way that Forster has. There is something about his approach, the lightness and yet the seriousness, and the possibility of handling all kinds of material in the way that he does. Nobody has made quite that impression. And of course he is a man of deep concerns and very strong emotional involvement with the happenings of our time, a man who is capable of great indignation and of really doing something about it, participating in this way or that in causes that he feels important.

Interviewer: I remember the comment that you have Chalmers making in *Lions and Shadows* where he has discovered Forster's use of the comic scene to relate horror.

Isherwood: Yes, that's quite true. Gerald Heard produced a very useful term, "metacomedy," the concept that there is a kind of comedy which is beyond both comedy and tragedy.

Interviewer: Yes, but is this Forster's comedy?

Isherwood: Well, I think that Forster has everything; he sometimes goes beyond comedy and tragedy. Of course, it's easier to see in certain plays of Shakespeare, particularly in *Lear*. It's quite easy to see in Dostoevsky, and then it's actually verbalized in the lines by Wilfred Owen: "Merry it was to laugh there when death became absurd and life absurder." One senses it too, I think, in the end of *Moby Dick* when the whale sinks the ship and you feel nothing except a tremendous exhilaration because everybody gets drowned. You feel that Melville is filling the scene with a kind of metacomedy. Don't you feel that?

Interviewer: Well, I have never thought of it quite that way. But to go back just a little to Forster, have you kept in touch with him since 1938?

Isherwood: Oh yes, I see him quite a bit every time I go back to England. He doesn't write many letters now, but I write to him on his birthday and this kind of thing. I saw him in 1961, the last time I was there, and he was visibly older but amazingly himself in every respect. His mind seemed completely unimpaired and he talked a great deal. I don't know whether he's writing. I haven't heard of that for some time now.

Interviewer: Do you have any theories on why he stopped writing after *A Passage to India?* Has he ever talked about that?

Isherwood: No. I very much doubt if one could talk about a thing like that. I don't think one would know. It's not the sort of thing I would know about myself. It's like when people ask me questions like, "Why did you come to California?" You can give superficial explanations, but if people go on about it, you just have to say that that's something which is done with another part of one's consciousness. Then again, it's perfectly true that he didn't write any more novels, but he has written a lot since then. He was by no means dried up, and he put a great deal of the passion and feeling that there is in his novels into essays and other things that he wrote, particularly that great essay "What I Believe." That's certainly one of his masterpieces, and one of the things that he'll be most remembered by.

Interviewer: I was going to ask you why you came to America, as a matter of fact. Would you rather skip that one?

Isherwood: Well, I was a great wanderer, you know. Actually I had spent very little of my adult life in England. I quite soon went to live in Germany. Then when the Nazis came, I began wandering about Europe. I kept coming back to London all the time, but I never really lived there. What amazes me more is why we all didn't have far more curiosity about America much earlier in our lives, because it is for English-speaking people so very much the other half of the coin. And really, what do you know until you have seen America? I was tremendously excited by my first glimpse of New York. And I still remember as the greatest possible aesthetic experiences seeing Yosemite for the first time and Monument Valley. These are moments when you simply burst into tears. When I first came out here, this place was absolutely enchanting. It was much sleepier and there was much more sense of the wilderness and sense of the spirit of place, of the mountains, and I loved that. I think all my life I have had a tremendous yen for the far west.

Interviewer: When did you first decide to settle in southern California?

Isherwood: I arrived out here about May, 1939, but I was first in New York for some time. I had been in the country the year before; that's when I really decided to settle in the States.

Interviewer: This was on your way back from China?

Isherwood: That's right—with Auden. We stayed in New York for a while.

Interviewer: Did you feel that transplanting to America had any effect on your writing? You use a great deal of dialogue in your fiction, for instance. Did you feel a change in accent?

Isherwood: Oh, very much so. But there is no problem as far as one is concerned personally, because whatever you are, you are. I simply became slightly more of a hybrid than ever before. I have always challenged the idea that writers have to have roots in the conventional sense. You have roots, of course, but they don't need the geographical context necessarily. I think that being a foreigner is very stimulating for a writer. Then too, it has to be observed that I am now sixty, that when I reach the age of seventy, if I do, I shall have lived half of my life in the United States; so that I am by no means a newcomer. California is preeminently a place that you don't have to belong to, in the sense of having been here since birth. If I had settled down in Maine that might be another matter, but here I feel very much at home and quite as much that I have a right to the place as anybody else I meet on the street.

Interviewer: Still, you haven't dealt with the American setting nearly so much as you did with Berlin, for example.

Isherwood: No. Well, I am just slowly starting to now.

Interviewer: Did you first meet Aldous Huxley out here?

Isherwood: Yes, I met him when I first came out here, in 1939. I had never known him in England.

Interviewer: Would you talk a little about your association with Huxley.

Isherwood: Huxley was a person who was at once seemingly remote and yet extremely loveable and even in his own way quite gregarious. It's a paradox about that man that he had such an enormously wide range of interests that there was nobody he couldn't talk to. You'd find him, after seeming so distant and shy, deep in conversation with the most unlikely people about their professions and problems and being very knowledgeable about them and, what is more, really anxious to learn more from these people and really succeeding in learning more and constantly adding to his stock of knowledge. He had the most tremendous kind of overall acquaintance with the doings and problems of mankind and the whole contemporary situation. It's particularly irritating to hear people talk about him as though he lived far off in a tower. My God, who wanted to go to Sacramento to save Chessman's life? Who spoke out about some of the strikes we've had down here? He was involved in all kinds of things, and you find that he actually did something about them. He was marvelous in that way. He was so concerned. He was tremendously concerned toward the end of his life about the menace of the population explosion, and he took the trouble to inform himself. He had all the facts and the figures, and he overwhelmed people who tried to put forward some kind of outmoded, prejudiced attitude, because he knew what he was talking about.

Interviewer: Yes, and he always had so much refreshing common sense about all these things.

Isherwood: He was a most wonderfully common-sensical man. He was very much against what he used to call the *Tiefe,* the deepness of mind of the German intellectual. And I recall—I put this down in my little article about him the other day—that one day toward the end of his life he came back from some college where they had all been discussing D. H. Lawrence, who as you know was a very close friend of Huxley's—I think largely because they were such polar opposites—and he said, "You know, I didn't understand one word they said from start to finish." And then he said a marvelous thing. He said, "You know, the trouble is that everything nowadays has to be regarded as a science, and so the professors of literature feel that they ought to have a technical jargon which nobody can understand." Well, of course it is terribly hard to write an English sentence and amazingly easy to create misunderstandings. I, being the sort of person I am, naturally tend, as I suppose we all do to some extent, to support my weaknesses with aggression. And so, since I can't understand the great mass of writing about ideas, I always say: "Well, that just means they can't write, it's all double talk, it's woolly, it's so vague, I can't read philosophy." And then I get very aggressive and talk about obscurantism. And my great ally in this was Huxley, oddly enough, because

Huxley, that most intellectual of creatures, never wrote a line in his life I can't understand. He had the most astounding clarity and could discuss the most abstruse subjects.

Interviewer: Was it Huxley who first got you interested in Vedanta?

Isherwood: Gerald Heard and Aldous Huxley were both very interested. They had heard about this Hindu monk, Swami Prabhavananda, who is the representative of a very large order of monks in India, an order which has had centers in this country for many years. There has been a center in San Francisco since just before the earthquake and centers in New York even before that, and Prabhavananda had come down here to open a center in Los Angeles about the end of the 1920s. I am not sure whether it was Huxley or Heard who first met him. They both took a great liking to him and conceived a great respect for him, and in due course introduced me to him quite shortly after I arrived. Then I got more and more interested in what Prabhavananda had to teach. But in a way far more than his teaching I was, as one would say nowadays, "existentially" interested in the fact that this man, who was obviously completely sane, very intelligent, and not in the least bit a crook, believed in the reality of mystical experience. By mystical experience I mean simply the possibility of contacting something other than one's self through a process of self-knowledge, through meditation or prayer, which of course is common to all religions. But I'd never met anybody who so completely convinced me that he believed in this possibility, that he had known people who had gone very far along that path, and that he himself had progressed quite a distance along it. This was what fascinated me about Prabhavananda, and we've remained close friends ever since. I see him constantly.

Interviewer: Are you still a Vedantist?

Isherwood: Very much so.

Interviewer: Has this had any effect on your writing of fiction? Don't you have a novelist in one of your books, Elizabeth Rydal, make remarks suggesting that mysticism and characters don't mix very well?

Isherwood: Well, of course *sub specie aeternitatis* that's obviously true, and the whole preoccupation with the individual ego and its manifestations is obviously in one sense a waste of time. But then again, what you always have to remember about the Hindu concept of life is this very important thing which they call *dharma,* which is your individual duty based upon your talents, capacities, and potentialities as of that particular moment. And there's such a thing as having the *dharma* of being an artist, just as there is the *dharma* of being the president of the United States, and in the context of this *dharma,* it's your duty and indeed the only way toward spiritual development to do your very best along those particular lines. This again of course is not at all exclusively a Hindu idea. It comes in the parable of the talents of Jesus of Nazareth, and it's something that is quite commonly recognized. By the way, I completely neglected to mention a biography of Ramakrishna I've just finished, a kind of popular life, which is coming out either next month or the month after in England, and in the States, I guess, quite soon afterwards. It's called *Ramakrishna and His Disciples.*

Interviewer: How did your translations with Swami Prabhavananda work out? You don't know Sanskrit, do you?

Isherwood: Oh, no, not at all. Prabhavananda is a very good Sanskrit scholar. As a Bengali it doesn't come too difficult for him to know Sanskrit because Sanskrit has to Bengali about the same relation as classical Greek has to modern Greek. And of course he has an excellent command of English. So we would simply discuss the whole thing, and then I would produce my version, and then it would be further discussed. Indeed our translations were also submitted to Sanskrit scholars in India.

Interviewer: This leads me to ask about your other collaborations—those with Auden in the thirties. I am very curious to know how you wrote those plays together.

Isherwood: Auden was once asked by a journalist, "How do you and Mr. Isherwood collaborate?" And he said, "With the utmost politeness." But really it wasn't like that at all. Auden had already written some verse plays before we collaborated. He wrote a very short play called *Paid on Both Sides,* which comes in his first book of poems. Then he wrote a play called *The Dance of Death* for a theatrical group headed by Rupert Doone, who was later our director; I think we may have even discussed a little how he should do this, but we certainly didn't collaborate. We sort of eased into collaboration. You see we were very intimate friends all this time. We saw a great deal of each other. We first met when we were seven and nine respectively.

Interviewer: I knew you had been in school together. I didn't realize it was that early.

Isherwood: It was early, yes. Then we met in our teens, and by that time Auden was a writer and so we had more in common.

Interviewer: And then you were in Berlin together.

Isherwood: We were in Berlin together. In fact, I wouldn't have gone to Berlin if he hadn't gone there. That was the whole reason for going there, and then once I got there it appealed to me and I stayed on. He went back to England and started in as a schoolmaster.

Interviewer: Where were you together then in the latter thirties?

Isherwood: He would come out and visit with me wherever I was. For instance, we did the final collaboration on *The Dog beneath the Skin* in Copenhagen. We wrote *The Ascent of F6* mostly in Cintra, outside Lisbon. As for *On the Frontier,* that was written all over the place, partly on a very slow old boat called *The Empress of Asia* coming back from China between Japan and Vancouver. We worked wherever we were together. The whole collaboration really amounted to this: here was Auden, who was obviously already a major poet, and all I felt I was doing was perhaps providing a slightly firmer framework on which these poems could be presented. I don't mean that Auden was incapable of dramaturgy because as a matter of fact he did a great many of the scenes. But my real function was very much that of a librettist, and he was the composer.

Interviewer: You made a comment in the thirties that if Auden had had his way he would have written something that was a cross between grand opera and high mass.

Isherwood: Yes, he loved these aspects of the theater, and he is a great opera fan himself.

Interviewer: There are a couple of ideas in the plays that seem to me particularly Audenesque, but they turn up in your work too. I wonder whether you shared them or whether they were Auden's or what. I am thinking of the Freudian interpretation of politics, which is fairly prominent, and then the idea of "the Test," and mountain climbing generally. This is an Auden metaphor, isn't it?

Isherwood: No. I would say that the idea of "the Test" is really more me and the Freudian interpretation of politics is more Auden. But it's very, very hard to say because, you see, quite aside from the difference in degree of talent, we were and still are profoundly different types of people. Auden has a tremendously strong intellectual grasp of everything, and I am much more a kind of intuitive person, a person who can throw off remarks, reactions, metaphors, little *aperçus* of this or that. But Auden really sees what it's all about, or anyway invents an explanation of what it's all about.

Interviewer: Yes, he's a great theorizer, isn't he?

Isherwood: Tremendous theorizer, a monumental theorizer. And this kind of theorizing is really a form of poetry in itself. He'll make with complete aplomb some remark like, "Of course *Coriolanus* is entirely about fishing." And you will say, "Fishing? Fishing?" But nevertheless somehow or other he proves it, you know.

Interviewer: After having thought of it.

Isherwood: Yes, sometimes, I think, after having thought of it. And the excitement of this kind of intellect is its poetic truth. He has this marvelous quality of flashing off these things and of grasping the whole structure. What he reads is amazing, his capacity for reading. I used to say, "But you're just skimming," but he always seemed to know what the book was about afterwards.

Interviewer: How about your collaboration on *Journey to a War*? Did I read somewhere that you wrote the prose and he wrote the verse?

Isherwood: Yes, but it wasn't quite as simple as that because we did in fact take turns keeping the diary—I've got it here in the house, by the way. One day Auden would do it, the next day I would do it. But it had to be done with an overall style. So I just took the entire diary and wrote the prose narrative. And when I prepared the text I tried to credit Auden with any bright remarks which he had made during his day.

Interviewer: That must have been an exciting journey.

Isherwood: Oh, it was a lot of fun. Really it was one of the most enjoyable periods of my life in many ways. It was so funny to be with a real, genuine explorer like Peter Fleming, because we couldn't help thinking of ourselves as somewhat absurd, especially since Auden through hell and high water wore carpet slippers because of his corns.

Interviewer: You managed to see everybody in China, it seems, and saw a good deal of the war too.

Isherwood: We really got around. There was a good deal of beginner's luck in that. I have never forgotten a fiendish young journalist, I think he was Belgian, who was always trying to arrange for us to go into action in a Chinese plane. I can remember quite well the roaring in my ears and the sick smile with which I greeted the news that he'd finally arranged it. At the very last moment something or other stopped it, thank God.

Interviewer: The plane crashed?

Isherwood: They almost always crashed. Yes, they were very unlucky pilots.

Interviewer: Is it because you were poets that you were welcomed everywhere by all manner of people?

Isherwood: Well, yes, and also, you see, it was very different from the Spanish Civil War. Almost nobody else had come out there just to see them and wish them well. And it created a lot of goodwill.

Interviewer: Yes, you were emissaries.

Isherwood: Well, they chose to think of us as such.

Interviewer: I would like to ask you a little bit about your work with the movies. I know you've done a good deal of script writing in the past. Are you doing anything now?

Isherwood: I have been working very recently in films, and I had an exceedingly happy experience just this very last year, 1964. Tony Richardson, the director of *Tom Jones* and some other extremely interesting films, asked me if I would work on his film *The Loved One,* and I did a certain amount of work on this, mostly of a structural nature, which is something that I have a certain talent for. But the person who was really working on the film was the author of *Candy,* Terry Southern. We worked a little bit together and got along very well. Tony wanted me to do another film, so I left that and Terry finished the screenplay of *The Loved One.* Then I worked on an adaptation of Carson McCullers's *Reflections in a Golden Eye.* This was in a way the most enjoyable film work I have ever done because the book was so marvelously right for the medium. It's simply astonishing when you examine this book how visualized it is and therefore it's absolutely unnecessary to indulge in a whole lot of psychological explanations. The people just do the things because they do the things, and that's that. The whole thing went into a screenplay with almost no changes whatsoever, just a little elaboration here and there. And I hope that can be made—the trouble as always is the question of casting. Tony liked that very much and then asked me to work on another screenplay based on a novel by Marguerite Duras, the woman who wrote *Hiroshima Mon Amour.* This was a very curious story called *The Sailor from Gibraltar,* rather like a non-tragic version of *The Flying Dutchman.* There's this beautiful woman who travels around in a yacht looking for someone who may or may not exist. And that one too I finished, just the other day. And now I am hastily doing this *Exhumations* book before I start work at UCLA.

Interviewer: What will you be doing at UCLA?

Isherwood: A Regents' Professor. I am going to be on campus there for the spring semester.

Interviewer: Regularly lecturing?

Isherwood: Well, no, there's nothing regular about it except I just keep office hours twice a week, and then if any of the students have manuscripts I read them. But I'm not going to make the mistake of having a creative writing seminar where the students' work is read aloud because when I did that I found that the other students tore them to pieces. It was so cruel. So what I do is I read the things then take the authors alone somewhere for a long walk around the campus, or in the office, or wherever, and we discuss it in complete privacy.

Interviewer: You have done quite a lot of lecturing, haven't you?

Isherwood: Yes, I have done a great deal of lecturing at one time or another, so I am quite accustomed to it. And I will give a lecture while I am on campus, but more just to get acquainted, to show myself there, than anything else. Then I'm supposed to give a series of talks about writing, one a week, but that entirely depends on the cooperation of the audience. If we can't create a group and have fun, then we will just stop.

Interviewer: Do you like teaching?

Interviewer: Oh, yes, very much. I find that it's a tremendous way of recharging oneself as a writer, and also I find that it's a lot easier to do it if you are in fact writing something at the time yourself.

Interviewer: Oh really, how is that? This is a comment very few writers would make.

Isherwood: Well, I feel that I have more to communciate somehow or other. Instead of speaking always of the past, I feel I am speaking of something that is going on right now. I have as a matter of fact got an idea for a novel, which I'll start tinkering with.

Interviewer: Would you mind talking about it?

Isherwood: Well, that's a little difficult, but it's somewhat related to my experiences last Christmas. I went with Swami Prabhavananda to India for a centenary of the birth of Vivekananda, and we all made speeches in a great hall to thousands of people. I don't know how many of them understood everything that was said, but nevertheless this was gone through. But what was very nice about the experience was staying in the chief monastery of the order, the Belur Math, which is outside Calcutta on the Ganges. And two of my friends, two members of this group, actually took the final vows while I was there and became swamis. This gave me an idea for a novel, but it is very vague at present. I find that the best thing is to start off with just absolutely free improvising, just saying, well somebody has got to go someplace, so let's have him go someplace, and then we'll see what happens, we'll see who's there.

Interviewer: Is his name Christopher Isherwood?

Isherwood: No, I doubt very much if I shall use that thing again. This fictional Christopher Isherwood got absolutely too big for his britches and became rather unmanageable, I thought. That's why I changed to this other technique in writing *A Single Man.* When I first sat down and began to think about *A Single Man,* I was really concerned with the character of the English-woman, and I was going to write a book called "An English Woman." I had the idea of this woman who had married a GI and came to this country. I had it all quite considerably worked out, her relations with her husband and with her son, who is of course purely American, and what happened and so forth. And Christopher Isherwood was going to enter the story quite indirectly as someone who is teaching at the college and meets the son; the son says to him, "You know, my mother is British too—you ought to meet her." And so Christopher Isherwood meets the mother and then learns about her problems and the marriage going on the rocks and the difficulty with the son. I was going to approach it entirely from that point of view.

Interviewer: Why didn't you?

Isherwood: When I came to start to do this, somehow nothing worked. Christopher Isherwood was wrongly placed. I couldn't get at the material from his point of view. You know, it's rather as though you were trying to fix something in a room. Something is wrong with the chandelier. The question of how the story should be told is like first of all deciding to stand on the table and then on the stepladder and then saying, well, I can really get at it better from a stool underneath. In a way, you mustn't be too near it, and then you mustn't be too far away from it. And everything depends on that.

Interviewer: Still, you found Christopher Isherwood a very handy character in most of your novels.

Isherwood: Well, you see, when I started off with him, I thought, well now, he'll just sit in the corner and keep his mouth shut and listen to all these people. That worked, more or less, in a way, for a while. He kept fairly quiet. But then this seemed unnatural. One asked, "Why was he keeping so quiet?" Now I'll tell you where Christopher Isherwood really worked best, in my opinion, is in my little *Prater Violet* because there he was up against a real talker, a tremendous dynamic behaver and talker, and a person whom at the same time, although he regarded him with humor, he could regard with great affection and genuine admiration.

Interviewer: Friedrich Bergmann was based on a real person, wasn't he?

Isherwood: Yes, it's no secret really now. He was based on a poet and film director named Berthold Viertel, and Berthold had come out here with his wife Salka before Hitler came into power. He was a Viennese Jew and she was a Polish Jew, but she'd gone to Berlin and had mastered German so perfectly that she was able to play very big, important roles in Ibsen and in classical drama in Berlin. Salka was a great friend of Garbo, she used to coach Garbo, and Garbo felt very much at ease with her because they talked German together and Salka had been a distinguished actress. Anyhow they came out to this very valley and to a house that you can see out of this window, and settled there, and Berthold directed some films. Then he was asked to go to England and direct three films for Gaumont-British and that's how I met him. There were three sons. One of them is Peter Viertel, the novelist. Peter married Deborah Kerr, the actress, and now they live in Klosters, Switzerland, and Salka lives near them. I have always kept in touch with them. It's been a great friendship.

Interviewer: I derailed you while you were talking about Christopher Isherwood in *Prater Violet*.

Isherwood: What I was going to say there was simply that because Bergmann is such a dominating character it doesn't matter that the observer is kept down, is not allowed to emerge. I think a great and amusing feature of the book is that right at the very end you discover that Christopher had a life of his own which he never even mentioned to Bergmann, which is the ideal relation between somebody like that and an observer figure. So I thought it worked there. I think this is the only time that it worked satisfactorily.

Interviewer: I thought it worked very well in *The Berlin Stories*. But Christopher Isherwood seemed to get rather out of hand in *Down There on a Visit,* particularly as the novel moved along.

Isherwood: Very much so, yes. That's where I saw it had to stop.

Interviewer: How much do autobiographical fact do you put in your fiction?

Isherwood: That's a terribly hard question to answer, without answering it scene by scene. It's not like a cookbook. I don't say I should have so much of that and so much of this. You see, I am always concerned with telling the reader feelings and emotions, how it felt to be there, how it felt to meet such-and-such a kind of person, what the physical existence of meeting them was like, the kind of effect they had on you. Now I am supremely indifferent how much of this is invented because my truth is the experience. On the other hand, it follows that I am not going to tell you about something I have never done in my life; for instance, I shall never write a book in which I'm taking part in an attack on a Pacific atoll during World War II. But I do try to convey, if it doesn't sound too pompous, the inwardness of experience. That's what the books are really about, and the experience of meeting certain kinds of people, the experience of the encounter, that's very important to me. And so, you cut corners, you invent, you simplify, you heighten certain lights and deepen certain shadows, as you might in a portrait. This may mean a very great divergence from the truth. I just don't worry about that. I naturally worry about the question of the book causing offense or pain, but by and large they never seem to have. I remember the only thing that my old landlady in Berlin objected to. She never in all those years had known that she'd been written about, and suddenly after the war she discovers that this goddam play is being performed, and then she read a German translation of the novel itself. The only thing she objected to was the one line which said that when she walked, she waddled. She objected strongly to the word "waddle." As a matter of fact, she didn't waddle, but somehow or other waddling conveyed her more. She wasn't nearly as fat as she's made out, but I felt that, by making her fat, her personality would become more vivid. So what are you to do?

Interviewer: How are the books received in Germany, by the way?

Isherwood: Oh, quite well. *Goodbye to Berlin* particularly was regarded with great interest. Germans have said to me very often, "You see, to us it's a kind of historical novel, it's so fascinating to go back to that period." I think it's all quite historically correct. I took great trouble, indeed I always do, with the historical aspects, the setting and the details. I like to get all that right.

Interviewer: To turn the question around, how fictional is *Lions and Shadows*?

Isherwood: Really very little. The only changes there are drastic simplifications. For instance, I left my family out completely because there didn't seem to be any particular reason for bringing all that up. No, I would say that's pretty much autobiographical. It's just that one or two people, I can't even remember who they were, objected to being named by their real names, so I finally changed all the names.

Interviewer: That's what creates the impression that it's like a *roman à clef*. And you say in a preface that it should be read like a novel; indeed *New Directions* once listed it with your fiction. That's what gives rise to this question.

Isherwood: Well, probably that was an unfortunate thing to say, but I suppose I was trying to cover up a bit in case people would think it was indiscreet in some way. But it's pretty much all true, as far as I know.

Interviewer: Then the real question in my mind is, what led you to write your autobiography at such an early age?

Isherwood: Well, it seemed like very much the end of an epoch in my life, the move to Berlin. And I wanted to get all this material down while I still remembered it. I suppose what I wanted to write about chiefly was my relations with Edward Upward and with Auden, the imaginary life in Cambridge, Mortmere and all that. I thought that I had better write this down or it would all be gone. Even now I deeply regret that I didn't write a great deal more about Auden's work. There was a time when I could have gone through all of his early poems and told you the genesis of almost every line, with endless reminiscences. I really knew and believed that Auden was a great writer, and I used to say to myself I ought to write this down.

Interviewer: To return to your latest work, what do you think of the reviews of *A Single Man*? Some of them have been quite fierce.

Isherwood: I must say with reference to some of the reviews in this country that I, rightly or wrongly, attribute a very deep-lying psychological motive to them. I think that the whole civil rights situation has exasperated a great many people who have been forced to behave more liberally than they're quite up to. It's now, except in the Deep South, virtually impossible to attack the Negroes or the Jews in public. And I do think that all of these other little minorities are really catching it. I'll be sufficiently Christian not to name names, but there was one review that seemed to me nothing but a kind of racist attack in which the homosexuals were a surrogate for this man's aggression, not only against them but against the whole tiresomeness of having to be nice to the others. There was a kind of hysteria there and a real fury which is simply not warranted by any piece of fiction. But the book has had very good reviews too, especially in England. I was particularly pleased that Walter Allen, whom I respect very much, wrote a very, very good notice. And then among my friends, Auden, who's extraordinarily difficult to please, thinks it's my best book. Quite a number of English reviewers thought so.

Interviewer: Didn't you feel that the American critics had very often missed the point of the novel? To treat this as a homosexual novel is to overlook a much bigger subject.

Isherwood: Well, yes, of course. In the first place, it's not about homosexuality. In fact, I have never in my life written specifically about homosexuality—not what I would call writing about homosexuality. What I have done in this particular novel is to write, among many other things, about minorities. And the homosexuals are used as a sort of metaphor for minorities in general. I could criticize the book quite searchingly in one respect: that the George character is a very uneasy amalgam of somebody else and of me, and doesn't hold together. What you have is a most unfortunate guy laboring under all kinds of disadvantages. I feel that if I were really George, I would kill myself. Poor devil, what has he got? Nothing! And for me, sitting here in all the snugness of my life, it's terrible to be told that I am George!

Isherwood on Hollywood
Charles Higham / 1968

From *London Magazine* New Series 8 (April 1968): 31–38. Reprinted by permission.

Christopher Isherwood has lived in California for almost thirty years, and has written five novels there: *Prater Violet, The World in the Evening, Down There on a Visit, A Single Man* and *A Meeting by the River.* His house is romantically situated above the plunging slopes of Santa Monica Canyon: red rooves nestling in green valleys, and beyond the bristle of television aerials the broad, beating surf of the Pacific. The house has a cool, California-Spanish flavour; white painted walls, informal bright carpets, a huge coffee table, framed European posters, mirrors and the kind of civilized clutter a man picks up over half a lifetime. Isherwood himself is small, neat, quick; his face is deeply bronzed by the Californian sun, and his eyes have the nervous brilliance of a bird's, blue and flickering, never still under the surprised tufts of eyebrow. He wears a white shirt, open at the neck, black slacks and slippers on this golden Californian summer afternoon.

His career in Hollywood has been felt by some to have damaged the quality of his fiction, but it is hard to find evidence of a decline in books like *Down There on a Visit* and *A Single Man.* He insists that the cinema has in fact sharpened the visual quality of his work, giving it a precision of outline it might otherwise not have had. As he talked about his films, from *Little Friend* in Britain in the thirties to *The Sailor from Gibraltar* in detail in an interview for the first time, one thing emerged very strongly: his passion for the cinema, and his confidence in its permanent value as a form of art.

Q: What was your first work in the cinema?

A: In 1933, I met the poet and film director Berthold Viertel in London. He was about to make some pictures for Gaumont-British and he asked me to work with him after we had been introduced by a mutual friend. Viertel had previously had working for him Margaret Kennedy, the author of *The Constant Nymph,* but she had become so involved with her dramatic version of *Escape Me Never* for Elisabeth Bergner, that she had to discontinue for the time being. Instead, I took over, and prepared the script of *Little Friend* to star Nova Pilbeam, who was at the time twelve years old.

It is a film not remembered today, but the experience of working with

Viertel at Gaumont-British was of inestimable value when I was writing *Prater Violet,* which is set in "Imperial Bulldog" studios. Fortunately, the writer Lesser Samuels—whom I have worked with since—was present there as well as in Hollywood, and he remembered the technical slang, the peculiarities of the studio equipment and so forth; because of this I was able to give a completely authentic account of that period. I met Robert Flaherty then, and again later in California at the Huxleys. I always remember him saying, "The film is the greatest possible distance between two points."

Q: And then what brought you to California, and to Hollywood?

A: I really made up my mind to come to America a good deal earlier than 1939, the year in which I actually settled here. In 1938, Auden and I went to the Far East, because we'd been offered some money to write a travel book, and we thought we'd go and see what was happening in the Japanese invasion of China. We produced *Journey to a War* as a result, and came back by way of Canada and the States. And we made up our minds then that we would come over and live here. But that was delayed by the Munich crisis, and we didn't in fact leave for the States again until January 1939. I came to California because I wanted to meet Aldoux Huxley who had moved here several years previously, and Gerald Heard, whom I already knew. I had always been very anxious to see the West, and I was simply stunned by the classic West. The first time I went to Yosemite and to the Sequoia forests, and to the desert, I was completely bowled over. Admittedly, the first night I arrived in Los Angeles was rather squalid, the hotel at the end of the bus journey was very bad, but that was only a momentary let-down, because Los Angeles in those days was enchanting. It wasn't very big, and there were marvellous orange groves everywhere, and the hills were almost untouched. I soon met Huxley, and Heard, and the Viertels, Berthold and his wife Salka, who later ran a great salon at which the Hollywood European figures gathered.

Q: How did Huxley adapt to life in California?

A: Huxley adapted very easily. He loved California as a physical place, the actual terrain. He adored the desert and he was a great naturalist, deeply interested in wild flowers and wild animals. He wrote some wonderful essays in *Tomorrow and Tomorrow* about that world. He had a faculty of interest in almost anything; perhaps he was supremely intelligent, and interest and intelligence are really synonymous. There was nothing that anybody could tell him that didn't interest him, and nothing which he couldn't relate to the whole structure of his knowledge, and add a brick to the wall. Of course, one's so apt to talk of this in a place of exile, just because some of the people in the movie industry were not the greatest intellects, but in fact the kind of people that Huxley and Heard knew here were every bit as extraordinary and interesting as anybody in Europe. There were some amazing scientists and people living here. For instance, Huxley was very friendly with Hubble, the astronomer, and he and Heard were constantly visiting universities and informing themselves about the latest breakthroughs in scientific fields. I don't think they felt at all deprived in California.

Q: How do you feel in a general sense about the relationship between the writer and Hollywood?

A: The person who matters in a film—whether it's in Hollywood, in Paris, Underground or what—is the director. If the director isn't a writer, there has to be a writer. The writer and the director should work in the closest possible collaboration. And in the last resort it should be the director who decides what he's going to use and what he's not going to use but these two should be together from the very first day. What was wrong with the old commercial setup was that you never saw the director at first, you saw the producer. And the producer and the director are not the same person. And however imaginative and marvellous the producer may be, and indeed I was deeply fond of Gottfried Reinhardt and we're very good friends still, it is not the same as working with a director, because you want to know, when you write something, will he go for that? Is it what he's going to shoot? Because if it isn't you like to invent something else for him. The whole essence of the Hollywood problem then was that in most cases the director came in too late on the picture. What does the director do when he comes in? Either he makes the best of a bad job or he starts tearing the script apart. But if he does that the situation is immediately one of crisis, because the picture's going to be shot in a matter of weeks, and here he is suddenly having the script desperately rewritten while you're shooting.

Q: Do you feel there's any truth in the statement that writers are ruined by Hollywood?

A: It's ridiculous. If you're going to be ruined, you're going to be ruined. Something will come along and ruin you if it can. I think it's very good in the first place for most writers to be forced to visualize: you have to learn to stop relying on the word and thinking in terms of possible silent sequences or sequences where the dialogue plays against the image and so on. And these things are very valuable to you. And you must remember that all my novels, or almost all, have been written post-screenwriting, as it were. Even *Mr. Norris* appeared after I'd worked with Berthold Viertel.

Q: What was your first work in Hollywood?

A: I first worked with Goldwyn on some kind of spy story, and then with Gottfried Reinhardt, who was a good friend of Viertel's, and was a producer at MGM. I wrote some parts of *Rage in Heaven* for him, a melodrama with Robert Montgomery and Ingrid Bergman, based on a novel by James Hilton. And I began to pick up the craft of writing for the screen. After that, I wrote some of *A Woman's Face* for Victor Saville. A Joan Crawford vehicle. I did some bits and pieces of *Crossroads,* a remake of a French movie about amnesia. My contract with MGM expired after a year in May, 1941. For some time I worked with the Quakers, and then I returned to Hollywood. I was with the Quakers at Haverford, near Philadelphia, helping refugees, particularly academic refugees, from Central Europe, and later with Swami Prahvanananda, the Hindu monk.

Q: And your film work after that?

A: In 1942, I started work with Lesser Samuels at Paramount on *The Hour Before Dawn.* What interested me in the film was that it told the story of a pacifist, what made him one and so forth. But they scrapped all our work in it and it came out as a story about a man who overcame pacifism as a temporary weakness. And then in 1945 I began working with Gottfried Reinhardt's brother, Wolfgang, on a version of Maugham's *Up at the Villa.*

The film was never made; a pity, because I think I wrote an amusing script for it. After that came some work on *The Woman in White,* from the novel by Wilkie Collins with John Collier, but unfortunately almost nothing of mine reached the screen. I left Warners, and didn't work again until 1948, when I wrote part of the script of *The Great Sinner* at MGM; that did reach the screen.

It was a version of Dostoevsky's *The Gambler* which put Dostoevsky himself into the story, and showed how he became a gambler himself. That was an idea of Ladislas Fodor, who had been on the script before I came in. You see, they have this unfortunate idea here that two people write a script, and that they will both have ideas and that then you will somehow amalgamate the ideas. Naturally there were divergences in Fodor's views of Dostoevsky and my own, and it made it very difficult for these two views to jell. Of course, the very best things in the film are Dostoevsky's own. The comedy of the grandmother, for instance, arriving from Russia and being amused by this childish, ridiculous vice of gambling, and then the next thing you know she's getting her nephew to show her how to do it, and then you dissolve and she's in the baccarat room and they're saying "The bank is five million." She's up to her ears, and she's gambling away all the family property on which the other members had depended on getting when she died. Marvellous stuff. A very funny thing happened on the film. There was an actor, Frank Morgan, who was supposed to speak with the voice of Christ when Dostoevsky robs the poor box in church. The voice booms down from the Crucifix. Morgan didn't show up, so they asked me to do the dubbing. To make the voice reverberate I had to speak the lines in a little concrete entrance hall leading to the studio. I had a mike and a long, long cable, and I was standing there. And there was a red light which went on. Suddenly the door opened and just as a signal to speak flashed red, a carpenter came in. So there was nothing to be done, I just spoke the line, and I looked him right in the eye, and I said in the loudest voice I could manage, "And they parted my garments among them, and they cast dice for my robe." I've never seen anybody as startled in my life!

Next came *Diane* a version of the story of Diane de Poitiers for Edwin H. Knopf. It should have been done in a high camp style, with a British cast. The lines were not designed to be said by people with south Los Angeles accents. For instance, Diane has to say to the king something like "Sire, God has lent you the greatness of his power. Show his greatness also in your mercy." It takes a professional to talk like that. It isn't much use if it comes out like "AW, Your Majesty, let him go this once."

I wanted Ingrid Bergman instead of Lana Turner as Diane, and Julie Harris as Catherine de Medici. They said, "Bergman is out, absolutely impossible." Six months later she'd come back, and she got an Oscar. Julie Harris said she'd be enchanted to do it, she almost humiliated herself, she came to the studio to have auditions even, but they weren't interested. We had great problems with the diction of both Pedro Armendariz and Marisa Pavan, who played Francis I and Catherine de Medici, although both were visually perfect. We would have been far better off with John Williams in the Pedro Armendariz role. A pity about the casting, because I had absolute freedom in writing the script, and every word of it was mine. The only time I have had this complete freedom. I took things from Dumas and Balzac, the whole field of French historical fiction.

Q: What happened to your project on the life of Buddha?

A: Robert Hardy Andrews wrote a script based on Buddha's life, and somebody from India, I think, managed to interest MGM in doing it. I wrote a new script based partly on him, but with a good deal of invention in it. Finally, nobody's script was made. My version was predicated on a perfectly simple kind of melodramatic problem; will or will not the prophecy be fulfilled, the prophecy that he would become a monk, that he would renounce the throne? We couldn't have anything about the enlightened Buddha, because that's not allowed on the screen in Buddhist countries. It was the story of how the young prince grows up, and if he sees these various people before he becomes king the prophecy will be fulfilled: the dead man, the old man, the sick man, and so on. I had the existing king living in a baroque Gordon Craig type of castle. In the back of this castle was a little door, a sort of *Alice in Wonderland* door, guarded by two tremendous men, one with a sword in his teeth and the other with a sword in each hand. And when you went through this door you came into a marvellous pleasure park, where everything was very Chinese, with little hills, and peacocks, and ivory pagodas, and here the young prince lived with his companions and girl friends.

I took considerable liberties with the Buddhist legend. In order to make the thing work dramatically, I introduced a pretender to the throne, who wanted the prophecy to be fulfilled and the prince to renounce the throne; he, the pretender, could then become king. Great methods were used by them to tempt the prince out of the palace and that created some dramatic situations. We had great difficulties when considering the casting, because the Asians would have objected to a non-Asian playing the part.

Q: What was your next assignment?

A: Nothing again in Hollywood until quite recently, when I worked on *The Loved One,* for Tony Richardson. I wrote the scene in the chapel, when the wedding is turned into a funeral and some single lines elsewhere but the main responsibility was Terry Southern's. I didn't like the novel. The ending isn't at all resolved, and you couldn't shoot it as it's written. The hero is such a boring kind of heel that it's really very distasteful. The book is very snobbish about California, and I didn't like his use of the Aunt Sally of Forest Lawn: it was far too trivial a reason for condemning the whole place. After that I did a picture for Tony I really, really liked the screenplay of. But alas when Tony didn't direct the picture they made a new version. That was *Reflections in a Golden Eye.* We followed the book down to the last syllable, but in such a way that it was totally cinematic. There were long sequences in which nothing was said at all. It's an absolute natural for the screen, in that the less you explain the better. At first you think Carson McCullers's people are out-rageously strange, but when you see them doing whatever it is they do, you understand them perfectly. My next version of a novel was of Marguerite Duras's *The Sailor from Gibraltar.* It hasn't, I hear, worked out very well, but I loved working on it. It was a very Pirandello idea. This woman on a great yacht with all the money in the world is looking for a man she once knew who is a murderer and in hiding under an assumed name. From time to time this woman acquires lovers, and the story is simply that the current man and she travel around looking for the lost murderer, the sailor from Gibraltar. And you gradually come to realize that looking for the sailor from Gibraltar is a way of life for her. And indeed that she can never stop, because otherwise she won't have anything to live for.

Q: What do you like in the contemporary cinema?

A: I admire Godard very much, and Truffaut enormously. I like the infor-mal approach they have; I don't like it when they get too tricky, that irritates me, but I like the way they bang open the door and kind of walk into the story and wander about and see strange, overall seemingly irrelevant things, which nevertheless are really all part of the pattern. But the person I admire tremendously is Antonioni. I was absolutely obsessed by *La Notte.* It seemed to offer a reflection of the way that experience really happens to you. Of course it's a terrible razor's edge you have to walk in this kind of art, because on the one hand you've got something so symbolic it's a bore and on the other hand you have a whole lot of irrelevancies which don't connect. But the wonderings of Jeanne Moreau in the earlier part of *La Notte,* the business with the rocket, and this strange, abrupt, bloodthirsty fight between the boys, which is suddenly over again and she wanders off, all this seemed to me quite extraordinary. And of course that brings me to Virginia Woolf. I was reading just yesterday *Jacob's Room,* and I thought, "My God, if you filmed it just the way it was written, with all these switches in time, it would make a marvellous picture." You see, I love unpredictability, strangeness in films. And that's what I want to see more of in the cinema in the future.

A Fortunate, Happy Life

Derek Hart / 1970

From *The Listener* 12 April 1970. Reprinted by permission.

Q: You've written a very great deal about your life from the time you were a boy onwards, and yet you write very little about your father. Why was that?

A: I didn't know him well at all. He was dead by the time I was ten—he was killed in 1915, at Ypres. Now I'm starting to write about him, because it is only very recently that I've read his letters and had a great added insight into him. To the Establishment—that's to say, the people at my school and so on—he was a hero. Normally, I would have said that anything they admired or liked was vile, and therefore he was not a hero, but I really did like my father very much. He was a marvellous person, so I think that I was working on a kind of anti-hero heroism that I could credit him with—in order to admire him, but admire him in a different way from the way the Establishment admired him.

Q: You've explained that as a young man you felt that you had to prove yourself, because you had been deprived of the opportunity of being in the war. Do you think that in this there were the seeds of your subsequent pacifism?

A: One of my favorite Shakespeare quotations at that period was from a sonnet: "No. I am that I am; and they that level/At my abuses, reckon up their own." I gradually realized that one should not concern oneself with what other people say, or what they tell you is your duty: your duty is what you find out for yourself. Having discovered this, whether I became a pacifist or not was another can of beans altogether. I might have decided to become anything.

Q: You don't feel that there is any conscious or subconscious rejection of the militarism that was embodied in your father?

A: It's very hard to say now, looking back at it, but I don't think I identified him with militarism, because I felt very much that it was his job, and while he was quite a good soldier, he was the least military creature. Even his undoubted herosim was kind of unmilitary. There is a marvellous story about how when the men were first under fire in the trenches, there was a bombardment, and my father, who was a major (he became a colonel before he died), sat down in the bottom of the trench and started knitting a sweater for himself.

Q: Your greatest fame has come through the things that you haven't actually written—from *I Am a Camera* and then *Cabaret,* both based on your *Berlin Stories.* Do you find this maddening, comic?

A: Oh, I don't find it maddening at all. Any ruffled feelings that I might have had have been soothed by checks arriving, like poultices laid on the throbbing wound, the wounded self-conceit. I was really very grateful indeed to John van Druten for writing the play *I Am a Camera.* It was really the doing of Dodie Smith. When she was out here, he came for lunch one day, and they were discussing things that you couldn't possibly turn into plays. Dodie, with a good deal of intention as she afterwards admitted, said "Of course you could never, never make a play out of Chris's Berlin stories," and Johnnie, who was a terrific eager-beaver and loved being set problems, said: "Oh, I don't know." And he went off, and I think it was that evening he phoned her and said: "I've already blocked out the first half of the play."

Q: In 1937 you and W. H. Auden were commissioned to write a travel book together—which was later published as *Journey to a War*—about China at the time of the Sino-Japanese War.

A: We'd promised to go to Spain with a whole bunch of writers and artists and people—the sort of delegation which used to visit the trenches and louse up the war while everybody was allowed to fire a rifle or something—but they put it off and put it off and put it off, and then the American publisher, Random House, said: "We'll give you money to write a travel book together." So we thought how marvellous, we'll go to China where we'll have a war all to ourselves. And there were we, with the whole atmosphere of our very old friendship—we met when we were small boys in school—with our own jokes and our own way of looking at things, travelling along and getting accredited and meeting famous people and finally wangling to go to the front and coming back again and air-raids and this and that. One time we were in a trench in the middle of a field, and a plane was circling around just behind the front line and Auden was busy taking photographs of me looking up at the plane and he said: "You look so wonderful with your great nose cleaving the summer air." We seemed to be in fits of laughter most of the time, and yet what we saw was often appalling and very serious, and these two things were going on simultaneously. There's always a tremendous sense of masquerade in my life, and I see, as it were, a masquerade in my friends' lives. By "masquerade" I don't mean anything false: I just mean that what the world does to them doesn't seem to jive with my picture of them. It was very strange, for instance, to see Auden preaching in Westminster Abbey recently.

I've always felt—and this goes back to my young manhood—that having opinions is a sort of art form, and has its own validity, quite aside from the validity of the opinions themselves, provided that they're cogently and forcefully expressed. For instance, Auden has opinions about the most unlikely things, and the most unlikely opinions. He might say: "Well, of course *Antony and Cleopatra* is entirely about cooking." And you say: "Cooking?" But, by God, somehow or other, he makes a case for it. When it comes to literary criticism, I'm not so drawn to the people who exhibit marvellous justice and perfect equity and good taste. I'd much rather read rampageous and, as many would say, wrong-headed criticism, like, for instance, D. H. Lawrence's *Studies in Classic American Literature,* because it has passion.

Q: But do you not have passionate opinions?

A: Yes, I do, but I don't seem to have this urge to express them in writing. It is, of course, something to do with being a novelist. You begin to see opinions as a kind of function of an individual and this makes you take a rather objective stand towards them.

Q: Do you have proprietary feelings about the screenplays you've written?

A: No, I don't think one could unless one were writer-director with very complete powers over the production. The best director-writer relationship I've been in has been with Tony Richardson and there it was absolutely ideal because he knows exactly what he wants and at the same time isn't at all autocratic. I'm obviously a frustrated actor, but who wants to act in some silly play where someone else wrote the lines? You can act all on your own, as I'm doing now. Of course, I have had a very fortunate, happy life. I almost invariably do what I want to do, or at least what I want to do at that moment.

Q: You have said in the past that you tend to write from the security of your own experience. How close are you to George, the central character in *A Single Man?*

A: It's extremely unwise to identify me too much with George, and I think if you really want to criticise George as a character the trouble is that he is rather badly joined together in places: the parts which are me don't altogether jive with the parts that are George. I see George as a person of enormous stoicism, and his kind of stoicism is quite foreign to my nature. Originally that book was not about George at all. One of my favorite American writers is Willa Cather and this is very much the attraction of opposites. I felt how wonderful it would be to write a tremendously simple, massive book about a character, and I wanted to write about a woman who'd married a GI and come to America from England. It was going to be called "An English Woman" and it was going to be all about this woman. I knew everything about her, and her marrige, and how she'd been attracted at first by the wild- ness of this GI, but as they got older they rather changed roles, and she became a kind of English eccentric and he became very respectable and finally he left her. He left her with an adolescent son, and this son was going to be the link with the narrator. In other words, the narrator is teaching in a college somewhere and meets the son, and the son says, "You're British. You ought to meet my mother," and so he gets to meet her and learns her tragedy. Well, I started to write the book this way, and then suddenly that voice—that sort of impatient voice from inside—said: What are you fussing around with this woman for? Let's get down to the interesting part. So, poor old Charlotte, she's still in the book, but she has only a minor role.

Q: You've written that you are enthralled by the sense of impermanence you get in Los Angeles. What particularly charms you about it?

A: In a way this country is fundamentally desert country. It has been adapted and planted and settled, but there is always a mirage about it. I like that. As a devotee of Hindu philosophy, to me it's very much like the Hindu account of the universe as being a kind of projection, or Maya. And some- times the great, noble, traditional buildings of Europe seem rather too solid in comparison. On the coast it's all rather dreamy and strange. It's very characteristic that when one travels in Los Angeles, there are streets you simply cannot recognise, because they've built other things on them. And since it always consisted of large billboards and signs and neon, more than buildings, you can change the whole place by just changing the lights. There's a sort of theatrical impermanence.

Q: There has been a considerable relaxation of all sorts of things in En- gland now, and the laws relating to homosexuality have, as you know, been changed. Is there now the same tolerant attitude in America?

A: If you take the whole of the United States into account, you'll find everything from the next best thing to making it legal all the way down to kids being sent to prison for ten, fifteen years. There are some absolutely barbaric statutes in some of the States—life imprisonment, and I'm speaking now of consenting adults.

Q: And in California?

A: Everybody says the law will be changed, but that's the maddening thing about human beings: people can all agree that it'll be changed, and then sit down under it for another ten years for no particular reason. Apathy really. The Hindus always say apathy is far worse than violence, because violence can always turn to its opposite, which is love and constructive action, but apathy is a kind of awful swamp in which we wallow until we're pulled out of it.

Q: You've made a great study of Hindu philosophy, haven't you?

A: I would never, never have taken even an interest in it, let alone been able to understand it, if it hadn't been that I met this very remarkable man who is a Hindu monk here, Swami Prabhavananda. That was quite shortly after I arrived and this was one of the major experiences in my life, and I've remained a very close friend of his and a student of his ever since.

Q: You say it was a profound experience meeting him. Can you explain what it meant to you at that time?

A: With anything like that, if it really means anything, it's simply that it provides you with a sort of ultimate resource—some kind of thing that you can turn to when what one calls one's own resources are exhausted: a reassurance that you won't just go screaming mad or flip under pressure. Or even if one does flip, this is sort of irrelevant. It's all part of this thing that my life is not intentional. I don't know any other way of describing my experiences except by saying that they happened to me.

A Very Individualistic Old Liberal

Len Webster / 1971

This interview took place at Christopher Isherwood's home in Santa Monica on Thursday, 10 June 1971. *Kathleen and Frank* was published that year and Isherwood started work on *Lost Years: A Memoir* on 26 August 1971.

Webster: First of all, I'd like to ask how, as a much-travelled observer and an involved Quaker sympathiser, you feel about current problems that the United States is facing—such as Vietnam and racism.

Isherwood: Well, as regards Vietnam—needless to say, I'm against the war—but then, you see, I'm a total pacifist, and I'm not particularly thrilled by opposition to a war which is such a mess from every point of view. I mean, it's no sweat to be against this war—everybody's against this war. This war, half the time, is being attacked not on pacifistic grounds but because it was a piece of very bad policy, is costing the nation untold losses in life and economic power, and so on. And so people are against it for that reason.

I'm against war, period. And therefore I sometimes find it a little bit, as it were, embarrassing to be shoulder-to-shoulder with people who normally wouldn't agree with me at all—they're only protesting against *this* war.

Webster: Have you taken part in any demonstrations?

Isherwood: No, I'm not a great demonstrator. I seldom take part. I've made myself *heard* from time to time, in one way or another. In general, I believe much more in doing it personally. I mean, whenever I speak in public or am asked questions, of course I come out very clearly on the various issues which interest me. But I'm not so much for general demonstrations largely because I feel that being a very individualistic old liberal, I always want to do it in exactly *my* way. I don't want the demonstration to be turned into something else, which large demonstrations almost invariably are. I mean, they have a militant tail and a passive-resistance head, or something. You never know if, suddenly, you're going to get stung in the back by the tail.

Webster: How did you become involved with the Society of Friends, and in particular the Wider Quaker Fellowship?

Isherwood: That really sprang out of involvement with Vedanta. And involvement with Vedanta sprang out of knowing Gerald Heard, who introduced me to Huxley. I'd always been very interested in his ideas and I came to feel that I was a pacifist, largely after going to the war in China in 1938 as a journalist. And Gerald Herald, whom I'd known in England, had gone to America—come out with the Huxleys—that is to say, Aldous and his first wife, Maria—and they'd formed already a community of people who interested them. Among other people, they'd met this Hindu monk, Prabhavananda, who's the head of the Vedanta Society here. He'd come out from a religious organization in India and they'd founded this little center here—it was then just a few people. And, as a result of being interested in this—because these things had really not concerned me before at all—I was completely non-religious up to that point—I became involved. I became involved by my interest in this particular individual, this Swami.

As a result of that, I became much more interested in all kinds of other religious groups and we had, sort of, a seminar, a kind of conference, here in the neighbourhood of town, at a place called La Verne, out in the valley, in 1941. It was during this that I decided I would like to do some social work with the Quakers. There was a Quaker there at the conference and I heard that in the East there was a hostel for all kinds of refugees—mostly professional people—who had come over from Germany and Austria. So I went and worked with them, and I wasn't there so long when came Pearl Harbor and America's involvement in the war. And so, in due course, I registered as a conscientious objector. But before I could be drafted to civilian service or anything, I was just on the border-line and they lowered the draft age because they'd got so many people into the forces that they didn't need older people. And so I was exempt anyway.

The Quaker hostel, meanwhile, came to an end automatically with the war, because, due to all the drafting of American citizens, an enormous number of vacancies for academic jobs were obtainable, and all our people got jobs. They were quite employable, brilliant scholars. Then I went and moved in with Prabhavananda for a while, and we got involved with making a translation of the Bhagavad Gita. I stayed up there for going on two years and, although after that I didn't continue living at the Vedanta Center, I've always remained in close touch with him ever since.

Webster: You were in Philadelphia, then?

Isherwood: To be strictly accurate, I was at Haverford, which is just outside. Haverford is often spoken of as "the center of Quakerdom." They've got a college there, a Quaker college.

Webster: Was it the central idea of the Wider Quaker Fellowship or the man, Rufus Jones, who appealed to you? Do you feel it was this person or the concept?

Isherwood: Oh, no. With the Quakers, it was much more the concept—I mean, what was valuable about the Quakers, to me, was the fact that they had the most marvellous way of doing things. In the first place, as you know, everything is conducted not just on a minority-majority basis, but every single person in a group meeting, if some project is being discussed, has to agree. And they have to wait until they get the sense of a meeting, that everybody agrees that a certain thing should be done—even if it takes a week. And they were amazingly cooperative, and extraordinarily free from hypocrisy, and they really mean business.

I've rather lost touch with the Quakers, unfortunately. I mean, I contribute to them, and so on. No, I belong to the Wider Quaker Fellowship, a kind of "friends of the Quakers," "fellow travellers of the Quakers"—I feel that one should always support them.

In fact, I have two organizations which I regard among the most admirable in this country: one is the American Friends Service Committee, which is the social action part of the Quakers, and the other is the American Civil Liberties Union. And those are the organizations which I most support. In a way, the American Civil Liberties Union represents my political life. I mean, in practice, I always vote Democratic, but I'm never very pleased with any of the candidates, and the only thing that really does seem satisfactory is the specific cases, and specific instances, where you can do something about some particular injustice. And that's what the Civil Liberties Union concerns itself with.

Webster: You mentioned politics just then. I gather that Gore Vidal—who is a friend of yours, is he not?—

Isherwood: Oh, a very good friend, yes.

Webster: —I gather that he's supporting Ralph Nader as a presidential candidate?

Isherwood: Yes.

Webster: Are you with him in this?

Isherwood: Oh, I think Nader is absolutely magnificent, but I strongly doubt whether a man like that could ever make it to be president because . . . I don't think he's nearly full enough of shit, you know. He's not the kind of—he doesn't talk that presidential talk. If he's anything like I imagine him, he's far too dedicated, too single-minded, to be president. The president has to appease such a lot, he has to straddle things, and he has to talk a lot of hypocrisy—there's no other word for it. And this is absolutely part of the job: it's the same in every country in the world. I mean, don't you agree?

Webster: Yes. I agree wholeheartedly, yes.

Isherwood: Nader is more of a one-man Civil Liberties Union, or something. He goes to work like a woodpecker on a certain point and hammers away and gets somewhere.

Webster: In a short essay—it was, in fact, reproduced in *Exhumations,* "Hypothesis and Belief"—you write: "Spiritual truth is, by definition, directly revealed and experienced; it cannot be known at second-hand." I wonder how *direct* do you feel your own "mysticism" is?

Isherwood: What I mean by "known" is in the ultimate sense of really, really saying, "I know," not "I infer," or "I've strong reason to believe," or "I have faith that it is so," but actually any mystic of any of the major religions, or minor religions, for that matter, would say the same thing. They would say that knowledge of The Reality is a personal matter.

However, what I think you can go a long way on—and that's certainly all the way I've been able to go—is, if you meet somebody who, quite obviously, has had some part of that knowledge himself, and if, after observing this person very carefully over a long period, you come to the conclusion that he or she is telling the truth, and is not self-deceived, and is not insane, is not a crook in any way—then, of course, it's a very serious matter. You begin to suspect that this way of knowledge is possible for human beings. Because unless you believe that the other being is supernatural, what he does, anybody else could do. Therefore, this is a tremendous guarantee of the truth of the whole religious hypothesis.

Webster: And this is what you found in the Swami?

Isherwood: Yes. Quite. You see. I've known this man now for over thirty years and we're very good friends—he's ten years older than I am—and all this time I've known him, I've seen him change. I've seen him go through all the phases of getting older, and I've seen this curious kind of certainty, which has nothing to do with dogmatism, but the certainty of his experience, growing in him. And this has just impressed me tremendously.

And, of course, it's not only just *he* but the people that he had contact with. He was a disciple of Brahmananda, who was one of the two chief disciples of Ramakrishna. . . . He joined the monastery as a very young boy and so that was very very impressive, to meet someone like that.

Webster: Do you understand much Sanskrit?

Isherwood: Absolutely not. Except for the technical words. The various translations that we've done together consisted simply in the Swami explaining exactly what it meant—he speaks very good English—and I just sort of touched it up, you know, and wrote it in a more fluent way.

Webster: How about the prose changes to verse? Was it your idea or his?

Isherwood: Oh, that was my idea. It was rather a curious affair, though, because what happened was that we worked almost a year on the translation, obviously taking it very easily. There were all kinds of things to do, and this just was something we picked up . . . a little bit every day. But when it was all finished, it was just another translation of the Gita and in those days there were already about fifty translations.

I remember we read it aloud to Aldous Huxley and to a woman friend of ours. And they were both obviously terribly disappointed. I was very flat-footed, and it was very like a whole lot of other translations. And, I don't know—it was one of those funny kinds of moments that occur, actually, very often in show-business when the director doesn't like the script and you go away and suddenly have an idea and change the whole thing. Suddenly, in a kind of flash, I saw that the whole thing would be quite different. I didn't look far ahead or think what I was going to do—I just suddenly thought of this kind of heavily . . . alliterative, vaguely Anglo-Saxon sort of verse. You know, which the thing opens with . . . yes . . .

> Krishna, the changeless,
> Halt my chariot
> There where the warriors,
> Bold for the battle,
> Face their foemen.
> Between the armies

There let me see them,
The men I must fight with,
Gathered together
Now at the bidding
Of him their leader,
Blind Dhritarashtra's
Evil offspring

Thump—thumb; thump—thump. And that went all right. And then I thought.
"Well, now obviously some of this thing should be in prose." The diadictic
parts of it, the teaching, should obviously be mostly in prose, because the
book is very mixed in style, or in content, shall we say.

It's no new idea. In things like the Bible designed to be read as literature,
they print some parts as poetry. And some of the things are quite obviously
too simple, too massive, to be put into poetry. It spoils the impact and extreme simplicity is what is so powerful. There's a terrific transfiguration
scene where Krishna appears in His Aspect as Lord of the Universe, which
is just absolutely poetic. Actually, the whole of the Gita is in verse, but trying
to put it all into verse—that's tedious, too. It seems just a way of keeping the
reader's attention.

And it was done very, very quickly. I think the rewriting of it, that is to
say turning it into this mixture, took something under three weeks. I felt I
could never stop. It was just all stored up.

Webster: And Aldous Huxley liked it then?
Isherwood: Oh, yes—yes, he was very encouraged.

Webster: How do you accept the concept of rebirth in Vedanta? I'm asking this question because, two years ago, in *Vedanta and the West*—in
1969—you wrote that, "If one suspected that Vedanta principles could be
true, and yet did nothing about them, then sooner or later you may be forced
to admit that you have been wasting your life," whereas I would have thought
that if rebirth is part of the Wheel of Life, one can't really *waste* a life.
Isherwood: Well, you can't really *waste* it, except in our Western sense of
"wasting time." Because, of course, the greatest saints of Hinduism have
said, "Well, after all, relax. I mean, if it takes a million births to realize the
Lord, nevertheless you will realize Him sooner or later." Though there's a
sort of doubleness there, I suppose you might say. Because, according to our
Western "hurry-up" thing, it's desperately urgent, and of course leading up

to this may be excessively unpleasant. But there is the idea that, if you reach a certain amount of Enlightenment, you won't be reborn, that you will simply exist in a kind of state of non-birth, during which you'll grow further and finally lose your identity altogether.

All this talk is really going around in circles because all philosophising is within *maya* and is all predicated on saying "I." But, at the same time, Vendantists belive that the "I" is only an illusion, only a false identification, because you are the Eternal, always were the Eternal, always will be the Eternal, and however much the "I" carries on like this and cavorts and plays around in various states of birth, consciousness, it never ceases to be the Eternal, in one sense.

Then, you see, you get to this curious thing that God Himself is said—I'm sure you've run across this expression—is said "to sport." That is to say, the whole universe, the whole of *maya,* with all its seeming horror and bliss, and beauty and ugliness, is all just His play, looked at in the last resort. It's really a question, you know, of, "Can you take it or not?" I mean, at what level you try to look at things and really to say, "His Will is our peace," or that "It's all Mother's play" when a million people die of cholera. It's very advanced.

There are always these two sides of the river. On the one hand, the absolute apathy of the person who has no sympathy, no compassion, nothing. On the other hand, there's the calm of the saint who's been through all that and sees that, nevertheless, in some mysterious way, all is well. And these two are polar opposites. And in the middle is the raging river in which the angry and the noble and the heroes in everybody are all struggling desperately trying to put the world right. The world will never be put right because it's just a continuum of *maya* and the dog's curly tail will always curl back again after it has been straightened. And although they predicate ages—the Golden Age, the Silver Age, the Copper Age and the Iron Age—although the millennium is supposed to come back every so often, it's only a phase in a cycle. So that, you see, is that.

What it all amounts to is, "Be still and know that I AM God," just to know your real nature, in which case you, of course, cease to be you and are what you are anyway, so to speak. This is something which just makes the mind boggle and people who like things very tidy and logical find it nauseating and say it's "Oriental nebulism." But it isn't, it's just when you get to talk about it too exactly, in this sort of way—I mean, at any given moment, it all seems so extraordinarily clear. But if you try to generalise it, to put it down in statements of this sort, you do of course make it into propositions which offend a great many people.

Webster: Tell me, do you remember your father at all?

Isherwood: Very little really. He was ten when I was—I mean *[laughing]*—I was ten when he was killed. I don't know, writing about my father has made me feel like he's my son. You know, the roles get sort of reversed because I'm the old one now. I'm older than he was when he was dead, so naturally I think of him as a younger man.

But I've never been one to bemoan the absence of parents or any of that kind of thing because it's always been my experience that, if you want a father, the woods are full of them—and I've had a number of them. And of course you might say, in a way, that Swami Prabhavananda is one of them. But I also felt very much that way, in a literary manner, about E. M. Forster, for instance. And I've lots of filial emotion ready to bestow on deserving cases.

I don't see why one shouldn't have several fathers and several mothers, for that matter, too. However, I got to be good friends—very good friends—with my mother in her last years. But I never saw very much of her after I was grown up. I was always away somewhere. I was, sort of, a bad son, in that sense.

Webster: At what stage do you think your writing changed from reportage-autobiography (which is a term Cyril Connolly has used, I think) to ideology-autobiography? Do you think it was with *Prater Violet?*

Isherwood: Well, those are sort of loaded questions because I would have said that there was a lot of ideology in the Berlin books. I mean, after all there was all this interest in the political situation—

Webster: But you're very aloof in the Berlin books, whereas in *Prater Violet* you seem a lot more involved.

Isherwood: Since I was trying to give the sense of a whole city—or, anyway, a whole world—I obviously mustn't be too involved with anybody. But this whole business of my being involved with the characters and trying to write under my own name was, I now think, not workable, in the last resort.

Webster: Was it drastically changed from the pieces you presumably took out of *The Lost?*

Isherwood: *The Lost* was very, very loosely written, that was nothing. I was always, you know, rewriting this stuff. I dictated a whole lot of it to my brother, and then sort of took it all apart and put it together again differently.

Webster: How closely connected were you with the Communist Party during your days in Berlin?

Isherwood: Oh, very little. You see, I never really joined the Communist Party in any way. As a matter of fact, the tremendous stumbling block to me personally was the homosexual question: the treatment of homosexuals in Russia—which was absolutely in contravention to their original declarations, that the private life was no concern—was always something which kept being brought up again and again with my friends. People would go to Russia and find out and say, "Well, of course, it's much exaggerated—" or "The laws aren't administered."

The point was that the Russians started to equate homosexuality with fascism. And this in itself was such a loathsome piece of hypocrisy that, while I hardly admitted it to myself at the time, I see now that a government that can lie like that about one thing is really profoundly rotten all the way through, and just like any other government, in fact—and not at all the Kingdom of Heaven! So that alone would really prevent me.

Then I began later to feel that the writers there were treated poorly because, while the ones that they liked were given everything, the others were persecuted and always were. Not merely persecuted but absolutely silenced.

However, none of my friends—with the exception of Upward—really joined the Party, and he later, while not by any means turning his back on all his principles, left the Party again. Stephen Spender, in some very brief way, got involved with them, but that was very soon over. He's described all that in *The God that Failed*. And Upward, of course, has described it in these novels that he's writing now.

Those were the two chief things, I suppose: the question of the private life and the question of the outlook for writers.

Webster: What made you become a U.S. citizen rather than keep British nationality?

Isherwood: Because if you're going to live in a country, I think you should have the right to vote, for one thing. Besides, I don't know, I wanted to. I'm really not a person who has these great feelings about nationalism. I think my feelings are much more racial, and after all, though God knows we're a mixed-up lot here, there is a kind of Anglo-Saxon segment, and I feel it's just as much my country as anybody else's, really. It's very different from other countries, you know, in that way, and I feel entirely British in a certain sense, but not nationalistically British. I feel very moved when I go back to England, and I must say that I'm received with the most extraordinary warmth.

Of course, this business of meeting Prabhavananda had a lot to do with rooting me here. It seemed to me a very important reason for staying—well, it still seems to me an important reason for staying.

Webster: You must have picked up quite a lot of languages one way and another while you were travelling around.

Isherwood: Well, it's disgraceful. I have very little talent for it. I speak German. I did speak German fluently—not correctly, not well, but fluently—and often spent long periods of time when I spoke nothing but German. My French is disastrous because I was taught it in school, and I've only the faintest smatterings of Spanish, that's all. No, German is the only foreign language I speak, and you almost never get the opportunity of speaking it now. You go to Germany, you can't find anybody who wants to speak German. They all speak perfect English.

Webster: Which is your favourite book?

Isherwood: Oh, *A Single Man,* I think. Simply because I think it was the most realised book that I've written, in the sense that I almost managed to do what I wanted to do. As a rule, books get so out of your hand—they run on.

I was in perfect paradise while I was writing *A Meeting by the River.* I thought that was just bliss. I wanted to go on rewriting it and rewriting it. I rewrote it three times. Or I wrote it and did two rewrites, and even so I really felt sorry, you know, to finish writing it. But, even so, I still think it sort of got out of control a bit, whereas *A Single Man,* due to the form and so on, said exactly what I wanted to say.

Webster: This might sound patronising, but when I read that, I thought, "God, we've reached the end of the novel. What can we do after this?" Because everything was there, in a very small, thin volume, and you couldn't do much more with it—a man and the world around him, and that was it.

Isherwood: Well, I don't call that patronising. That sounds very agreeable. Since one can't begin the novel, one may as well end it! No, I don't feel that. I really, in a way, rather wonder if I'll ever write another one, or if I won't write some quite frankly autobiographical stuff. What I have are enormous mountains of diaries covering the whole of the American experience. And I might publish some of that, except that there's always this eternal question of discretion, the anecdotes about all sorts of people.

I found a great pleasure in writing my part of this latest book, *Kathleen and Frank,* where I was writing with the utmost frankness in a non-fictional manner, and I really enjoyed doing that. I don't quite know what you lose by doing it, or what you gain by making a novel. The sort of thing, whatever it is, I do have to contribute as a writer I feel I can do just as well about real people and by telling what's called "the truth": that is to say, my version of it. Because, you know, you can describe—you can describe character, you philosophise, you can do all these things—you can present the material in this way, or that. What else is there? So I rather wonder, in a way . . .

Webster: You were always tipped as "the great hope of British writing" after the thirties. Do you think you ever met the hopes of people?

Isherwood: Evidently not. Otherwise I should be a hundred times better known than I am and be, sort of, a famous man. But I do think that I've had what I really, in a way, much more wanted—a body of extraordinarily affectionate readers. I get such nice letters. The people who do dig my work seem to really dig it, you know, and to enter into it more.

Webster: So you think perhaps you've had more of a contribution to make to certain people.

Isherwood: I think that I've had recognition of the kind that I—the only way you can measure a contribution, I suppose, is by the recognition—I've had recognition of the kind that I like. I do feel that, yes.

Webster: What is your best-selling book?

Isherwood: Obviously this Berlin material, because of all its side-effects: the fact that it was made into a play, into a film, then into a musical, and now into another film—

Webster: Another film?

Isherwood: A film based on the musical. They're making it right now.

Webster: Where?

Isherwood: Germany, I'm happy to say. So perhaps it will be a little bit more convincing.

Webster: Are you going over?

Isherwood: Oh, no. I think it's almost finished. But Michael York is in it, and Liza Minnelli.

Webster: Do you find that real-life people you know become completely submerged beneath the fictional characters that you create?

Isherwood: They do and they don't. The real-life people go on living, the fictional characters sort of carry off some part of them. I find it frightfully hard to remember what really happened after I've written a fictional account because of course it's just in the happenings that the greatest fiction takes place in my books. Often I invent complete scenes and situations and whole plots, which are quite untrue, about true people, because I always regard happenings in fiction as simply the best way of showing off your animal. It's like taking a horse over jumps, or something, and so the jumps are adjusted to show the horse off in the best way.

Whatever characteristics the character has that you want to display, you create incidents which will best display those characteristics. The action is made for the man, not the man for the action, in other words.

Webster: Gerald Hamilton said in his autobiography that he was sympathetic towards Buddhism. Did he mention this at all to you?

Isherwood: Yes, he talked about that a lot. But in actual fact, in his later life, he joined the Catholic Church. That was his great thing. He'd been in China a lot, you know.

Webster: Did that have any influence on you going to China?

Isherwood: No. I always wanted to go to China. I've always been a desperate dreamer of travel. I used to look at the river and imagine going down it on a ship commanded by Joseph Conrad, and finding myself in this place or that place. To this day, if I go somewhere exotic, I can't help repeating to myself, "I'm in New Zealand," and then it all becomes different and marvellous and exotic, and all these very Scottish boys and girls in the streets . . . New Zealanders seem like "magic people." And of course the expectation is quite matched by the reality. Some of the country around is magnificent, and when we went to Australia, it was just too wonderful for words.

My father always dreamed of going to stay with the Stevensons—it was wonderful to go to Samoa and go up the hill where he's buried and look out all over the ocean and the islands and the great forest below, and everything—wonderful! But I am a terrific travel-snob and the only way I could get across Siberia on the railway would be by saying every minute, "I'm in Siberia, I'm in Siberia." That would take me quite a lot of the way.

Webster: One of the ironical things that Gerald Hamilton does mention in his autobiography is the fact that the only real spy that he ever met—or "really successful spy"—was introduced to him by you. I think it was Guy Burgess.

Isherwood: It probably was Guy Burgess. Well, would you call Guy Burgess a spy? I don't know what to call him. I knew him, of course, from quite a different angle, he was just a sort of boon companion whom I didn't know very well. I was amazed and incredulous and wouldn't believe it when this scandal broke. I said, "The Russians would never touch him, what would they want him for?" He was the most unreliable, drunken creature . . . I said, "No, it's nonsense—their agents are of sterner stuff than that, surely."

It is amazing. To this day, I don't know. He's not my idea of an agent: he never seemed to be responsible enough to be one.

Webster: When Burgess and Maclean disappeared, I think both you and Stephen Spender were interviewed, weren't you?

Isherwood: Well, every soul who'd ever met them was interviewed. And especially out here where, in those days, the FBI had very little to do. They used to come down and see me quite often about it, you know, and I would say, "I don't know anything more, I can't tell you anything more—I've nothing to say about it, I'm far more surprised than you are."

Webster: You never met Maclean?

Isherwood: No, I never did. My idea of a spy is somebody like Philby, who really, you know, functioned.

Webster: I could never understand why you didn't follow through the "Mr. Norris" idea and do a proper "spy" book. Can you think why?

Isherwood: Because I don't know about espionage. I don't believe in writing about things I don't know. Which reminds me, there was a marvellous aside, talking of espionage. I can't remember who wrote it . . . but one of the London journalists, a well-known one, was writing about "camp." And he said how I'd defined "camp" in *The World in the Evening,* and he said that Isherwood had said that ballet was "camp" about romantic love and that Baroque art was "camp" about religion. "In the same way," he said, "espionage might be said to be 'camp' about war, and the mini-skirt 'camp' about rape." Wasn't that brilliant! I thought it was marvellous.

What I want to do really is to try and get down to the inwardness of my own experience of life in my time, because I know that, if I can do that, I shall touch other people's experience. I mean, it's when you speak out of your most personal areas that, suddenly, other people say, "By God, that's exactly what I thought!" And that's when you really light things up for people. Because I mean, after all, art is, in so far as it's "functional" in that sense, illuminating your experience for you so that when you have a similar experience it's all that much better because of something which was put into your head by something you read or got from art.

By the same token, I think art gives reassurance. I mean, you say to yourself, "Well, whatever it is that happens to me other people have been through it, you know"—and therefore you feel sort of strengthened by it. Of course, I don't like the idea of art being "useful," in that kind of way. I don't like to push this as an idea, but I do think it's true, nevertheless. It's true for me, reading other people, you know—well, one knows how the poets are some of the greatest reassurers.

Webster: Talking about poets, do you ever feel a little bit—perhaps not resentment, but just a tinge of jealousy that Auden is so well-known, so famous, and that you—as you said—have got a small, if loyal readership?

Isherwood: I don't know. Auden is so extraordinary, so wonderful, and somehow or other a poet perhaps should be more famous, don't you think? It's such an event, a poet—a real, new poet. Such a tremendous event. When there's a good batch of novelists around, the most that one is is like one of those peaks in the Andes at Lake Titicaca—they are, in fact, twenty, twenty-one, twenty-two thousand feet respectively. But they're all just little hills, rising above the twelve-thousand-foot plain—at least they look big, but not very big. A poet is alone, somehow. He seems to stand out. You see these tremendous towers, like Yeats or somebody, who stand right out there.

Webster: Do you ever wish you'd written more poetry?

Isherwood: No, because I would be a different person then. It's impossible for me to wish to be other than I am. I don't wish anything really, I don't feel any regret. I realize I wasted a fantastic amount of my life in stupid anxieties and laziness, or the kind of laziness that arises out of anxiety when—because you're in a flap—you don't do anything at all. I can't really understand "regretting" one's life.

Webster: Do you ever get a little bit afraid to look back on your life, to go back into the past?

Isherwood: For what reason?

Webster: To try and recreate it, because you can't completely recreate your own experience.

Isherwood: Oh, no. Of course, you don't recreate your own experience, you make a sort of poem based on your experience. Art isn't a recreation of one's own experience—that you can get nowadays easily enough by shooting a great many home movies and having the tape-recorder on all the time, and we'll have even more sophisticated machines before long. We'll be photographing ourselves all day long, if we want, in some quite inexpensive manner, and no doubt it would be amusing to dwell on these things. I would simply adore to see home movies of all of us in the thirties, for instance—or even in the forties or fifties or sixties. You know, life goes by so quickly and even ten years ago seems extraordinary. We have a few home movies, and we look at ourselves fifteen years ago—it's amazing!

Webster: What do you think you'll be remembered for?
Isherwood: Oh, that old Berlin stuff, I suppose. It's always the way.

Webster: Would you like to be remembered for that or for something else?
Isherwood: Well, "remembered"—what does all that matter, really? I mean, it's good in a way, and it's nice, and so on, but if you don't get recognition while you're alive, it's a cinch you don't want it afterwards. I hope I shall be wiser—no, I suppose I should like some thumping recognition in my old age, particularly when I'm quite ga-ga and past it, you know. It would be nice to be suddenly recognized in a very big way, because that's about all you've got then.

Trade Winds

Cleveland Amory / 1972

From *Saturday Review* 19 February 1972: 10. Reprinted by permission of the estate of Cleveland Amory.

Christopher Isherwood is a man to whom one addresses questions about himself at one's peril—or at least at the peril of betraying an ignorance either of one of his earlier, largely autobiographical works; his real autobiography, *Lions and Shadows*; or of his latest book, *Kathleen and Frank,* an extraordinarily complete story of his mother and father, largely in the form of their own diaries and letters. Could he, we wondered, be accused of overacting?

Mr. Isherwood, a quick, gentle fellow, smiled. "I think," he said, "heredity is deeper than we give it credit for being. I know about the modern theory of it. There are great ideological forces that try to push us into the all environment thing. Socialism comes along and says, 'We can make anybody over into anything. Heredity.' And the Catholic Church says just about the same thing. All I say is it's an open question. I cannot believe there's an absolute answer, and I am exceedingly dubious when anybody says one or the other makes no difference."

We asked Mr. Isherwood when he came to this country and learned he was first here on the way back from China (with W. H. Auden)—a trip that resulted in his book, *Journey to a War.* What, we pursued, about China?

"About China now," he said, "I'm extremely interested but very ignorant." He paused. "However," he continued, "I'm sure the feel of it is the same. The Chinese are Chinese first and everything else second. They're supremely Chinese. They've been at it, don't you know, for so long."

"It's quite a cheerful feeling, really. In the tiny villages which Auden and I were hiking through, even the feeling of being among them was a cheerful one. They had humor even though there was a terrible trouble passing over them in great waves."

What about the Japanese? "I know they did terrible things," he said, "but in the past I saw that at least all of them weren't atrocity-minded. I remember they always bombed the railroad stations in those towns. But the Chinese knew it and they seemed to know even exactly when they were going to do it. They would come out and sit on the side of a hill and watch. The bombing of the station was like a show—a traveling show which went from town to town."

Mr. Isherwood, too, traveled a great deal.

"I never lived in England much," Mr. Isherwood continued. "I was always roaming about." Why, we asked, did he settle in, and on, Hollywood? "I had friends here," he replied, "and they got me a job at MGM. The first picture I worked on was James Hilton's *Rage in Heaven*. Ingrid Bergman was in it, and I used to show up in the dressing room with the script. To me, she was the most beautiful—the complete star. She was absolutely fresh—like breakfast!"

Breakfast? We queried. "Yes, and I'm afraid she might have heard of my comparison. Because, years later, I met her and she said, 'I wouldn't have recognized you. You look so *old*.' She, of course, still looked absolutely smashing."

Why, we wanted to know, was a writer of his stature satisfied with Hollywood? "Actually," he said, "I never got seriously involved. I did once sign a contract, but I got out of it after a year. I never felt I was a miserable slave. The fun was considerable, and even some of the fellows at the top were all right. I remember the day Dore Schary took over. He came around and said hello to every single writer. Mayer, on the other hand, had never said hello—we never even met him. I thought that was disgusting."

What about film writing in general? "Films are different," Mr. Isherwood told us. "They really aren't writing, at all. They're visual. You're setting visual situations. Even the lines of dialogue aren't real lines. They're lines bounced against the visual image."

Did he ever feel corrupted? "No," he said. "I used to say, 'You can corrupt yourself, but you can't *be* corrupted.' I had a secretary, and I used to say to her, 'Now today you're going to get on with your novel'—she was writing one, too—'and I'll get on with mine.' And we would."

Mr. Isherwood has been keeping a diary ever since he can remember. "Whenever I teach," he told us, "I always say, 'Keep a diary.' But I really recommend more of a notebook than a diary. Put something down about what you read—anything. You don't know whether it will turn into fiction or what—that isn't the important thing. What is important is that you must find out what you're interested in—the essence of your interest.

"So many young writers start writing what they're not really interested in. So their books aren't either—I mean interesting. To be interesting, your book must be your *burning* interest."

An Interview with
Christopher Isherwood
David J. Geherin / 1972

From *Journal of Narrative Technique* Volume 2 (September 1972): 143–58. Reprinted by permission.

The following interview took place on 17 March 1972 at Mr. Isherwood's home in Santa Monica, California. The interview, as it appears here, has been corrected and emended by Mr. Isherwood.

Q: One of the most interesting aspects of your fiction is the use of a character named Christopher Isherwood in several of your novels. I'd like to begin by asking what prompted you to use this Christopher Isherwood persona in the first place.

A: Simply this: I felt that the story could only be told from the point of view of myself as the narrator. The reason being that I couldn't really project myself into anybody else and tell the story through his or her eyes. I found it a very unnecessary bypass because if you are going to tell the story through somebody else's eyes, you first of all have to imagine the person through whose eyes the story is being told. I felt this was absolutely unnecessary and tiresome, and I don't really trust my ability to know what anything looks like through anybody else's eyes anyhow under any circumstances in life whatsoever.

I therefore said to myself, I'll tell the story in the first person. Then, of course, the question was, who is the first person, and the answer was, the first person is me. Now at first, in *Mr. Norris,* because of a kind of coyness, or goodness knows what, I gave myself an assumed name. It was in fact my two middle names, but nevertheless it was an assumed name since I have never called myself William Bradshaw.

When it came to beginning to write the pieces which formed *Goodbye to Berlin* (the other half of the omnibus volume, *The Berlin Stories*), I thought to myself, how silly this is, this William Bradshaw. If I'm telling the story, let me call myself Christopher Isherwood. But when I did this, I began to realize that the person who tells the story is also a character in the story. This set up a kind of conflict because I didn't really want to be a character in the story and, furthermore, I was a little bit embarrassed with my own name and all, getting too deep into the story and fictionalizing about myself. It's why the stories that have the Christopher Isherwood persona have something odd about them, in my opinion.

In starting to plan and construct a novel, one of the major questions is how are you going to approach the subject. Are you going to approach it in the first person, or in the third person? Are you God looking down at everybody? Are you inside one of the characters, or are you inside various characters in succession, as in *The Memorial,* where the viewpoint is changed from one character to another? (Incidentally, in that novel it is always passed on by touch, like the baton in a relay race, from one character to another who then takes over the narration.) I liken that to trying to fix the electric light. Something is wrong. You wonder, now how should you get at the fixture. Sometimes it's more convenient to go up the stepladder, sometimes perhaps you should come down through the attic to get at it from above. Or perhaps you should stand on the table and get at it sideways because if you're right under it you can't see properly what you're doing. I've often got on the table when I should be on the stepladder, or got in the attic when I should be on the table, with the result that I had to start all over again because I realized that I wasn't approaching the thing in the right manner to get the maximum result.

Q: Deciding to use the persona device was obviously the right choice for many of your novels, particularly the Berlin novels. However, putting a character with your own name into a novel brings up the whole question of the autobiographical nature of your fiction. What is the relationship between autobiography and fiction in your work?

A: I was always concerned primarily with live models. But I was trying to show the inwardness of the models that I was using for my characters. That is to say, I was trying to show what it was about them that really interested me, why they seemed to me more than themselves, why they seemed to me to be almost archetypes, and therefore why I was writing about them, what was magic about them, what was numinous about them. In order to show that, I didn't hesitate to alter actual facts and create scenes which never actually happened, invent circumstances of all kinds. The analogy I usually use here is that of a horse that you're showing off at a show. You want to put it through its paces. In the same way you want to put a character through its paces, provide scenes which will make it behave in the way which is almost characteristic of itself. Therefore you very quickly get away from what really happened into what might have happened—that is to say, you get into fiction.

Q: Do you think that some critics have become too concerned with the autobiographical aspect of your work and have not paid proper attention to the artistic, the creative, the purely fictional quality of your novels?

A: Why that should excuse the critics from paying attention to anything, I don't know. After all, a lot of autobiographers are terrible liars, which means that what they write is fiction. There are many, many famous writers of memoirs who are extremely untrustworthy, as has been discovered later. Why shouldn't the critics still like what they write?

Q: You advised the readers of your autobiography *Lions and Shadows* to read it as a novel, suggesting perhaps that it wasn't all true. Is the Christopher Isherwood persona in *Lions and Shadows* really any different from the persona in the novels?

A: Well, yes, obviously, because in *Lions and Shadows* he at least holds the center of the stage, more or less, and therefore is seen in much greater depth. The whole endeavor of the Christopher Isherwood persona in the novels is to be in the background as much as he can because what he is trying to do is tell a story. He's not telling *his* story really at all, or only incidentally, and only just to explain why he was there with those people and what he was up to. But in all cases, fundamentally, Christopher Isherwood is in the background. Whereas *Lions and Shadows* is about Christopher Isherwood. Only there are certain reticences which to my mind, now anyway, rather constrict the whole thing. The principal one is that I didn't come out and say I was homosexual, which really colors a tremendous lot of one's value judgments and of attitudes to other people.

Q: You once said that what strikes you today about the Christopher Isherwood persona in *Mr. Norris* is its heartlessness. Do you think if you had emphasized or developed the persona's homosexuality, this would have helped to explain his behavior more?

A: Well, it would have made the persona more human and, insofar as somebody is more human, he is less heartless. What one means by heartlessness is indifference, a characteristic of robots. The Christopher Isherwood persona is more than somewhat of a robot.

Q: Would you say in a later novel, such as *Down There on a Visit,* the Christopher Isherwood persona is less of a robot and more of a character with feelings and emotions of his own?

A: That's quite true, but I think in doing that I rather upset the apple cart in the book itself. I mean I think he became too rambunctious. It didn't really help. It was like getting somebody drunk in order to make him talk. But it wasn't really as good as having a character. There was always some kind of inhibition in my use of this device, this Christopher Isherwood thing. I don't find it satisfactory.

Q: This confusion between the persona as device and the persona as character does create some problems. Do you think, for example, that some critics have put too much emphasis on the "I am a camera" statement at the beginning of *Goodbye to Berlin* as a statement of your technique?

A: Yes, very much so. What I was simply trying to do was describe my mood at that particular moment. Obviously, the description does not fit Christopher Isherwood in many of the other sections.

Q: In which of your novels do you think the persona device works best?

A: In *Prater Violet,* simply because the main character, Friedrich Bergmann, talked so much and dominated the stage so much that it was natural for the Christopher Isherwood character to stay in the corner and listen. As long as he was listening he was a perfectly efficient pick-up machine and scanning device, and nothing more. Therefore, it was all right because he wasn't pushed out into the middle of the stage, wasn't compelled to act, to behave as a character, so this problem didn't arise. I discuss the use of this persona in a brief statement which can be found in a book by Leon Surmelian, called *Techniques of Fiction Writing: Measure and Madness.*

Q: You originally intended *Goodbye to Berlin* to be a huge epic novel in the Balzacian tradition. It didn't work out that way. What happened?

A: It was too plotty. I am much, much more concerned with character than plot, because a little plot goes an awfully long way.

Q: Are there any unpublished sections from this lost novel still extant?
A: I don't think so.

Q: Do you consider *Goodbye to Berlin* to be a unified novel, or just a series of loosely connected sketches?
A: The latter.

Q: Have you seen the film version of *Cabaret?*
A: Yes.

Q: Are you pleased with it?
A: No. Not altogether, by any means. But it's quite entertaining, I think.

My criticisms are the usual ones, the ones that many people have made. The moment you have a cabaret, you're going to have performances which are somehow amusing in it. I mean, you can have one song sung badly, like Marilyn Monroe in *Bus Stop*. She's marvellous when she sings the song in that. But she's meant to be a bad singer. You can't do that when you show as much of the cabaret as they did. I think the whole idea of having this cabaret throws the rest of the story off balance.

Now what are they stuck with? You have this little girl saying "Oh, I'll never make it. I haven't really any talent." Then she comes on the stage and you realize that she's every inch Judy Garland's daughter. And Joel Grey comes on the stage and he's simply fantastic. The truth is that this cabaret would have attracted half of Europe. You wouldn't have been able to get in for months on end.

Q: What is it about Sally Bowles as a character that has made her so popular all these years, first in your story, then in the stage and screen versions of *I Am a Camera,* and now in the stage and screen versions of *Cabaret?*

A: Well, I understood her first when I saw Julie Harris play the part. Julie Harris played her as though she were Joan of Arc. It was the whole idea of militant bohemia, so to speak. One of the best theatrical moments when the play was first produced was in the last act where Julie is believed by Chris and everybody to be completely under the thumb of her British mother who has come over to Berlin. But as a matter of fact the mother has given up in despair and has left for England. Julie, as Sally, comes in in this terribly frumpy, respectable middle-class coat, which the mother has given her. She takes it off and appears in the dress that she wore in the first act, a sort of bohemian uniform, a tight-fitting black silk dress with a flaming scarf. And the audience shrieked because what it meant was that squares are defeated, the establishment has gone down in ruins, and Greenwich Village is triumphant over all. Julie had the power, quite unconsciously because it was so much her own character, to project this. And there was a great scene, which would have meant nothing with another actress, where she pours the champagne and raises the glass and says, "Even *warm,* it's wonderful!"

Q: Is the model for the character of Sally Bowles still alive?
A: Yes.

Q: Is she living in England?
A: Yes.

Q: There was the note at the end of the story about Sally where you asked her to get in touch with you if she ever read the story. Did she?

A: Oh well, that part was all made up. We kept in touch always. I had lunch with her and her daughter the last time I was in England in 1970. It's just that she's a private citizeness and I've never, never given out her name. Some journalist got hold of it, found out who she was, and asked her. She said, "Yes, and now go away." And that was that.

Q: All your characters are so realistic, so lifelike. Are they all based on real people you have known?

A: Yes, I would say that. Very occasionally an amalgam, but I could always identify at least one person with any major character. The minor characters are very often invented. I always draw on my experience in one way or another.

Q: Many critics, beginning with Cyril Connolly's famous comment on the "fatal readability" of your prose, have noted the clarify of your writing. Is it as easy for you to write as it is for your readers to read, or do you take great pains with your style?

A: Great pains, yes.

Q: Do you normally work from diaries when writing your novels?

A: It's not as direct as all that. What I mean is, there is this material in many cases available, and when I'm feeling on unsteady ground, then I often turn to the diaries to look and see if I can get some kind of hint from them. I don't think there are any long passages of direct quotes from the diaries because a very little will set me off. If I get half a dozen lines of dialogue which are characteristic of a certain character, then I feel I can make that character speak indefinitely. It's just a matter of getting the rhythm of speech, or getting a few little details of how a place looks, or something of this kind. Most of it really is simply to give me confidence. I mean, I can do without it but I don't think I can and therefore the diary gives me just that little bit of confidence. I say to myself, well at least *this* part of it is authentic.

Q: Your most recent book, *Kathleen and Frank,* is constructed almost entirely from the diaries of others—your parents. Were there any particular problems you faced in writing that book?

A: The chief problem was to wade through this material and pick out the bits which seemed to me to describe the characters most succinctly and things that I thought were good that they had written. There was a tremendous lot of this stuff. My embarrassment was that there was too much good stuff.

As for the writing of the commentary on it, that was extremely simple, relatively speaking. I did a great deal of research on the Boer War and various other areas, historical and social. I had an enormous amount of help from Robert Collison, the head of the research department of the library here at UCLA. It was all great fun, really. It all came together quite easily.

Q: You conclude *Kathleen and Frank* with the statement, "This book too may prove to be chiefly about Christopher." Do you plan to write an autobiography which will more obviously be "chiefly about Christopher"?

A: Maybe.

Q: In another section of your commentary in the book, you credit your mother with being the counterforce in your life, the impetus which helped you to become the person and the writer you became.

A: All that's perhaps kidding, to a point. But in a sense it was true. Somebody had to be and she was. There's always a kind of counterforce, isn't there? In Vedanta philosophy, they say the physical world is made up of these three forces, which they call the gunas. There is the idea, the inspiration, and there's the principle of force, and there's the principle of inertia. Now you need all of these in order to get anything done. And the inertia is just as important as the force, because the inertia is the counterforce. You must have a fulcrum for your lever. You must have an interaction of force and resistance. And one can always find someone to thank, for playing the part of this force of resistance.

Q: One of the most interesting things to me about *Kathleen and Frank* is that you seem to have devised a whole new approach to biography, letting the characters literally tell their own stories.

A: What is amusing about it structurally, I think, is this: the extracts of the diaries and the letters are all in strict chronological order. But darting around them is the commentary, which starts at the present day and goes back and forth and sideways and all over the place, and keeps coming back to the present and comparing it with the past, and darting back to the past and comparing it with the present. In that way it's a somewhat Proustian kind of structure because the past is literally recaptured and certain things which were already stated at the beginning of the book are restated in the end.

Q: Do you think this particular biographical technique could also be used effectively as a novelistic device, by inventing letters and diaries and providing a running commentary?

A: Oh yes, you certainly could do it. There is a little bit of that in my novel *The World in the Evening* because there you have one character, Stephen Monk, commenting on his wife's letters a long time after her death. He gives extracts from the letters and then comments on what she said in them, which involves darting about in time.

Q: The first section of *The World in the Evening* was published separately a few years before the whole novel appeared, wasn't it?

A: Yes, the first chapter appeared in the first issue of *New World Writing,* April 1952.

Q: Many of your novels—*Goodbye to Berlin, The World in the Evening, A Single Man*—all started out to be quite different from their final form. Do you find you usually discover your true subject only as you begin writing a novel?

A: Oh yes, almost always. And ideally what I do is, I like to write whole drafts. I don't like polishing things until right at the end. With *A Single Man* and *A Meeting by the River,* I wrote three complete drafts right through from beginning to end, picking up things as I went along and making alterations and gradually getting into the theme.

In the case of *A Single Man,* I started off with my experience on California college campuses, and of two friends of mine, an Englishwoman who had married a G.I. when they were both very young and he was over in England right after the war, and how they came to this country and what her life had been in this country. The book was originally called "An English Woman" and I was meaning to write it in a sort of Willa Cather manner—very, very simple and describing this woman entirely in the third person. Then of course the question arose, how to get at the electric light. Well, I think to myself, I'm teaching at a college and I get to know this kid, and he's having a lot of trouble at home with his mother. And he says, after he and I get to know each other, "you're British too, you ought to go see her. Maybe you could talk some sense into her, maybe you could explain I'm not ungrateful. I simply want to go and live with Loretta. And she must understand that."

And so, that's how I started off. And then I realized by progressive stages that I wasn't primarily interested in the boy or in this woman. I was interested in the professor character. But nevertheless, this woman and, very far in the distance, her husband, and the son, who isn't her son after all—he's called Kenny—all appear in the book.

Q: Have any of your novels presented themselves to you almost whole, so to speak, so that there was little difference between the original conception and the final product?

A: No, I couldn't ever really say that. If such a thing happened, I would absolutely hate it. I don't think I would write it. I love the exploration of writing. That's exactly what appeals to me. When I was working on *A Meeting by the River,* I used to think, I wish this would never end.

Q: *A Meeting by the River* is unlike any of your other novels in that there is no narrator at all in the novel, just the letters and diaries of the two brothers. Was this the best way of getting at the light fixture in this case?

A: Yes. Of course, it can be criticized, and has been, because it's like a court and all the evidence for the prosecution and for the defense is presented and you suddenly realize there isn't going to be a verdict. There isn't any jury or judge and, at the end of it all, it ends with a deadlock.

Q: By presenting it in this form, by eliminating the narrator, the reader is forced to become the judge, isn't he?

A: Which of course I intented. Certain qualities in that book come out much better in the stage version of the novel, which Don Bachardy and I have written and which will be produced soon here in Los Angeles. It is a religious comedy which ends up with both sides thinking they have won. At the end of the play Patrick, the worldly brother, thinks to himself, "It's very amusing the way Oliver has gone to this monastery, he thinks he's so humble. But I know exactly where that will all end." And he foresees a future in which Oliver will be a kind of English Gandhi. His last lines are, "Twenty years from now he'll be running Asia."

On the other side Oliver is hugely amused because he's had this vision in which he saw that Patrick is already completely under the swami's protection, and that he is saved. And that he will simply hate being saved because he will suddenly start being completely dissatisfied with his life, get into the most awful mess with it.

Q: Do you find yourself more sympathetic with the position of one brother over the other?

A: Not really—except that I'm far more Patrick than I am Oliver.

Q: What are your thoughts about getting back to the theatre again after all these years since you and Auden collaborated on the three plays in the thirties?

A: Well, I have worked in the theatre in one way or another since then. I did a thing some years ago at the Mark Taper Forum, an experimental theatre here in Los Angeles where *A Meeting by the River* is being produced. They asked me to do an adaptation of Shaw's novella, *The Adventures of the Black Girl in Her Search for God.* By just putting it on the stage in the kind of wandering way in which you make a play nowadays, and having a very good director, Lamont Johnson, and a perfectly marvelous actress, Susan Batson, I think we produced a very remarkable show. It went wonderfully and I had the greatest fun down there.

Q: I'd like to raise the question of what might be called "minority literature"—that is, literature written by and perhaps for blacks, Jews, homosexuals, etc. What are your thoughts about the value of minority literature?

A: Well, you see, if you're really going to plead the cause of your minority, I think it's much better to do it in political literature, in pamphleteering, in articles and speeches, for the very simple, very obvious, but very much overlooked fact that your statistics are all faked in fiction. All the people who die in *The Grapes of Wrath* are killed by Mr. Steinbeck. He may say, well I killed exactly the proportion of Okies who would have been killed according to the figures on the Okie migration, but it's not the same thing. Therefore fiction is really not a very good vehicle for propaganda.

If, however, with great good humor and aggressiveness, you state an extremely slanted position, that I find delightful. I adore the prejudices of Tolstoy and the outbursts of Dickens because they are humanly fun and kind of invigorating, as all protest is. It strengthens all of us, just as moaning and whining depresses us.

Q: Would you call yourself a homosexual novelist?

A: Oh no, I haven't written about homosexuality, at least not very much. I've introduced some homosexual characters, but that's not the same thing. *A Single Man* is about minority feelings, but really most of the stuff in it is quite generalized. It would apply certainly to blacks, and probably to Jews too, but to a lesser degree because obviously here in America the Jews are in a very much better position than either the blacks or the homosexuals.

Q: Do you think the homosexual writer, or the black writer, or the Jewish writer, have special insights which might be of value to the majority audience?

A: Well, I think it's good for the majority to be reminded from time to time that there's a great underlying resentment on the part of the minority. Minorities want to be given their rights and also in a sense want to be allowed to live their own lives. These two things are very important and it's worth reminding people of them.

There's an old story told about the gold rush days. There's this fellow who doesn't know what to do—he can't get any sex. Finally he says to a friend, "What does one do for sex?" He's told there is this Chinese cook in the camp. The man in need of sex is terribly shocked, but finally says, "All right. I'll do it. But nobody else must know." The guy he's talking to says, "Well, that's a little difficult. You see, four other people must know." *"Four!"* the man cries. "That's right," his friend says, "the four men who hold the cook down. You see, he doesn't like it any more than you do." That's a wonderful civil rights story. It's very good sometimes as a minority member to remind people that you don't like it any more than they do.

They think it's very charming, for instance, that they can neck all over the place but you're not allowed to kiss your boyfriend in public. A married couple, ever so liberal and nice, will ask a homosexual for dinner, and then impose and project their domesticity in every possible way. It never occurs to the married couple that they're being the least bit tactless. Little things like that are amusing to point out. You don't have to get nasty. When you have a serious statement of your wrongs, then I think political writing with facts and figures is better.

Q: You have been a Vedantist now for over thirty years and have written about it extensively in essays. Would you also say you are a religious novelist?

A: Well, yes, I think *A Meeting by the River* is a religious novel. Very much so.

Q: Would you include any other novels written since your conversion?

A: Well, there are religious elements in them. There's not an awful lot in *A Single Man.* That's another thing I leave out of the character of George, that he really has no spiritual resources. In that way he's a kind of old-fashioned stoic. He's absolutely backed up against the wall. This is another reason he's unlike me personally, just as his predicament is unlike mine, because I don't live alone or suffer from those disadvantages, I'm happy to say.

Q: In his recent book about you, Alan Wilde concludes that as a writer, you can best be described as an ironic moralist. Would you agree?

A: Well, I think I'm ironic, yes. Perhaps *was* rather more than *am*. There is a kind of irony in my work. And my humor, I don't know how to describe it. It has a sort of double edge thing to it, very often.

Q: Directed inwards and outwards, at the persona as well as at others?

A: Yes, a little bit. It sort of makes fun of the persona.

Q: You once described yourself as a "serious comic writer." Do you still think of yourself in this way?

A: Yes, I have no use for out and out comedy writing or out and out tragedy writing. They bore me to distraction equally. I think both pictures that they give of life are false in the most heartless way. I don't know which is worse— the triviality of the total comedian or the superficiality of the total tragedian.

Q: E. M. Forster was your model for this kind of serious comic writing, wasn't he?

A: Yes, very much. He was my great, great shining example.

Q: I know that Forster was a long-time friend of yours. Did you ever try to convince him that he should have published *Maurice,* his posthumously published novel about homosexuality?

A: Oh yes, we talked about it constantly, ever since I first met him, which was quite a long time ago, in the early 1930s.

Q: Why didn't he ever publish it?

A: First of all, it would have upset his mother. There were other people who felt it would have caused a disturbance. I think it would have, too. It's very nasty from their point of view, very subversive. It's a partisan book, it's a very slanted book. There's no question about that. It's really an absurdly militant book. But that, of course, is also its charm.

Q: Haven't you donated the royalties from *Maurice* to a fellowship fund for English writers who wish to visit America?

A: Yes, but that isn't nearly as noble as you make it sound! It was always understood that I should use the money in this way. Forster and I discussed this many years before he died. I was extremely lucky in that I had this marvelously simple way of doing it. It was very easy for me to hand the whole thing over to the National Institute of Arts and Letters, of which I am a member. I wouldn't have known how to set up a fund, or decide who should receive the awards, or anything. They have vast experience of doing this sort of thing.

Q: What are your feelings today about the uproar caused when you and Auden left England together for America in 1939? Do you think that perhaps some readers and critics responded negatively to your later works because of your leaving?

A: I don't think it lasted very long. I don't think the English are very vindictive in that sort of way, to start off with. Also, I think they tended to see, as time passed, that all of this was really part of a life-pattern. You see, I had hardly lived in England since I was an adult. I went to Berlin when I was twenty-five. I was always roaming around all over the place, coming back to England just for visits. Also, at the time I left, they hadn't known about my pacifism.

Q: You have done a lot of teaching and lecturing about writing at various universities. Do you find this beneficial to a writer?

A: Well, I get very tired of it very quickly. I like it for just a little while. I get tired of hearing my old songs again. I get bored with them. I have a few tapes that people made and I think, oh dear, I said that much better ten years ago, why say it again, and not so well.

Q: Would you say you are a disciplined writer? Do you, for example, set aside a particular time each day to write?

A: No, it's not a question of setting aside time. I do make a kind of act of the will every day. I mean I do something with it and if you do that, even if you do only a very little, it all gradually adds up. And then there are days you do a great deal. And of course as you get nearer to the end of something you always do more and more and more. That is my experience.

Q: Are you a slow worker?

A: Yes. I always like to say to myself, "Well, you've got all the time you need. Don't fuss. Just keep on."

Q: Although many of your novels are distinguished by the use of the Christopher Isherwood persona, many of your other novels are quite different from these. Would you consider yourself an experimental novelist?

A: I think in the very, very beginning, yes. *All the Conspirators* is full of little jazzy tricks, including a good deal of imitation of Joyce in *Ulysses.*

Q: There are some other parallels between Joyce's novel and some of your other novels. For example, there is the relationship between the young artist and the Jewish father figure in *Prater Violet,* the question and answer technique at the end of *A Single Man,* and the single day aspect of that novel.

A: In neither of these cases was this kind of thing conscious. Possibly yes, in the case of the single day unit, but of course that had been used by people long, long before Joyce. It's very seldom that I actually say to myself, I'll do it in a certain way because somebody else did it.

Q: I'm almost hesitant to bring this up, but there is a character named Joyce in *Prater Violet.* Was that purely accidental?

A: I should say that is absolutely and totally accidental, yes. Joyce, after all, has quite a different connotation when it's a woman's name. It suggests a certain kind of person to me.

Q: Which of your books gave you the most difficulty in writing?

A: *The World in the Evening.* The reason for that was that I was up the wrong tree, trying to get at it in different ways, and never could. I wish now that I had taken it apart. I often think that I would like to have written it from the point of view of a minor character and begun it like Ford Madox Ford in the beginning of *The Good Soldier*—"This is the saddest story I ever heard." I would say, "This is a story about the two most unpleasant people I ever met."

I believe it would take the curse off Elizabeth and Stephen completely if you admitted that there was something unpleasant about them. In fact, Don Bachardy and I started to write a play years ago based on *The World in the Evening* which we called *The Monsters,* and the monsters were Elizabeth and Stephen.

Q: Is the problem with Elizabeth's character the fact that she is presented as being almost perfect?

A: In a way. I wanted to have a woman who had sort of a legend. But of course underneath you showed a whole life going on between them, full of friction. I mean, they were beautiful people on the surface. Everyone thought, what a beautiful relationship they had.

Q: Which of your books pleases you the most?

A: *A Single Man.*

Q: Why?

A: Because everything fits. It sort of keeps going, and it's varied. Something is happening under the surface. And it's all very much out of my experience, very close to my experience . . . I don't know . . . It's hard to say.

Q: It seems to me that *A Single Man* would make an excellent film.

A: Oh yes, it's very often been considered as a film. As a matter of fact, we have every intention of making it into film, sooner or later. But you've got to have the right director.

Q: I suppose you would hate to see the novel damaged in any way by transferring it to the screen.

A: Well actually, one would begin by departing very much from the book. One thing right away which occurs to me which I would like would be that the dead lover ought to be seen every so often, just sitting about in the room, smoking, lounging with his feet up, quite solid. Or he would be coming down the stairs and they would pass each other, or he would be seen looking in at the window. In other words, the thought of this person is quite solid so you would see the person. I think there should be a considerable period before you realize that the person isn't alive.

There are many, many other things. For example, the way the fantasies are treated, the sex fantasies, and the fantasies of destroying the high-rise buildings. There's a sequence toward the end where George is masturbating and has these sex fantasies and keeps changing the actors in the fantasies because they don't function properly. This could be an extraordinary scene of comedy which I have never seen on the screen. There would be new people like players in a football game continually running out onto the field.

And I think maybe this detached narrative voice could actually lecture at certain points. I'm not sure, for instance, that toward the end, just when George is going to die, there shouldn't be an actual chart shown, with animated diagrams where you see the formation of the plaque, showing exactly what happens. You see the heart working and have this explained in a very flat voice by a sort of lecturer.

Q: You have used a number of different narrative forms over the years—in novels, biographies, plays, movies, etc. Do you find the narrative problems essentially the same in all forms?

A: Oh no, certainly not. After all, with film, the whole business is to create the image, to clear the way for the image. All the talk is nothing. If you want to talk, use the theater. If you want to show, use the film.

Q: What about the novel?

A: Oh well, the novel, my goodness, the novel is much subtler to my mind than either of these media because you can have all this dialogue. Description is all very nice and none of us can resist it, but actually it's not very powerful as a rule and doesn't take us very far into the way things look. But, you see, you can also analyze everything in the novel. You can stand back from the conversation and say, "Yes, now you watch those two. Isn't it funny. You see, he's the one who keeps waving the knife, but it's perfectly obvious he's not going to stab her. He has no intention of it." Why hasn't he? Does she know that? All these kinds of things are impossible, I don't care who is writing, for the stage and the screen. You can't show that in the same way. You can show it perhaps in another way, but this is what the novel is all about to my mind. It cuts much deeper.

Christopher Isherwood: He Is a Camera

Anne Taylor Fleming / 1972

From *L.A.* 9 December 1972: 14–16. Reprinted by permission.

If people recognize the name at all, they probably think he is dead or at least quietly awaiting that event in his homeland, England. They would be wrong twice. In fact, they might have even seen him jogging at Will Rogers State Beach or working out at Bruce Connors Gym in Westwood, one or the other of which he tries to do every afternoon, or at a Hollywood party buried between beautiful people and would-be artists. Unlike them, his name can be found in the appropriate directory under Isherwood, Christopher 145 Adelaide Dr., Santa Monica. He lives in the same house in the Santa Monica Canyon where he has lived for the past thirteen years. He calls Los Angeles his home. "I'll be seventy next year. I have spent half my life in the United States. Los Angeles is a great place for feeling at home because everybody's from someplace else," he says, curled like a small grey-haired pixie, in khaki corduroys and an army shirt, legs crossed in front of him, on his narrow bed. Under him is an Indian throw of muted brown and orange; a similar one covers a small rectangle of the white-washed wooden floor—so California—that runs throughout the house. The room is spare. The only other color is in the jigsaw faces behind Isherwood's head, recent paintings by the man he has lived with "twenty years come February," Don Bachardy. There is the bed, two chairs, a long desk in front of a window facing the sea, and a night-table smothered in books with titles like *Stravinsky, Mind Games, Scientology*. Books cover every wall in neat rows. Frequently while he is talking, Isherwood looks at them, hopping up from his perch from time to time to stand in stocking feet, thumbing through a volume to find a lost name, a lost phrase, his milk-blue eyes—that particular English blue—sparkling wildly.

He talks today of Auden and Huxley; he has known them, lived beside them. He talks of hashish and mescaline, he has taken them. He talks of Hinduism and of God; he believes in both of them. He talks of Hollywood; he has been starstruck like most people. He talks of Jung and Forster, of Venice Beach, of his latest play *A Meeting by the River* which will open a trial run in New York, December 18; of McGovern, of ecology, of death and euthanasia, and of California, his home since May, 1939, his final home.

Earlier he had written of it in an essay on Los Angeles in *Exhumations*: "California is a tragic country like Palestine, like every Promised Land. Its short history is a fever chart of migrations—the land rush, the gold rush, the oil rush, the movie rush, the Okie fruit-picking rush, the wartime rush to the aircraft factories—followed, in each instance, by counter-migrations of the disappointed and unsuccessful moving sorrowfully homeward." Although he calls himself "the most unsuccessful screenwriter in Hollywood," Isherwood is not disappointed with his chosen land. In fact, he not only calls Los Angeles home, but in a quiet, unannounced way he has become its poet-in-residence, writing about the evils and beauties of the city with equal excitement and compassion.

The place he finds most beautiful is the shore, "the stretch of ocean running five or six miles south from Santa Monica Canyon to Venice, partly inside, partly outside the city limits of Los Angeles." He wrote of this stretch in *Exhumations* that ". . . most of this beach district is down-at-heel; it has little to do with the Los Angeles of legend, city of movie studios and tycoons, stars that shed no light and searchlights that seek for nothing, glamourized graveyards, oranges and advertisements equally large and tasteless. This is not so much a waterfront as a backyard washed by waves." In the three and a half page essay, Isherwood writes about Santa Monica Canyon, Marion Davies's house, Santa Monica Pier, Muscle Beach, Ocean Park Amusement Pier, the boardwalks and the bungalows that fill the spaces between them, and of Venice: "Today, Venice is a quiet shabby little place at the edge of an oil field which extends for a mile or two along the shore. But you can still see the hotel where Sarah Bernhardt stayed. You can still live at an address on the Grand Canal (though a garbage raft will float past your window instead of a gondola); you can still admire the pure curve of a bridge which would not disgrace Italy, except that it stands among oil derricks, is made of wood and plaster and is apt to fall down soon."

He says of the same stretch today: "I think you can still find elements of everything I talked about. You feel the pathos of people who have come out to the very edge, who are living far from their base; the pathos of people who couldn't drag another inch and have created a far away model of the home-place; people living on the westernmost point looking out. It's impossible to stay here and not go to the Islands, take off for the Orient. It's very romantic. Of course it's ridiculous to talk about California like that now," he worries

aloud about the way we abuse this shore, the object of his love, about so
many more "cardboard and spit" houses going up, about the pollution of the
water, about the tearing down of the Santa Monica Pier. He made appearances on behalf of Proposition 20 . . . and voted for McGovern. And yet it is
the impermanence of the city that seduced Isherwood and that has kept him
here. "And which," he writes at the end of his essay on "The Shore," in
Exhumations, "of all these flimsy structures, will be standing a hundred years
from now? Probably not a single one. Well, I like that thought. It is bracingly
realistic. In such surroundings, it is easier to remember and accept the fact
that you won't be here either."

Today he says: "It suits me very well. In Los Angeles, the old aren't made
a tremendous amount of. In England I feel I'd be embalmed. I'd be paid more
attention to, but it's the kind of attention used for putting on mummy cloths,
getting ready for the tomb. I hate the dark breath of the tomb which is often
mistaken for death. In England I'd be inclined to die," he says with the same
mixture of seriousness and detached amusement with which he might talk
about the weather. "The institutions, those big heavy monuments—I feel I'm
free of that here."

Isherwood arises at 7 A.M. each morning in his small white bedroom, facing the shore, where he now sits, and returns at nine after breakfast to sit
down at the typewriter, a ritual of many years. "I try to write something
every day. It doesn't matter how much as long as you make that effort of the
will. We (Don and himself) always work in the morning—the top of my head
you know. That's when the thoughts are thought, the ideas had . . . morning
is when I invent things I mean." At the moment, his daily writing includes a
movie script he and Don are writing together about a mummy and his diaries,
"from which most of my writing is based," in which he is trying to recon-
struct the "eight year bald patch between 1945 and 1952." The author of at
least eight novels, three plays, and assorted essays has composed at the typewriter for many years because "it gives you a certain distance. When I start
something I keep after it as a rule. Sometimes there are broken bits of stuff
left dangling which I'll later put into something else, but usually I write a
whole draft through, then another complete one, then another. It's usually the
third that's the one. When I was young I would advance chapter by chapter
securing my reader. It's not as good; its inorganic. Now I write quickly—after
all, that's the way it comes. I don't stop if something's not right, to fix a
character. If something is tricky, a bit of dialogue or something, I'll write it
down longhand on scribbling paper first." The first draft of *A Single Man,* a

small book about one day in a man's life which Isherwood calls "my most achieved work," took him eight months working every day, the finished product took two years.

If *A Single Man* is his favorite of his own works, E. M. Forster is his favorite writer or the "one I most modelled myself after." Forster, "not Forester," he says in gentle correction, "was revolutionary. He wrote in an extremely informal, low-keyed tone, never melodramatic, but extremely melodramatic things happen. Up to the point at which something happens and after that point, you can hardly believe your eyes. In one of his books," continues Isherwood, chuckling to himself as over a private joke, "he wrote about a young man who died. He simply said 'He was broken up on a football field.' The next scene the young man is in the dying shed with a girl leaning over him. When I was in Berlin, somebody gave him one of my novels and he liked it, not very much, a bit. I thought well my career's over. Now I'm a writer. That was fame on my terms," says Isherwood smiling. Of Forster as a person, Isherwood says: "He was absolutely adorable, so concerned . . . a real uncle."

To anyone who has read *A Single Man, Down There on a Visit* or *The World in the Evening,* the author proved himself a remarkable imitator on his own terms. That is to say that his prose is as wonderfully simple and his plots as quietly dramatic as any of Forster, in fact as the best of Forster. Isherwood lived his early years in the English literary salon presided over by Forster and Lawrence, and they became his gods. "I liked D. H. Lawrence because of his brute subjectivity. For so many of us he gave the wonderful feeling that your subjective impressions were the best you could offer the reader. When Lawrence didn't like Florence, Florence was hideous. This was incredible . . . not having to say what something actually looked like."

Isherwood does not at all believe that the novel is dead in this country—that oft heard cry. In fact, according to him, we're retracing Lawrence's steps. "We're right back to Defoe. He raised journalism to the power of art. Mailer does this. He takes reporting that little way beyond and starts being subjective. He sees the whole thing—like the Miami experience—in a flash. It's in the classic tradition. That's what Zola was trying to do," he says easily.

Like many of the serious writers before him who came to Hollywood, Isherwood got into the habit of supporting himself by writing screenplays, "an exercise in ingenuity" but one he does not resent. "I'm a storyteller," says Isherwood who has written dozens of scripts, among them his favorites, *Reflections in a Golden Eye,* from the Carson McCullers story and *The*

Great Sinner taken from Dostoevsky's *The Gambler.* He'll tell you in loving detail the intricacies of each plot. All of his screenplays have been overshadowed—at least for the moment—by *Cabaret,* the musical-movie of his first big book, *Goodbye to Berlin,* the script this time not his. *Goodbye to Berlin* was published just before World War II. It was made into a play, *I Am a Camera,* by John van Druten in 1950, became a movie, then a musical, *Cabaret,* and finally a musical movie. "All of them were out of my hands," says Isherwood who did not become fabulously rich from any of them. "All negotiations were shared with the Van Druten estate. I just get my fraction of that, which is shared with the people who put *Cabaret* together and the lawyers. I'm well fixed; I don't have great expenses, just the house, and no dependents. I have no particular security but what one wants with security I don't know."

The movie *Cabaret* was not overwhelmingly to his liking but "you know how it is when you're working with a studio," he says without bitterness. "Liza is so . . . positive. And the sex is done in a way that makes it dirty . . . oh, la la, snickering. The boy in the movie is fashionably bisexual. Towards the end, he and Sally (Bowles, the heroine) try to pretend they're in love. It's all so half-assed. The sex never came out of anything; it was caprice, shadow-play. A person could go to bed with a Newfoundland dog and make an audience respect it if he could make them believe that he cared about the dog or the dog cared about him. I respect lust completely—lust for lust's sake—but these people don't even feel lust let alone anything else. It's like these nude shows in the theater where men go around jumping on everybody without even having an erection. I'm in favor of liberty. Theaters should never be closed; one can always walk out on them, but the sex is often trifling, a bore."

"I've always had the feeling that I could only really know my own personal experiences; I'm a born existentialist. I put myself in the book to talk about Sally—there was a real one. It didn't matter what I was or was not. I was a perfectly normal 100 percent homosexual. You couldn't say that then. We were like brother and sister. I shared her bed when I was broke. There was never a cross word between us. Homosexuals do embrace and kiss girls. They do go to bed with them sometime for the fun of it . . . just like men fall into bed with other men. This talk of perversion is nonsense. There can only be perversion when there's cruelty."

Patrick, one of the brothers in *A Meeting by the River,* says it this way: "What I want is a life beyond their taboos, in which two men learn to trust each other so completely that there's no fear left and they experience everything together in the flesh and in the spirit. I don't believe such closeness is possible between a man and a woman—deep down they are natural enemies—and how many men ever find it together."

If Forster and Lawrence were Isherwood's literary models, Aldous Huxley and Gerald Heard were his spiritual mentors. When he first came to Los Angeles in the late '30s, they had introduced him to their friend, Swami Prabhavananda, a Hindu monk of the Ramakrishna Order who had founded a small Vedanta center in Hollywood. Isherwood helped the Swami to refine some Sanskrit translations and gradually became his disciple. "I gradually ceased to be an atheist because I found myself unable to disbelieve in his belief in God. By seeing this man vividly as an individual two or three times a week over a long period, I knew he was not insane, that he had had the mystical experiences he said he had, that his resource was open to me," says Isherwood. Isherwood has attended the center since then—at present, two or three times a month—and meditates daily. "During your daily reverie, things keep popping up, like the traffic ticket you got, whatever. Into this reverie, you introduce the concept of God which then begins to pop up regularly. It's better than saying 'cancer, cancer, cancer.' If you say cancer enough, you'll probably bring it on yourself."

If Heard and Huxley were ahead of everybody about religion, they certainly were, in Isherwood's words, "aware of psychedelic drugs long before most people knew what the word meant. That was the wonderful thing about them. They were open to everything," says Isherwood, eyes alight, hands in motion. Huxley first took mescaline in Saskatchewan, Canada in May, 1953, in the presence of a Dr. Osmond who had been using it on schizophrenics and wanted now to try it on "the most sane man he knew." "Huxley wrote about it in his books *(Doors of Perception),*" says Isherwood, moving to pick up the appropriate volume, and excitedly, as if the moment were now, quoting his friend: "I took four-tenths of a gram of mescaline and sat down to wait for the results."

"Naturally when I heard about it, I was thrilled to the teeth. In 1955 when it was still legal, I walked into a drugstore in New York and bought some mescaline. I took it in a hotel in London. I had had some hashish in Morocco—both majoun which you eat and kif which you smoke—and seen horrors of a major sort. Now a month later I was taking mescaline. I thought, you idiot, what have you done." Isherwood hopped a cab to Westminster Abbey to see if God was there. "He absolutely was not." When he had taken the hash in Morocco, Isherwood had seen "an enormous possibility of terror, loneliness, the abyss." "But," he says, "I always knew which end was up, even though I was in another kind of reality. It was just a matter of whether or not to panic. It doesn't upset your system of philosophic values or your view of the universe. But I did see the possibility of a temporary Hell."

"Huxley took it dozens of times always in extremely controlled situations. In fact, he went out on a low dosage LSD trip. When he was very far gone but still conscious, he asked his wife for some LSD. The doctor said it could make no difference so she gave it to him. He made a few more remarks. Huxley died the same afternoon President Kennedy was shot. I saw him maybe two weeks before he died. He was never in undue pain. His mind was sharp until the end."

"Sure I miss them," says Isherwood of his dead friends. The afternoon sun has left the room; he has been talking with small pause for two hours. "But," he said, "life is an immediate predicament. We live quietly here. We do go out a great deal at night—to movies mostly, or to see friends. I'm not mad about parties. There are people in Hollywood I like who happen to be stars. I'm tremendously fond of Jennifer Jones. I've known her since back in the David Selznick days. I was a pallbearer at his funeral. There are others but I never remember names. There are actresses we're terribly pleased to run into. But you know how it is in Hollywood. You don't see someone for two or three years and you're still friends and when you run into them, it's a fiesta. And Don has his own friends. He's brought artists into the house. There are some extraordinary ones here—Ed Moses, Billy Al Bengston, Ed Ruscha," each of whose work is hanging in Isherwood's very simple living room.

"You were asking 'didn't I miss all sorts of things?'; which is perfectly natural. There is something I want to make clear. My life is really by all odds much happier than it ever has been. It's not a question of resignation. I'm perfectly happy in my life. I'm less tortured by anxieties now than I ever have been."

"I'm terrified of an unpleasant passage but I cannot possibly feel fear about the after-experience. I am strongly in favor of euthanasia. My generation's fathers who were doctors all killed people—freaks, misbirths—as a matter of course. I would sign a paper right now, this minute, requesting that it be done to me. Heard had a succession of strokes that left him more crippled each time but never killed him off. I wouldn't shoot myself, because I have a feeling the instant is prolonged. I would take an overdose of morphia in my own time. My religion's opposed to it—they say it interferes with Karma. But I'd do it myself to people I cared for. I'd do it to myself.

"We can't really know what comes after, but if there is a continuity of consciousness, then everything else I believe is true. In the abyss, there will still be that resource. It is obviously unimaginable because we lose all sense of identity as a noun."

Christopher Isherwood Interview
Winston Leyland / 1973

From *Gay Sunshine Interviews* Volume 1. (San Francisco: Gay Sunshine Press, 1978): 199–206. Reprinted by permission.

Two separate interviews are printed here: Interview I was taped in summer 1973 by Winston Leyland, editor of *Gay Sunshine,* and originally appeared in *Gay Sunshine* 19 (September–October 1973). This interview is copyright © 1978, 1984 by Gay Sunshine Press Inc. Winston Leyland (San Francisco) is the publisher of Gay Sunshine books, information on which can be accessed at www.gaysunshine.com. Interview II was taped in San Francisco in December 1976 while Isherwood was touring with his book *Christopher and His Kind.* It was conducted under the auspices of Fruit Punch, gay men's radio, which broadcast an edited version over KPFA (Berkeley) in February 1977. The late Roger Austen, who conducted the second interview, authored the book *Playing the Game: The Homosexual Novel in America* (1977) and wrote the introductions to the two books of writings by turn-of-the-century California writer, Charles Warren Stoddard: *Cruising the South Seas* (Gay Sunshine Press, 1987); and the novel *For the Pleasure of His Company: An Affair of the Misty City* (Gay Sunshine Press, 1987). Both interviews are reprinted with permission from the book *Gay Sunshine Interviews Volume 1,* edited by Winston Leyland, Gay Sunshine Press, 1978, 1984.

Leyland: In the introduction to your *Berlin Stories,* you say that you destroyed your past and that the real Christopher Isherwood disappeared. What did you mean by that statement?

   Isherwood: Well, that's a literary phrase. My religion, Vedanta, encourages me to believe that there isn't one single, *real* Christopher Isherwood, in a personal sense. There are many, all equally real or unreal. When I started writing about Berlin, I found that the story would be more coherent and indeed *truer* if I fictionalized it to some degree. And so I started rewriting my life and therefore manufacturing a different Christopher. But the story never departs from my own essential experience. It's still Berlin as I saw it. I never gave my fictitious Christopher any characteristics or virtues or vices which I didn't have myself. I agree with Hemingway—one should only write what one knows.

Of course, the Berlin experience seemed different to me then. While I was there, it didn't seem as glamorous to me as it now does. As a matter of fact, there were long periods which were dull and quiet, when things went on much as usual. Nowadays, people often say to me: "Jesus, if only I had lived in those days! If only I'd been with you there!" I smile to myself, because I think how bored they'd have been a lot of the time. And yet, the funny thing is, I can look back at Berlin through their eyes—looking through the telescope of my stories, as it were—and see Berlin as they see it.

Leyland: Don't you think that people are romanticizing the San Francisco beat period in the fifties in the same way?

Isherwood: Of course they are. But there *are* periods in one's life which one finds romantic at the time as well as afterwards. For instance, my trip to China with Auden in 1938 seemed just as romantic at the time as it does now. But Berlin—because I stayed there several years—became simply a way of life. In the winter it was a very dark and drab city; heavy buildings. I gave English lessons, day after day. A boyfriend would come by in the evenings and we'd go to the movies. It was enjoyable but certainly not a scintillating or brilliant period. It was appetizing, because I was young and full of life and tremendously happy to be away from all the restraints which England represented—above all, to feel completely free sexually. Also, it was a great freedom to be able to speak a foreign language. I could say things in German which it would have still embarrassed me to say in English: things about love and sex, particularly. And that made me feel like a new person. Nevertheless, at the end of three and a half years, I had gotten pretty used to all that. It was no longer a thrill.

Leyland: Were your characters in *The Berlin Stories* taken from real life?

Isherwood: Yes, certainly. No important character in the Berlin books is without a model from real life.

Leyland: What about Baron Kuno von Pregnitz? He's almost a caricature of the Prussian homosexual.

Isherwood: The imaginary island where he lived with all the boys—I took that from another character, actually. This sort of baron—I mean, someone who put on the airs of being an aristocrat, even though his title was often invented by himself—was a stock figure in the Berlin homosexual bar world.

I suppose I was always aware, in the back of my mind, of an intention to write about Berlin, even while I was there. That was why I kept a diary. It was very terse and fragmentary, but it helped me to remember a lot of things later.

When I started to write the novel about Mr. Norris in 1934, about a year after I'd left Berlin for good, I was very much under the spell of another experience I'd just had. In 1933, I got a job—the first of that kind—writing for the movies, in England. (That's all described in my story *Prater Violet*.) Because of this job, I became intensely cinema-minded. I had always been a great movie fan, anyhow. Now I was in love with plotting, action, and trying to tell a story in visual terms. Even while writing this novel, I kept thinking how its scenes would look on the screen. That was good. But the effect of my plot-mindedness was that I put my portrait of Mr. Norris into a primitive, pre–Eric Ambler story, with some absurd melodrama about espionage. I adore spy stories, both in books and on the screen; but in this case the two styles of story-telling didn't blend very well.

Leyland: But the character of Mr. Norris certainly does come alive.

Isherwood: Yes, he has managed to exist independently, outside the book itself, as it were, in the minds of many readers. The original of Mr. Norris also existed independently—alas, he's dead now—and often did things which I could never have invented in my wildest dreams. But he was very conscious of the fictitious Mr. Norris and even wrote a book called *Mr. Norris and I.* His real name was Gerald Hamilton.

I'm often asked if I regret that I didn't say outright in *The Berlin Stories* that I was homosexual. Yes, I wish I had. But I should have had to say it very *casually,* if I *had* said it; otherwise, I would have made the Christopher character too odd, too remarkable, and that would have upset the balance between him and the other characters. Christopher is the narrator, so he mustn't stand out too prominently. To have made him homosexual, in those days, would have been to feature him as someone eccentric. I would have made a star out of a supporting actor. That's a valid literary reason. But I must also frankly say that I would have been embarrassed, then, to create a homosexual character and give him my own name.

Leyland: Do you think you could have gotten an explicitly homosexual book about yourself published in the thirties?

Isherwood: Oh yes, I could have got such a book published if I hadn't gone into too many details about homosexual lovemaking. But I must come back to what I've just been saying: in those days, people expected you to announce the theme of homosexuality with a flourish of trumpets. By the time I'd finished introducing and explaining and apologizing for Christopher the homosexual, there would have been no room in the book for my other characters. It would have overbalanced the boat.

Leyland: It's difficult now to get interviews with some well-known writers and poets who are gay in their private life but have never let the gay dimension into their writing. Some are uptight about being interviewed in a journal like *Gay Sunshine.*

Isherwood: If a writer doesn't want to admit to his homosexuality publicly, that's his affair. But to refuse specifically to do so in the gay magazines, that's sheer snobbery. That means he's ashamed of his brothers and sisters.

Leyland: In *The Berlin Stories* you yourself came more to the surface in the Peter and Otto story. Did you have an affair with the boy Otto when you were in Germany?

Isherwood: Yes. In that story, I took a real person, a friend, and described him in the character of Peter, an English homosexual. As a matter of fact, it wasn't Peter who was living with Otto Nowak on Ruegen Island; it was I myself. Otto and I were lovers for quite a long period and lived together some of the time. Actually, there were only two boys who were really close to me during the whole time I was in Berlin. First Otto, then another boy who left Germany and traveled with me. To some degree, the other one is described as Waldemar, in *Down There on a Visit.*

Toward the end of my stay in Germany, I became much more conscious of the political situation. The Berlin books were written with a good deal of political hindsight. I couldn't resist posing as someone who had been deeply concerned with the fate of Germany right from the day of my arrival. That simply wasn't true. To begin with, I was both indifferent and ignorant. And even as late as 1932, I find that I wrote to my mother and spelt Hitler's name wrong!

In the working-class world of Berlin, every young attractive man was under economic pressure to become a hustler; nobody was getting enough to eat. These hustlers were apt to become gang-minded; they joined political parties which fought in gangs against other rival political gangs. These boys were pretty vague about the political part of it. They just wanted some action to relieve the frustration of their lives. They switched sides continually. Many of them who had called themselves Communists became Nazis when it was obvious who was going to win.

Leyland: Were Spender and Auden in Berlin at that time?

Isherwood: Not nearly as much. Auden came before I did, to brush up on his German because he intended to become a schoolmaster. But he soon left. We were old friends; we'd met at school when he was seven and I was ten. We met again in our teens and I discovered to my amazement that he wrote poetry. Then we became really intimate. Later, Stephen Spender came to Berlin from Hamburg, where he had been living. (You can read all about that in his autobiography, *World within World,* which is pretty frank about both our lives.)

Leyland: There is an unfavorable mention in *The Berlin Stories* of the German Youth Councils of that period. What were your feelings behind that comment?

Isherwood: I don't like that passage and I don't know why I put it in. It strikes an insincere, rather puritanical note. I may have written like that because I felt that these people were in a fair way to becoming fascists. But that in itself has an unfair implication and a very dangerous one. I should have discussed the whole question fully or left it alone. Does homosexuality predispose you to join group movements of young men and hence, in certain historical circumstances, to become part of a totalitarian group? Maybe so. But that isn't the whole story. An awful lot of homosexuals who were conned into doing this in Germany later discovered to their cost how totalitarian regimes deal with homosexuals. At the time of the Roehm scandals in 1934, there was an out-and-out attack on homosexuals as such, although the real reason for the liquidation of Roehm was entirely political. And in Soviet Russia, about the same time, homosexuals were being denounced as fascists. Both Communists and Nazis regarded them as potential traitors.

Leyland: And, of course, gay people ended up in Nazi concentration camps. We had a short article on this in *Gay Sunshine* 18. A lot of people associate homosexuality in Germany in the early thirties with Roehm's SA gang. A caricature of homosexuals has been built up, as exemplified in the movie *The Damned.*

Isherwood: Yes, there's a strong suggestion in *The Damned* that homosexuality is a factor in the damnation. People ask me nowadays, "Wasn't it kind of decadent there?" meaning, actually, homosexual. It's infuriating; it's such a vicious oversimplification to say that pre-Hitler Germany was decadent and so a Sodom and Gomorrah punishment fell upon it through the Nazis who in their turn of course were decadent too. You end up by saying, "It's those

Germans; they're all decadent anyway, whatever party they belong to!" [*Laughter.*] As a matter of fact, I think Germans, when they're homosexual, make very good homosexuals. They're not in the least decadent, as far as my experience goes. They're simple and natural about it, and they have a strong natural capacity for tenderness and unashamed sentiment. I have often thought that I detected some of this same quality in Americans.

Sometimes I'm asked about my relationship with the girl who was the original of Sally Bowles in my stories—and of the Sally Bowles in the play and the film *I Am a Camera* and in the musical play and film *Cabaret.* My relationship with the real Sally Bowles was the simplest imaginable. She knew that I was fond of her like a sister and that I was a contented homosexual. We had no problems. Never were there any coy suggestions that I might be partly in love with her or secretly longing to go to bed with her. That's what I found a bit dirty about the film *Cabaret.* First the boy's supposed to be gay, and then he isn't, because he can make it with Sally, and then he is, after all, because he plays around with the Baron; and then he wants to marry her but she reminds him that he may lapse at some future date and run after boys again. His homosexuality is presented as a kind of indecent but ridiculous weakness to be snickered at, like bed-wetting.

Leyland: When did you first come to a realization of your own gayness?

Isherwood: Quite early—by the time I was ten or so, in the sense of being physically attracted to boys at school. I managed to have orgasms with them while we were wrestling and I guess some of them had orgasms too, but we never admitted to it. I fell in love a lot during my teens, but never did anything about it. I was very late in getting into an actual physical affair. That happened while I was in college. There was no question at all in my mind about my homosexuality. It was like a choice which my mind-body had definitely made. I was even willing to agree that I might have become heterosexual if I had decided to. I tried it a couple of times. It was quite workable. But I preferred boys and I already knew that I could fall in love with them. I have been perfectly happy the way I am. If my mother was responsible for it, I am grateful.

As I have said, coming to Germany was a psychological release for me. It was in Berlin that I first came in contact with an organized homosexual group. It was centered at the Institute for Sexual Science which was run by Dr. Magnus Hirschfeld. He was a great pioneer and himself a homosexual. He had managed to re-educate the Berlin police and liberalize their attitudes to sex. He and his associates were deadly serious about their work in a typically German way which often seemed funny to a foreigner. I laughed at them often, then. Now I see them as heroic and noble. (Their institute was later wrecked by the Nazis.) Many people came to see Hirschfeld from all over Europe.

I remember how Hirschfeld put on a special scientific demonstration for André Gide. Among other exhibits, they brought in a boy with two perfectly formed female breasts. Gide sat there judiciously holding his chin. He had a very pragmatical attitude toward the whole thing and didn't want to listen to a lot of theories. Gide liked very young boys. At the bar he visited (it was one of my regular hangouts) they couldn't find anyone young enough for him, so they produced a boy who was actually about twenty-three but looked fifteen. There were no complaints. Gide was rather grand and gracious, with a cape. He liked to be called "maître." I didn't appreciate his greatness then as I do now. I thought him a snob—but then I thought anybody was a snob who didn't live in the slums.

Leyland: Isn't that an upper-class English romanticism—an idealization of the lower classes and a desire to associate with them?

Isherwood: Typically upper class, yes. My own snobbery was simply inverted. Upper-class homosexuality in England tended to fixate on working-class boys. I didn't really recover from that state of mind until I began to live in America. When I found myself living in the working-class section of Berlin I felt I had transposed images and was playing the role of my own lover, so to speak. I had enough money to live in a more respectable part of town if I had wanted to, and I did, later. I moved into a slum tenement because of this boy Otto. I lived with him and his family.

Leyland: What was the attitude of your contemporaries in England to homosexuality?

Isherwood: Most of my friends were either homosexual themselves or very relaxed in their attitude toward it. They had been to upper-class schools and were therefore quite accustomed to it. But then, I instinctively avoided people who I thought might disapprove of me. I never allowed anyone I knew intimately to be under any misunderstanding about my own homosexuality.

I came to the United States to live in 1939. I was very drawn to the Quakers because of their pacifism. And, more recently, they have put out an admirably positive statement about homosexuality. It was maybe a little condescending in places but it did say flatly that homosexual love can be, under certain circumstances, just as worthy of respect as heterosexual love.

Leyland: Were they idealizing monogamous gay love in a typically liberal approach?

Isherwood: That's probably so. I agree that it's very dangerous to equate a homosexual relationship with heterosexual marriage. You drag in the whole bourgeois system of obligations and the concept of ownership.

I would very much like to write a novel about gay life itself, but it's terribly hard to do so. I have never written much about homosexual relationships— just some references to them in *The World in the Evening* and *A Single Man*— although I myself have lived much of my live in a series of quite long relationships. In my diaries I've tried to examine my fantasies about sex and how they relate to the kind of relationships I've had. One of them is incestuous, the desire for a brother who is also a lover. A younger brother.

Leyland: Have most of your relationships followed this pattern?

Isherwood: Yes. All the relationships I've had have been with younger people than myself. I say "brother" rather than "son" because I don't like to think of the person I love as being a reproduction of myself. The idea of a brother suggests a greater polarity between us.

In my novel *A Meeting by the River,* and even more explicitly in the play which Don Bachardy and I have made out of it, there is a good deal of metaphor surrounding the two brothers who are the principal characters. One of them becomes a monk in a monastery in India and therefore has "brother" monks. The other, a married man, takes up with a California boy because he yearns for an ideal brother who is also a lover—a sort of Walt Whitman camerado. The two actual brothers have a love-hate relationship which binds them in spite of themselves until it is resolved at the end of the story.

Leyland: Do you think that the deep relationships you've had during your life have been satisfactory and fulfilling?

Isherwood: Fulfilling, yes. I'm a bit shy of the word "satisfactory." It suggests that something has been delivered as ordered, according to specifications. It suggests the phrase "fit and forget," as applied to something absolutely reliable and predictable; you install it and it functions from them on, no need to worry. With love there *ought* to be a need to worry, every moment. Love isn't an insurance policy. Love is tension. What I value in a relationship is constant tension, in the sense of never being under the illusion that one understands the other person. When you fall in love, you feel you've discovered the bird of paradise, the magic person from the Other Land. You suddenly see a human being in all his magic extraordinariness. And you know that you can never understand him, never take him for granted. He's eternally unpredictable—and so are you to him, if he loves you. And that's the tension. That's what you hope will never end.

In my novel *A Meeting by the River* the married brother's romantic feelings go out to men; he regards his marriage as a kind of fortress. He sallies forth from the fortress to have adventures. Then he rushes back into it and his male lover is left standing outside in the cold. This kind of bisexual interests me a great deal. I have met many of them during my life. I describe another of them in *The World in the Evening,* but the one in *Meeting* is far more convincing, I think.

Leyland: Do you feel that such people are really bisexual or basically homosexual?

Isherwood: It seems to me that the real clue to your sex orientation lies in your romantic feelings rather than in your sexual feelings. If you are really gay, you are able to fall in love with a man, not just enjoy having sex with him. That's the test I would apply to such people.

Leyland: In the gay world a dichotomy is often set up between the sexual and the romantic resulting in the one-night-stand syndrome. It's very hard (but very important) to integrate friendship and sex.

Isherwood: Yes, that's true. Some people I've talked to have been very amazed when I told them I have sometimes been to bed with friends. Auden says somewhere in his writings: "Awareness of likeness—kindness; awareness of difference—love." Friends have this awareness of likeness. The combination of sex and friendship can be beautiful, but it's apt to be short-lived because excitement doesn't last when you feel the awareness of likeness. The love remains, but it's a love without tension, a different kind of love. How could you fall in love with someone about whom you could say, "He's exactly like me"? That would be sheer narcissism. Once, when I was in my early forties, I met a boy who was at least fifteen years younger than I was. Everybody noticed how alike we were physically. "He could be your younger brother," they said. And I found him wildly attractive! He didn't take the slightest interest in me.

Leyland: When did you first feel the need for this creative tension?

Isherwood: When I was young. I didn't philosophize about it, but the need was undoubtedly there. When there was no tension, I wasn't really in love. But sometimes I tried to kid myself that I was, because the person I'd met was so "suitable" in every other way. I mean, he was somebody who would have done exactly what I wanted and never interfered with my work and waited for me when I went out and stayed home with me when I wanted to stay home. That was one side of my character, and it demanded a kind of chauvinistic marriage relationship. The other side of me knew it had to wait for the magic person, who would awaken real love and consequently tension and the destruction of convenience.

Leyland: You were tempted to isolate yourself from relationships by devoting yourself to writing?

Isherwood: Yes. When I was young in Berlin and apparently engaged in sowing my wild oats, I was terribly sensible about working. I got up early in the morning and wrote. At night I did go round to bars, but I always returned home early, with or without company, and managed to have a good night's sleep, sex or no sex.

Leyland: Have you been able to maintain this discipline?

Isherwood: Yes. I do keep at it. The important thing is that you do something every day, no matter how little. If you form the habit of work when you're young, it makes things easier later.

Leyland: Was the character of George in your novel *A Single Man* autobiographical?

Isherwood: Yes, to a large extent. But there are important differences. Unlike poor George, I've never had a lover who has died on me. Then again, George is a stoic and an agnostic, without any religious faith to help him through his life. He defies fate. He fights with bared teeth up to the last moment. I'm not a bit like that.

Again, George is a professional college professor. When I lecture at a college, I do so as a guest speaker. Therefore I can allow myself a great deal of freedom in what I say. I am expected to behave like a celebrity, not a professor, to amuse rather than instruct. The things I make George say in the classroom are the things that I would say. Coming from him, they are a bit out of character. But I feel *A Single Man* is the best thing I have ever written. This was the only time when I succeeded, very nearly, in saying exactly what I wanted to say.

Leyland: In his book *Homosexual Oppression and Liberation*, Dennis Altman quotes you talking about the "annihilation by blandness" which liberals adopt towards gays. To what extent have you been exposed to this in your own life?

Isherwood: Well, I've never been annihilated by it. But I've been very conscious that I was exposed to it. At one campus where I was lecturing, I asked a friend, "How many of my colleagues know I'm gay?" He answered, "All of them." I wasn't surprised. But, just the same, it was kind of spooky, because not one of them had ever given the faintest sign that he or she knew. If I had spoken about it myself, most of them would have felt it was in bad taste.

I suppose my own role as a gay is to try and get people out of their closets. When you're elderly and well known, closety types are apt to approve of you. Your books encourage their fantasies of freedom.

Leyland: What was the attitude of your parents to your gayness?

Isherwood: I've written about my parents extensively in my recent book *Kathleen and Frank.* I always felt that my mother had a built-in defense against the whole idea of homosexuality. She was unable to believe that a relationship without a woman in it could be serious, under any circumstances. She thought it was a sort of pose, a mental game that I played. I told her that I was gay, very soon after I grew up. She appeared to accept the situation. She was always polite to the young men I brought to the house, and in one or two cases she genuinely liked them. But I believe her imagination refused to accept the fact that I was actually having sex with them. Sometimes my mother's attitude made me furious. I think it even helped to confirm me in my homosexuality. I had to *prove* to her that there really is such a thing as a homosexual! But since she lived to be ninety-one, I had time to outgrow my antagonism; we ended by accepting our misunderstandings.

I think it would have been much harder for me to tell my father that I was gay. But that crisis never arose, because he was killed in World War I, when I was ten years old. I realize now that I was sexually attracted to my father, in my childhood. I used to go into his dressing room in the morning while he was doing physical exercises almost naked, in his undershorts. I can still remember liking the hardness of his muscles and the smell of his body.

I had a gay uncle with whom I had an amusing relationship after I grew up. He used to invite me to dinner at his flat and we would talk about boys. At the end of the evening, I would get a kiss from him which was rather too warm and searching for any nephew, even one's favorite.

When I started to write *Kathleen and Frank,* it was obvious to me that I couldn't tell their story without making my own gayness absolutely clear. So I kept stating this fact throughout the book. And this led naturally to similar statements on television, in public talks and in press interviews. So now I have officially "come out." Those who have always known that I was gay can now no longer pretend that they don't know. Those who have been prejudiced against me as a homosexual will now be confirmed in their prejudice. My fellow gays will mostly say "So what?" I don't risk being fired from a job, or sent to prison, or run out of town. Society can afford to overlook the deviant behavior of an elderly, otherwise respectable literary man who has sufficient savings in the bank. It may be that what I have done will inject a little courage into the souls of a few timid brothers. If so, good. If not, also good, because I at least feel a certain satisfaction.

About eighty percent of my friends have always been gay, and I feel curiously ill at ease when I have been away from gay people for long; it's a feeling almost like a lack of oxygen.

Many of my brothers have suffered terrible guilt because of their nature. Many more have been made to suffer because of it, by others. My life has been extremely lucky. To quote from *Kathleen and Frank:* "Despite the humiliations of living under a heterosexual dictatorship and the fury he has often felt against it, Christopher has never regretted being as he is. He is now quite certain that heterosexuality wouldn't have suited him; it would have fatally cramped his style."

The Wandering Stopped:
An Interview with
Christopher Isherwood

Carola M. Kaplan / 1973

From *The Isherwood Century: Essays on the Life and Work of Christopher Isherwood*. (Madison: University of Wisconsin Press, 2000): 259–79. Reprinted with permission.

The following interview took place in Christopher Isherwood's home—a modest, one-story, ranch-style dwelling in Santa Monica. The house, where he lived with Don Bachardy and where Bachardy still lives, is tucked into a hill on a quiet residential street above Santa Monica Canyon. To reach the house, which was virtually invisible from the street, I descended a steep staircase to a wooden gate, rang the bell, and proceeded down more steps, then along a stone patio to the entrance. Isherwood came to the door. His manner was cordial, relaxed, and welcoming. Small and slim, he looked tan, fit, and considerably younger than his almost seventy years. He ushered me into the large living room, whose walls were covered with paintings by contemporary artists. The most striking feature of the comfortable room was a large picture window, which looked down on the canyon and at the same time commanded a spectacular view of the ocean.

I had met Isherwood previously, after a talk he had given at one of the colleges in Claremont, a town some sixty miles to the east. I had rather shyly introduced myself and told him I was writing my dissertation on his work, focusing particularly on the novels he had written since his emigration to America. To my hesitant request for an interview, he had responded with alacrity, inviting me to call him at home, informing me that I could find his telephone number in the directory. On the day of the interview, I arrived, unsure of how to proceed, interview questions in one hand, tape recorder in the other. Isherwood was warm and reassuring. When I asked him if I could tape-record the interview, he replied, "Of course," and proceeded to help me set up the microphone for best reception, saying, "I have a lot of experience with these things." We sat opposite each other on two soft white contemporary couches, the tape recorder on a glass coffee table between. I had the flattering sensation that I had all his attention, while I was aware at the same time that his sharp eyes, startlingly blue against his deeply tanned, still-boyish face, missed nothing. He was dressed casually, his sport shirt open at the collar, revealing his body to be as tanned as his face. Throughout the interview, I was struck—and immensely touched—by his friendliness, his openness, and his apparent vulnerability that seemed to be strongly supported by an underlying surety. Listening to him, I had the feeling that he drew upon deep resources he had been long in acquiring.

Before the interview began, Isherwood told me that he had just finished writing the screenplay of *A Meeting by the River* in collaboration with Bachardy. He was very pleased with the result, which was an adaptation of the play version, on which they had also collaborated. Both of these adaptations are based on Isherwood's 1967 novel, a religious comedy about two brothers whose lifelong rivalry leads to a final confrontation and ambiguous resolution. Their crisis erupts when the younger brother, Oliver, a formal social activist, informs Patrick that he is living in a monastery in India and is about to take final vows as a Hindu monk. Patrick, a charming hedonist, currently juggling his marriage to Penny and his affair with Tom, whom he met while negotiating a movie deal in Hollywood, rushes to India to attempt to persuade Oliver to change his mind.

I was pleased to begin the interview with a discussion on this particular book and its adaptations because *A Meeting by the River* was the first book I had ever read of Isherwood's. I had picked it up in paperback, as light holiday reading—or so I mistakenly judged it to be. Since I knew nothing about Isherwood or his work, I had the rare and delightful experience of "discovering" him. I so loved the novel, which proved both profound and provocative, that I proceeded to read all of his fiction with an avidity I had not known since childhood. What made *A Meeting by the River* particularly attractive to me was the fact that it is a religious novel, and I admired immensely Isherwood's deftness and humor in handling this difficult form. Since I had then decided to write my dissertation on "The Search for Belief in the Novels of Christopher Isherwood," much of my interview with him centers on this theme.

I came to the interview feeling a strong kinship with the person who had emerged for me through autobiographical characters in Isherwood's novels. Of course, I feared I might be disappointed in speaking to the actual man, but the reverse was the case. I had a feeling of great rapport with him: there was an ease and flow in our conversation, and I was aware throughout that he was sincerely concerned to respond to my inquiries with care and honesty. At the time I was in a period of spiritual searching in my own life. I believe he picked up on that and took great pains to answer my questions, to allay my doubts, and to encourage me in my quest.

As I read over the interview, after the passage of twenty-five years, I am struck by its personal quality. Isherwood's responses seem to me wonderfully straightforward and unself-conscious—his remarks not at all delivered for effect, but simply as one side of a conversation between two people with a compelling common concern: how one may come to spiritual insight, and how this insight changes one's life and work. It seems to me extraordinary that he was willing to speak with a virtual stranger about so many intimate aspects of his life—in particular about key relationships and decisions and the ways in which these had entered his writing. Most of all, I can now see that Isherwood himself exemplified in that interview the qualities that he told me he had admired so much in E. M. Forster: his ability to care tremendously about the other person, even more perhaps than that person was able to do, and his concern to give reassurance. For me, this interview remains remarkable in its immediacy, warmth, and intensity—and in its vivid evocation of Isherwood as a singular man.

Isherwood: *A Meeting by the River* was really quite different from any of my other works.

Kaplan: You mean because you really didn't have a narrator—because *A Meeting by the River* has a different structure?

Isherwood: Yes, because it's all written in letters, and documents, and because there's no real point of view. It's just as I always say: it's like a trial where both sides give evidence. But there's no judgment, no verdict, no summing up, nothing. You just hear all of the evidence.

Kaplan: Do you feel that you didn't in any way slant that evidence? You don't think that the scales are weighted at all in favor of Oliver?

Isherwood: They are only weighted in favor of Oliver in the sense that what he's pushing is much more practical than what Patrick is pushing. But I wouldn't say that they're weighted otherwise. As a matter of fact, one's sympathy and the sympathy of most readers goes strongly to Patrick, I find. . . . You see, I have now approached this material three times, and every time the two characters change very subtly in certain ways. When we made the play, Oliver luckily was played by a very good actor, Sam Waterston, who gave it great energy and a kind of conviction and even a sort of sexiness, so that he held his end up very well. But otherwise, it's uphill work for Oliver, because onstage all that sort of skullduggery of Patrick's is very charming. It has a kind of eighteenth-century appeal, this villainy. Anyway, then you see more and more that one comes to something else in the material, which is that Patrick is doing this in a very sincere way, that's to say he is genuinely horrified by the monastery. This is something we bring out much more in the screenplay. For one thing, on the screen you'll be able to see the place and see the whole atmosphere of Calcutta and of India and everything and the scariness of it, the feeling of somebody actually doing these things. When you really see the room where he slept with all the other monks on the floor, it kind of brings it home to Patrick what Oliver has done to himself. And also, of course, in the play, and even much more so in the screenplay, matters are complicated by the fact that the other characters appear; the wife especially has come out very strongly in the screenplay.

Kaplan: She is a very interesting figure in the book as the brothers evoke her. Of course, she is seen so differently by Patrick and Oliver.

Isherwood: We have a rather amusing situation in the screenplay, which is a sort of nontriangle. That is to say, both the wife and the boyfriend come to India. They get along very well. And the wife, unlike all women who appear in dramas about monasteries, goes to the monastery and tells Oliver to stay there, not to come out. [*Laughter*] It's a very curious kind of anti-temptation scene—in which she comes to India to tell Oliver to, for God's sake, stay in there and not let Patrick upset him again. She makes a rousing speech telling him he absolutely should stay there. And also the conclusions that the two brothers come to about each other—that of course does appear in the play—comes out very strongly. At the end of the play, Oliver says of course the truth is that Patrick is really terribly influenced by this place and by the mahanta [the head of the monastery] and that he will in the end have an appalling religious conversion, which he will hate and think that he is having a nervous breakdown; he'll probably go to a psychiatrist about it and so forth.

Kaplan: Do you believe that it is possible for someone who isn't obviously or actively seeking a religious experience to have one nonetheless?

Isherwood: Well, of course if you get down into the inwardness of the story, the whole thing is sort of psychosomatic. In a way you might almost say that the monastery is a sort of psychosomatic event in Patrick's life.

[*Laughter*] I'm not being very precise in my use of words, scientifically speaking, but you know what I mean. Quite aside from being a real place by the Ganges and being a place that Oliver lives in, it represents a problem of Patrick's.

Kaplan: One that existed even before he went there, you mean.

Isherwood: Yes. And therefore he doesn't go there really entirely just to see Oliver but from an awful kind of fascination to see how he would feel if he did go. And then of course both the brothers at the end are smiling and delighted because each thinks that he knows something about the other one. In the film we have this nice scene, after the bowing down, which was the end of the play. When you become a swami, a sannyasin, when you've taken sannyas [final vows], according to immemorial tradition, you have to go out for three days and beg your food. Now of course this is only a convention because in fact all kinds of pious people around you are only too delighted—they come out with enough food for a church picnic. But nevertheless you do go out in your robes and you have to go barefoot and you go to these houses. And the last scene in the film will be that Oliver and his fellow swamis, his brother monks, are all out there; and what they give you is a sort of gooey kind of soupy stuff with a lot of beans in it and so forth, which they empty into the fold of your cloth, so you have to hold it like this and then people dip in and taste it—which is extremely unappetizing if you're not used to it. All right, so here is Oliver in the dust by the side of the road, barefoot with the other monks, and they've got this stuff. And Patrick and Penelope are driving to the airport and they see Oliver there; so they tell the car to stop and they get out and they rather gingerly partake of these alms which are very holy and then say goodbye and they get back in the car. It's then that Patrick makes his final speech. He lights a cigar and he says, "Of course he will stay in the monastery. Little does he realize where his humility is leading him. In that yellow robe of his, he'll preside at international conferences, he'll march into palaces and confront dictators barefoot. Twenty years from now he'll be running Asia." [*Laughter*] Meanwhile, Oliver has taken Penelope aside and said, "Look, Penny, I want you to look after Patrick for the next few weeks because he may begin to act very strangely." Penny says, "What on earth do you mean?" He says, "Well, he may think he's got something wrong with his stomach, or he may feel he's having a nervous breakdown; but do try to reassure him because, as a matter of fact, the only thing that's wrong with Patrick is he's in a state of grace and he doesn't know it." [*Laughter*] And she's utterly bewildered by this statement. So then they go off, these two. And that's the essence of the comedy. It's meant to be quite balanced, really, because the real moral of the story, if it has a moral, is a sentence in the Bhagavad Gita which says, "God is eternally perfect. What does he care for our righteousness or for our wickedness?" *Sub specie aeternitatis,* it's absolutely immaterial, isn't it, because there isn't any such thing as righteousness and wickedness. It's all *maya* [illusion], and he's God, we're God, everybody's God, there's nothing but God anywhere; and all the rest is this strange playing on the surface of life.

Kaplan: Then there's nothing necessarily preferable about Oliver's choice over Patrick's?

Isherwood: It's relatively preferable, but not from an eternal viewpoint, no. I mean, it's symbolic, in other words. Yes, it's preferable, because after all not only is all this happening, but this play is being written from within *maya,* not from outside, so one can't say. You can't dare to say, for instance, that enormous massacres are good or are the same as any other kind of behavior. This attitude is only possible in the moment of complete union with the Eternal. You couldn't say it from any other point of view. It would be just completely heartless and insane. But nevertheless, in a certain sense, it's true. In a certain sense, the Eternal is either nonexistent or it's everywhere, by definition. If it's everywhere, then Hitler is God, then everybody is God. But as Ramakrishna said, everything is God, but Tiger God is to be avoided. [*Laughter*] In other words, I mean, sometimes from a distance you can say, "Yes it's God, all right, but. . . ."

Kaplan: And isn't there a distinction between that part within an individual which is God and that part which is *maya,* that is, the working of his illusion in terms of his ego, of his own distortions?

Isherwood: Yes, from the relative standpoint, but the absolute standpoint of Vedanta is that there is no difference, that this multiplicity is all contained in oneness. In other words, in the last analysis, from the highest view, all action is symbolic. But that doesn't mean that you shouldn't do your best. [*Laughter*]

Kaplan: One has the distinct feeling in the book that Patrick isn't doing his best, especially for his brother.

Isherwood: In the original book, I was very far from understanding exactly what I was writing about. There is so much in this theme as you get more and more into it. I was interested on a much more superficial level. Do you know that novel *Les Liaisons Dangereuses* or *Dangerous Liaisons?* Well, this kind of mischief for mischief's sake interested me. But I never thought of Patrick as being really bad exactly; he's just sort of a tease. I mean, he wouldn't do anything really fiendishly bad like Madame de Merteuil or whatever her name is, the woman who was really evil.

Kaplan: Just gratuitously evil.

Isherwood: Gratuitous evil is obviously the worst kind. People who are sincere who are evil because of some sort of drives are not as bad as people who just do it for no reason. When you get the late Roman emperors who were just bored and had some slaves killed in front of them—besides people like that, somebody who sincerely had drives, like Hitler, is not nearly as bad, obviously. The worst thing of all is this kind of passionless evil-doing. Where it's just utter lack of feeling.

Kaplan: I was thinking as you were talking that not only have Patrick's actions not been gratuitously evil, but from Oliver's point of view, Patrick has really done him a favor by the end.

Isherwood: Oh, yes, really a great point is made out of that. Very much more in the play, I think, than in the novel. But it's funny—it is all in the novel, in a sort of way.

Kaplan: I was thinking in terms of the novel. Of course, Oliver invites Patrick—that first letter is clearly an invitation.

Isherwood: He wants Patrick to come, of course, because he wants Patrick to approve of him.

Kaplan: Do you think he has some doubts that he wants allayed by having Patrick there?

Isherwood: Of course he has doubts. It's terribly, terribly hard to do anything that is against the usual concepts of your culture. It is very, very painful and embarrassing, and doubts come—always.

Kaplan: I am remembering the essay you wrote on "The Problem of the Religious Novel," in which you said something about wanting to show that, although ultimately a saint is so very different from the average man, in the beginning that saint was simply Mr. Jones. And I have a sense that that's what you have done with Oliver. Because if Oliver were somehow certain, I don't think we could deal with him at all. His doubts and the vestiges of all the earlier feelings for his brother make him understandable to us, but not fully, because he's advanced beyond that too.

Isherwood: I don't think of Oliver as being by any means a saint, yet he might become one. The Hindus have a very different way of using the word: they don't use the word "saint" really in the sort of Western convention. What they mean when they say "saint" is quite specifically somebody who has received some degree of spiritual illumination, in other words, who has actually seen the Eternal in one way or another, cognized it, been aware of its presence. Whereas here we tend very much to dwell on the moral aspects. We say, "he's so good," "he's so charitable," he's this and that. The Hindus would reply, yes, it's quite true that having seen the Eternal, this brings you to the conclusion that the Eternal is everywhere in everybody. And therefore naturally it makes you much less antisocial than most of us are because we see they're all my brothers—whether you like it or not, they are. [*Laughter*] Let's face it, that's my sister and that's my brother and that goes for the cobra and for the dove and all creatures and everything and human beings of all sorts. Now, that's the Hindu idea, as I say—the idea that some degree of enlightenment has been reached. I really tried to make a saint, to describe my idea of a saint much more in the not very satisfactory novel of mine called *The World in the Evening.* [In] Aunt Sarah, I tried to describe what I think of as a saint a little bit more with her.

Kaplan: Did you have a particular person in mind as the basis for Sarah?

Isherwood: It's very composite. I met a lot of Quakers when I was working with them, and many of them were, I think, very advanced. But you see, one doesn't know really. There's a wonderful story about when Claire Booth Luce became a Catholic and she immediately was very gung-ho, really going after being a Catholic in the biggest way; and she went down to see a very remarkable priest who lived downtown—I think he's dead now—who everybody said was quite extraordinary. And so she gets down there and she begins talking to him and she says, "Father, it's so sad that nowadays there are no saints at all." And he said, "Oh, I wouldn't say that." He said, "That old lady out there (he was pointing to a Mexican lady who was sweeping the floor outside), Mrs. Martinez, she's a saint." Of course, Mrs. Luce was all shattered because that wasn't at all what she meant by a saint. But probably he was right. I met people like that, yes.

Kaplan: I know that for me the scene in which Stephen looks at Sarah and sees her not as this old, fuss-budget aunt, but really sees what's there—well, that really came alive for me. So I felt that you had to have seen that in someone or through someone.

Isherwood: Yes, I felt that in a few people. [The English mystic writer] Alan Watts always liked that scene so much. He told me about it one time, how he often read it to people.

Kaplan: I found that scene very powerful—and the scene at the Quaker meeting too. The silence was extremely evocative.

Isherwood: That's all based on experience, of course. I lived with them for quite the better part of a year.

Kaplan: One of the things that the book implies through Stephen is that there is a reality greater than yourself, even if you are not actively seeking that or actively wanting to know that. It really is there, everywhere all around you; and there are people who embody it or know it, and so you can find it in all kinds of experiences—and you seem to suggest that throughout the book.

Isherwood: I do—I believe that.

Kaplan: It seemed to me that you were suggesting this possibility in certain daily states, such as, for example, when Stephen just wakes up in the morning and doesn't really feel that he is himself.

Isherwood: It's why I don't like the book. I made a terrible mistake in telling the story through Stephen, and I don't think I should have. I think I should have done it in some other way. I don't exactly know, but . . . it gave me more trouble than all the rest of the books put together, and I was working on it and messing with it for years and years, and it never came out right. Finally, I think, I should have sat down and taken it all apart and done it once more. But he's wrong. Stephen is sort of fakey in some way.

Kaplan: Do you feel that at that point you were trying to describe some sort of new and exciting discovery? It seems that there is much more overt statement in *The World in the Evening* than there is in the following books, in which religious experience seems to be a possibility for the characters, but it's more subtly hinted at. And when they do arrive at it, they do so in a way that's understandable in terms of their character.

Isherwood: It's very glib, I think. I don't like it. As a matter of fact, while I was staying at the Vedanta Center in Hollywood, I was writing *Prater Violet* and this thing [*The World in the Evening*] I wrote later. But I think there's something deeply wrong with it. It's fakey. I like it the least of my books. You'd be surprised at the number of people who like it, though. To this day I get letters about it.

Kaplan: I think it is a very interesting book because it has tremendous energy and so many new ideas. You begin to explore them in that novel but do so with more ease in the later books. For example, in *Down There on a Visit* there are three episodes in which Chris is not involved with any kind of religious experience, but in the fourth he is. The character of Paul puzzles me in that novel. He's played off against Chris in that last episode, and Paul seems so much more of an absolutist than Chris, especially at the end.

Isherwood: I don't think Paul altogether works. What I was trying to do was to write about somebody who is a kind of touchstone. Everybody he comes in contact with, he almost unconsciously reveals any kind of falseness in them. There are people like that; and it's not that they're very nice themselves at all, but they just have that kind of truth. Some kind of truthfulness, a rather sinister kind that sort of unmasks people. I'm actually engaged at the moment in just starting a book which is, as you might say, an autobiography, that is to say it's absolutely true, not fiction at all. And I'm covering a good deal of the same ground. It's a sort of book of the period of my life which Germans call *Wanderjahren*. It's about going to Berlin and covers the time until I'd been in this country about four or five years and it became kind of my home. I don't mean that there is a great big thing about that, but it's that the wandering stopped.

Kaplan: Do you think that had to do with your adoption of Vedanta philosophy?

Isherwood: It had a great deal to do with it and various kinds of roots that I put down and various relationships that I had formed and one thing and another. But it involves going over some of this material from a different angle. It's very interesting to me, at least, doing it, because quite different things come out. Now, the Paul character will probably hardly appear in this book at all, but there will be a great deal about Gerald Heard and Aldous Huxley. Gerald Heard is of course Augustus Parr. But then again he's caricatured very much in *Down There on a Visit*. What I'm really much more concerned to do in this new book [*Christopher and His Kind*] is to write almost entirely about people who really turned me on, as remarkable, inspiring people in one way or another. That doesn't mean they weren't absurd, ridiculous, bad, or anything, but really very positive sort of types, all the way from hustlers in Berlin bars to the swami or anybody, Ingrid Bergman.

Kaplan: Do you see them as having certain things in common?
Isherwood: People around whom one can form a myth are the people who

actually turned me on personally. I was tremendously struck reading Jung's autobiography; and he starts by saying, I'm going to tell the story of my myth. I'm not going to go into a lot of detail or gossip or stuff, but I'm going to say what the themes were that sort of turned me on and excited me, not the facts so much as the tale, the way the whole thing unfolded.

Kaplan: And this is what you're trying to do?

Isherwood: Yes, but not about my extreme youth, and not about my later life either. It's just this period, it's roughly speaking from 1929 to, let's say, 1943.

Kaplan: You have gone back to periods that you dealt with earlier to deal with them again. It reminds me of what you talked about in *The Memorial*— the idea of the dynamic portrait that you go back to again and see more and more in it. The most dynamic portrait is Chris.

Isherwood: What else does one know? One doesn't have much but one-self, certainly. The last book I wrote was *Kathleen and Frank,* which of course was the facts behind *The Memorial* and the characters. Only there they did the work themselves because of all the diaries and letters.

Kaplan: When you created this persona, "Chris," did you see him and yourself as essentially the same person, or did you separate yourself from him?

Isherwood: I have really no idea of what I'm like totally. I mean, I have no sense of myself as a person exactly, just as a lot of reactions to things. I know from experience that as one gets older one can produce certain kinds of effects. And one knows things that one can do and things one can't do. One knows certain weaknesses, obviously, very well. But it's very hard to know—and if you start watching this thing, trying to watch it as you do in art, you're quite at a loss really. The trouble is to make fun of it too much, to make it absurd. That's the temptation one has to resist. Which is really a kind of inverted vanity, this clowning about.

Kaplan: I see you've gotten very interested in nonfiction and particularly in depicting yourself in a nonfictional way. Is that because you feel that fiction oversimplifies life too much?

Isherwood: I'm more interested, you see, in the comment, as it were, and the comment you can have just as well in nonfiction, as long as the thing very closely concerns you.

Kaplan: Don't you have less room for comment in fiction in that it has to be implicit in what's dramatically happening?

Isherwood: Yes, because you have to keep getting on with all the invention of the business, the interplay. And sometimes that's fun: I enjoy, of course, writing movies and that sort of thing. And I've enjoyed it in the past in books. I really enjoyed writing *A Meeting by the River* more than anything—I really wished it would never end. And I kept writing it and rewriting it and rewriting it. But when you really come down to it, what fascinates me is thinking about the given material and trying to see what it meant, making it into a sort of poetical shape, trying to find the inwardness of it, the myth, in fact, what it expresses. And that's difficult.

Kaplan: I'm sure it must be. Especially if the myth changes, as it did for you with *A Meeting by the River*—and as, in each medium, you said the characters did change.

Isherwood: Yes, they change, of course, all the time.

Kaplan: Does that have to do with the fact that people have illusions about themselves, so that even when you come to look at a literary character, you must see that character in terms of his illusions? But also as you change and your illusions about yourself change, that character too must change?

Isherwood: Yes, I'm trying to do that. I'm trying to contrast, for instance, the Christopher who entered that period in 1929, the Berlin period, with the Christopher who came to the United States ten years later—as far as I can judge, a considerably different person.

Kaplan: In what ways?

Isherwood: More hard-boiled, more cynical, more careerist, I think. But then, on the other hand, luckily that didn't work out very well—so all was well. [*Laughter*] That was the story of it. But then, you see, the element that goes very, very deep in the material, which is never satisfactorily expressed in any of these books and which now I am expressing, is the homosexuality, not so much from the point of view of the question of sexual preference as the whole thing of belonging to a rather small minority, a tribe, which is sometimes overtly persecuted but always sort of subtly slighted. And what this means, the boiling rage underneath the nicey-nice exterior.

Kaplan: You do a marvelous job of bringing that out in *A Single Man.*

Isherwood: It was so funny, you know, S. N. Behrman wrote about that. He found it so shocking, this feeling of oppression. But really I was speaking to every minority. How could he as a Jew say that one never feels mad at people who are non-Jewish? I mean there's a certain moment when you think, well, fuck them, you know. . . . That was absolutely said on behalf of every single minority, those passages. In fact I wrote it much more about being a minority than about being homosexual, really. It was deeply involved in the psychology of minorities in general.

Kaplan: One of the most moving things in *A Single Man* is George's rage. He says that it's the energy of middle age—but on the other hand it's a thing that wraps you up in our own ego, so it's hard for him to break out.

Isherwood: Oh, it's very bad, yes. And of course, that was where you might say, in a way, I was sort of, not cheating . . . but being alone has not been my life experience, I'm happy to say. Therefore I was perhaps loading the dice a bit, but I just didn't feel up to juggling a domestic homosexual relationship on top of all the other factors in the book. Just to sort of clear the decks a bit, I wanted to have George by himself.

Kaplan: But at the same time you have suggested very well George's relationship with Jim throughout the book.

Isherwood: Yes, I tried to. I think perhaps it might have been strengthened a bit, perhaps that would have helped. But the very last thing I wanted was to create a kind of pathos around this man, and yet of course there is some. Another thing that was depriving for him was that he had no real kind of philosophical support.

Kaplan: In some ways it seems to be waiting for him at points in the book, for example, in the classroom scene where he's teaching *After Many a Summer Dies the Swan.* One has no sense that it really means anything to George.

Isherwood: Well, that's why one comes back to wanting to write nonfiction. Take George—I was always juggling a little bit. There was George on the one hand, and there was me on the other. When I start clowning like that in the classroom and carrying on, this is much more me than it would have been George. My whole experience academically, of course, has been as a guest lecturer, and it's a very different thing if you're a known writer and you go to one of these places. Not that I didn't teach, really. I gave regular courses and did lots of homework, and my colleagues said, you know, you do it all right. Nevertheless I was a privileged person, and I was expected to amuse primarily, rather than instruct. . . . In the classroom, kids expect you to. I mean they have no use for somebody who doesn't. In fact, I am really more at my ease with the college generation, the succeeding college generation, than I am with any other age group of Americans. I feel so very relaxed with them all that I never feel any problem. Partly because I don't try to be young or any of that stuff, but I just go right ahead and talk to them. You can talk to them, and I see a great many of them. They come here, and we talk. But, anyway, that is the trouble—that George and I didn't quite make one person there. There are times when it begins to slip out of gear.

Kaplan: If George's life were happier, or fuller, you wouldn't have the sense of his need for philosophical support—which is present no matter how happy one's life is.

Isherwood: Oh, of course. The more intense the happiness, the more poignancy one feels in the fact that it can only be for a certain while, that things change, and that one is separated from people by death and circumstances. All that is very true.

Kaplan: Did you see George as avoiding understanding himself when such an understanding might have been possible? For instance, when Kenny asks him if he's ever taken mescaline and speaks about his friend seeing God after having taken mescaline, he does not consider the possibility of seeing God under any circumstances. It almost seems like an evasion, that it was possible for him to consider it and yet he wouldn't.

Isherwood: I think there is an evasion there. I agree with you. I was trying to write a poem, you know; I mean, it could be one of those days, like Virginia Woolf's *Mrs. Dalloway.*

Kaplan: I was wondering if you had *Mrs. Dalloway* in mind as you wrote the book.

Isherwood: That, and a thing you'd never imagine that there could be any connection with, but which made a tremendous impression on me: I was obsessed by Antonioni's *La Notte* at that time. I didn't take anything from it, but there was something about the feeling of *La Notte.* Those things are very individual, why one's turned on by something. But that picture meant a great deal to me.

Kaplan: I also thought there were certain things in *A Single Man* that were reminiscent of *Ulysses* as well.

Isherwood: Everybody has been influenced by *Ulysses.* But it's a little dry emotionally for my taste. It's too mental, it's not my scene. But as an overall thing it's obviously a masterpiece. There are amazing things in it, and the ending is tremendous.

Kaplan: I have the feeling that in *A Single Man* there is an ongoing theme that has to do with the metaphor of life in the Upanishads, that life is a chariot race. Did you have that in mind?

Isherwood: Possibly, yes. Somebody said that the image of the road ran all through the book.

Kaplan: I saw the freeway scenes and the details throughout of Los Angeles as being used to emphasize the isolation of life here.

Isherwood: You know, the funny thing is I didn't mean to write that book at all. I meant to write a book which is called "An English Woman."

Kaplan: You wanted to focus on Charlotte?

Isherwood: The whole book was about Charlotte, but I couldn't get at her properly somehow. I had all sorts of devices, but they didn't work. It was Don Bachardy who suggested the title for the book.

Kaplan: It's a good title because it seems to mean so many different things.

Isherwood: He's a very good critic of things; and we just got to work on *A Meeting by the River.* In the play there were a tremendous lot of his suggestions, of all kinds.

Kaplan: What are we to make of Oliver's religious experience at the end—when he sees the swami? It isn't as if his experience were unmediated, but he does have an experience through the swami. Can we take that as disingenuous, something he desires and therefore sees?

Isherwood: I don't regard that as an evasion. It's absolutely necessary if you're playing a fifty-fifty game. Everything must be susceptible to two explanations. In other words, Oliver was in a jam psychologically. He was terribly bothered by his situation. He found a way out, which nobody else could find—having a vision which explained to him that, as a matter of fact, Patrick had just as much right in the monastery as he did. Now, this is very sound from every point of view, but at the same time it can all be explained away, as they say, by any San Fernando Valley psychiatrist, who just says, "Oh well, what else could he do? He had to resolve this." As a matter of fact, we've gone much further in the existing draft of the screenplay. In the existing draft, Oliver has the vision, and he sees the swami sitting on the seat, and then two absolutely identical poodles jump onto the seat, one on one side and one on the other. And he pets them and laughs. Then they turn into Patrick and Oliver, meaning that in the sight of the swami—we don't belabor the point. [*Laughter*] So the scene is kind of farcical. I always think that one of the best ways of conveying these sorts of states is through something on the very edge of farce because it so often is in these descriptions that people give of visions.

Kaplan: I remember your saying something about that in "The Problem of the Religious Novel."

Isherwood: A funny thing happened when I was with the Quakers in Haverford. Somebody produced an apparently authentic picture of George Fox in ecstasy—he was the founder of the Quakers. So everybody said, how nice to have a picture of George Fox having a religious experience. And what you actually saw in this little painting was—he was going like this [Isherwood crossed his eyes]—the eyes, you see, were centering, and his tongue was out. Somebody had really dared to paint exactly what he saw happening to this man. I believe it's in the Haverford College Museum, but I don't think it is displayed. There's an aspect of all this which is embarrassing to people who imagine things in a kind of sweetness.

Kaplan: People who are not believers are very demanding in what they expect from people who do believe.

Isherwood: Very demanding. Some saints are particularly farcical. Saint Philip Neri, the founder of the Oratorium, was just full of practical jokes. He used to sit in the pope's lap and pull his beard. He took the injunction of Christ, "Suffer the little children," quite literally, and so he allowed them to play all over the altar, and they were always knocking over the blessed sacrament and absolutely outraging everybody. And of course the great scene of Ramakrishna, when he was conducting a worship—and there were these very devout people, including this woman who paid for the temple, who believed in him. And this cat came in, and Ramakrishna suddenly realized that the cat was also the mother of the universe, and he bowed down in front of it and gave it the food. . . . They nearly threw him out of the place, but he was simply being the most orthodox Vedantist of all. [*Laughter*]

Kaplan: One of the things that fascinated me in your biography of Ramakrishna is not only that he himself seems to have had a great sense of humor, but that he could see that even really religious people were funny a lot of the time.

Isherwood: Because you still retain what's called your character. Ramakrishna was an extremely volatile, lively, amusing, charming person. Other people become great saints who are by nature quiet and meditative. The Bengalis are fantastically animated. When I went there, I went to the theater, and of course I couldn't understand a word, but I never wanted to leave. They were so funny on the stage. The clowning and the brilliance of the sort of mockery that they convey was fascinating. You could go on watching them for hours.

Kaplan: When we read or watch *A Meeting by the River,* maybe we needn't take sides at all. Perhaps each is right in all the things he sees in the other. For example, perhaps Patrick is really right in seeing this desire for power in Oliver. It may very well be a strong part of Oliver's personality.

Isherwood: I certainly intended that it should be something that was there. I really don't apologize at all for not having a kind of solution. I think it would spoil the whole effect.

Kaplan: And is the open ending perhaps a commentary on the either/or Western tradition? That one must be right, one must be wrong.

Isherwood: Yes. One time we were at a religious service and a very sacred moment had occurred right at the end when Swami [Prabhavananda] got out some Ganges water and he was sprinkling it—and suddenly he roared with laughter and said, "You all look so funny." And everybody in the place just laughed and laughed, quite spontaneously. That happens sometimes—it's just beautiful. Of course young people now, they understand all that much better. All those things they understand so well, instinctively. You don't have to spell it out. That's marvelous.

Kaplan: There's always been this pull for Western writers toward Eastern traditions. You see this from the beginning of the twentieth century. Did you have any interest in this, for example, when *The Waste Land* came out?

Isherwood: No, I felt that Eliot had sort of sold out. I didn't like this religion thing. It bothered me. But I thought it was kind of a camp, you know. I didn't really take it very seriously, in some curious ways. I thought it was a kind of poetic attitude. But I see more and more that so much of all this dissension is a question of semantics.

Kaplan: So you didn't really feel, at least until you came here, much of an interest in, say, Forster's interest in Eastern religion?

Isherwood: No, I didn't. It didn't really mean anything to him, I don't think, in the same way.

Kaplan: No, he doesn't ultimately come to believe.
Isherwood: No, no.

Kaplan: In other words, your interest really dates from . . .
Isherwood: From meeting this man, this individual.

Kaplan: Gerald Heard or Swami Prabhavananda?
Isherwood: Well, Heard very much prepared this thing from a kind of
intellectual point of view. He got me very much straightened out semanti-
cally. I mean, a lot of my categories were simply based on being frightened
of certain words; and by rephrasing things he got me into a receptive mood.
But it was really basically meeting Prabhavananda. Of course, once you get
into that sort of area you in fact meet other people rather easily who are
equally impressive in a somewhat similar way. But my whole approach was
entirely existential in that way. It was just a question of meeting this person
and observing him over a long period.

Kaplan: Do you feel that that is really the only way that you can get on
the track of this kind of thing, that you must meet a person who somehow
strikes you in this way—that he has found something? Or could one come to
it in a somewhat more spontaneous way?
Isherwood: I talked to a young swami in India whose parents were
strongly atheistic. He had done it entirely by reading the works of Vivekananda. He became absolutely convinced and took off and joined the monastery. But that's not my idea. I must say Vivekananda was a remarkable
person.

Kaplan: Do you think that personal religious discovery is a possibility, or
do you think that really it has to be through direct knowledge of the religion?
Isherwood: Oh no, of course it doesn't! It could be in any manner or way.
And I think that you could even be an atheist, you see, and you could have
something. There again you come to this thing of what words you use. It's
quite clear that a lot of people who are under the impression they don't have
any religious belief have got some kind of insight. I felt that about Forster
very much. He never would say that he was anything more than a kind of
agnostic. He was interested but that was all. He was so marvelously open.
When he became quite old, I really used to think sometimes he had that baby-
like quality which Ramakrishna had. He was like a child, you know. Not that
he was the least bit gaga or anything, but he was just very joyful. I was with
him about a month before he died, the last time I saw him, when I happened

to be in England. Everything he said to me was trying to reassure me. He said, "I realize I can't write anymore, I can't invent things." And he said, "It doesn't matter, it's all right, it doesn't matter." And he was very gay, very cheerful inside somehow.

Kaplan: He was trying to reassure you, on his behalf, so that you wouldn't worry about him?

Isherwood: Also to give reassurance, which is very important, of course, toward the end. To keep telling people, "Look, don't worry; it's not as bad as they tell you; it's nothing like they say."

Kaplan: He knew he was going to die soon?

Isherwood: Yes. But he was quite extraordinary, because while he was surrounded by people who were fond of him, he in some ways led a rather solitary life. He lived at King's College. And people went to see him all the time. But he spent a good deal of time alone and had a couple of strokes and fell down. One time he was unconscious the whole night, lying on the floor, and nobody found him till the morning. He was very lucky his head didn't go in the fireplace. He fell right by the fire. Things like that happened, but he kept going, and he was cheerful again and amusing. He wasn't just being stoical either; he had a real resource.

Kaplan: You felt that he had some kind of insight.

Isherwood: Yes, I'm sure. He was wonderful. It was tremendous, his capacity for caring about other people and minding what happened to them. His empathy was extraordinary. How he felt things, felt things terribly, felt things that happened to one more than one might oneself. You know, he'd really mind, you'd see the pain in his face. That's very advanced, all that stuff.

Kaplan: That reminds me of your thirties novels and the concern with finding some political commitment. In *Goodbye to Berlin,* I recall Chris's conversation with Bernhard Landauer, in which he says to him, "You know, you really have to be committed to something." Did you feel that way yourself at the time? Did you feel the necessity for some sort of commitment, to Communism, for example?

Isherwood: I think it was very superficial. I mean, it seemed so; but, on the other hand, I was always stubbing my toe over this business of the way Soviet Russia really let Marx and Engels down completely, with regard to the private life. When they started persecuting homosexuals, I realized that I could never possibly be a Party member. It just seemed to be a kind of self-immolation that was being asked of you, that you should just sort of give up everything. I didn't really think about it enough, but deep down I'm sure I felt that, after all, politics exist for man, not vice versa. I mean, one cannot just sacrifice oneself to the state.

Kaplan: So you did not really see Communism as a viable alternative to Nazism? There is such a sense of despair in *The Berlin Stories*—do you think it's because you saw no political alternative, no real solutions?

Isherwood: Oh, I think I was dumb, you know, and didn't really think very much. I didn't think nearly deeply enough about it. I've never been very intellectual in that way—I didn't analyze things in that sort of manner. I repeated, I went along with people. And Auden, of course, really didn't agree with them, I don't think. And then by degrees he began to say so. But it was unthinkable for me. And then I became also increasingly a pacifist, which had some relation to going to this war in China, where one saw this thing that happens in all wars, that a most awful lot of people who couldn't give a damn get killed. When you actually see a whole lot of civilians who've been bombed, it occurs to you very vividly that it's all a lot of shit. [*Laughter*] All this stuff is sort of monolithic patriotism. Most people want out when the going gets rough.

Kaplan: But then the individuals really don't have the ability to get themselves out.

Isherwood: Exactly. In all wars you find out later, when it's too late, the most appalling economic forces that have been at work, which brought the whole thing about. Somehow or other, goddamn it, you find the same people are in charge at the end of it all—way back of the front men, the people who own the factories. They get them rebuilt and things go on and people manage; they survive.

Kaplan: In your recent novels, do you ever feel that you are proselytizing?

Isherwood: I never do consciously. You mean about Vedanta? No, because I really am just enchanted whenever people have any kind of belief, anything which supports them.

Kaplan: I didn't necessarily mean for Vedanta, but for belief, for at least testing out the possibilities of experience beyond just what we can see in our daily life.

Isherwood: I do think that's important. For that I would proselytize, certainly—to ask people to ask themselves what's it all about. Every artist does that—they have to, in one way or another. But I just meant that I didn't think that this particular brand of things is important at all. I mean, you have to swallow such a lot with anything that you do. There's all the trappings. Hinduism is exceedingly off-putting to a lot of people; it's very alien and odd. But then again the Quakers are simply marvelous. But then again there are things about them that bother some people terribly, their sort of plainness and kind of wholesomeness. What's great about the Hindu thing is that it's very lively and kind of campy and fun.

Kaplan: Do you think one must accept the trappings?

Isherwood: No. No. No. No. I mean, I don't tend, for instance, to take part much in their general religious doings. I've made it a more personal and more private thing, as far as I'm concerned. A lot of people get immense support out of going to pujas and sitting for hours and ringing bells and chanting and so on. Sometimes it's very exciting and really marvelous—and then again, you know. . . . The great thing is just to remember that the thing exists—that's what it's all about, and you must keep reminding yourself of that.

November 1, 1973

When Isherwood asserted that "the thing exists," I understood him to mean "God." What he seemed to be saying was that the most important understanding to come to is that God exists, but it really does not matter by what path or through what words one comes to this understanding. Thus, while Isherwood had not been at all reticent in discussing his religious beliefs, he remained somewhat reticent in the language he used to explain them. This restraint, it seems to me, is very much in keeping with his emphasis on the varieties of religious experience and the different paths to spiritual insight. He knew, from his own experience, that semantics often gets in the way of understanding, especially of religious understanding. Throughout our talk, he took pains to suggest or open up possibilities; and he seemed carefully to avoid conventional religious language, either because he himself found such terminology constricting, or because he felt such language might prove an obstacle to spiritual insight or personal discovery.

To Help along the Line: An Interview with Christopher Isherwood

Sarah Smith and Marcus Smith / 1975

From *New Orleans Review* Volume 4, Number 4 (1975): 307–10. Reprinted by permission.

NOR: There seems to be a general fascination today with the Weimar Republic. Not only are scholars studying its collapse, but one also encounters a rather widespread popular fascination with that period of German history. Could you reflect, in terms of your own experiences, on the state of society and politics of that time and the United States as you see it today?

Isherwood: To tell you the truth, I don't see very much relation between the two. I never have. I'm constantly asked, "Do I think the Nazis are coming?" The answer is no, not in any way which could be compared to the ending of the Weimar Republic. Perhaps this is due in part to a sort of irritation I feel toward doomsayers. My experience in life has always been that while you're watching one mouse hole, the mouse comes out of another. Since I'm not in any sense a political observer, and wasn't in those days, I only go on a kind of instinct. But I find the capacity of this country to remain more or less afloat almost infinite considering the things that have happened.

NOR: Is this merely economic luxury, the fact that we can afford stability, or is it because of some cultural or spiritual quality?

Isherwood: It must always be something psychological. It must be something in the inhabitants. I remember so well, for example, in Colombia, when I was there in 1947, several Colombian intellectuals said to me, "Our respect for the Constitution and for the principles of democracy is the only thing that makes us superior to Paraguay." Barely four months later there was the most appalling civil war in Colombia. General Marshall was visiting and had to get out of Bogotá, along with other American representatives. A very popular politician named Gaitán had been murdered, and as a result, there was a tremendous slaughter in the streets. I always felt in South America this could happen to any of the countries that we were in. I don't say that North Americans are necessarily more law-abiding. It may be partly a sort of saving streak of apathy. I don't know.

NOR: What about the young people today who have such a deep hunger to believe? It seems that anything can be packaged and sold to them.

Isherwood: I have been appearing on campuses for many years, and something has developed in the last fifteen years or so. The young are constantly asking about religion. They want to know. And I never try to push it. I never try to say more than I dare. I never try to seem holy or pretend to have knowledge beyond the absolute basic thing about which I can say, "Well this—I really promise you—I believe this much." If you try to fake anything, they see through it instantly. Stalin was in a theological seminary when he was young, and needless to say, he left. Gerald Heard used to say what an awful tragedy it was that there hadn't been anybody really spiritual at that seminary. Obviously Stalin had seen right through the whole lot of them and had therefore decided that religion was indeed just the opium of the people. I think it's frightfully important, and this is really much more difficult than it sounds, only to say what you *absolutely* believe. I mean, never to kind of skate around difficulties; if you feel that there's a difficulty you say honestly, "I don't know—I would like to believe that or think that but I'm really not sure myself."

NOR: How does one communicate to others a sense of mystery without specifically saying this is the mystery that one ought to believe in?

Isherwood: Well, I'm absolutely sure that everybody has a natural sense of the numinous, of something mysterious, something that awes you, beneath the appearances of things.

NOR: How does this relate to your interests in Vedantic studies?

Isherwood: I cannot say too often that I am not in any sense a guru, anything of this kind. I never set out to be. I am simply somebody who is able to write the English language a little better than a lot of people, and as such, put my know-how at the service of this monk, Prabhavananda who is also my guru. This is a very, very different thing. I mean I never did anything except just put into rather more readable language what *he* said, what *he* taught me, and everything that I ever wrote about it was very carefully passed on by him and indeed by the head of the Order, and all sorts of people in India (in the case of the book about Ramakrishna). So that you can hardly call that independent writing in the sense of making something up or even thinking something out.

NOR: Do you then regard yourself as simply an editor?

Isherwood: Well, really, yes—not much more than that. I mean, the only Vedanta book to which I contributed anything of my own (other than in a purely stylistic way, such as in the choice of words), was *How to Know God,* the commentaries on the Yoga aphorisms of Patanjali. In that book from time to time I would think of illustrations, examples, things that would appeal to Western readers, or make comparisons with things said in other literatures on the same subject. That was about the extent of my contribution, really. You see, Prabhavananda speaks very good English. And he's also spent almost all of his adult life in the United States. He came to the United States when he was just thirty, has been here ever since, and he's now over eighty. So naturally, he has quite a way with the English language. He has very little opportunity even to speak Bengali except to his two assistants; most of the time he's speaking English.

NOR: You mentioned that you did not regard yourself as a guru, and even suggested that you disliked being cast in that role. Do you see yourself as a seeker? Are you pursuing mysticism? Have you achieved what you think is a . . . ?

Isherwood: What I've achieved is open to question, but there's no doubt in my mind whatsoever that I am a believer and a disciple, and that's only strengthened with the years. The degree of my involvement is apparent when I try to imagine myself without it. That would be like taking away the whole frame of reference from my life.

NOR: Do you practice Yoga, and if so, what type?

Isherwood: Oh just a very simple form of meditation. I don't practice Hatha Yoga, the exercises, although I have done them in my time—I took some lessons. The general attitude of our particular group toward the Hatha Yoga physical poses is that they are okay—many of them are like the exercises you are given in a gym. But we very much frown on the breathing exercises, because if you really practice them hard—that means *hard*—you may very well bring on hallucinations and psychic, as opposed to spiritual, visions, and this may lead in its turn to your becoming mentally unbalanced.

NOR: You mentioned a particular group. Which group is this?

Isherwood: It's the Ramakrishna Order, one of the largest orders of monks in India. The Hindu monks I'm associated with are members of the Order who have come to teach here, not as missionaries, but simply in an informative capacity. You see as a matter of fact you could quite well be a devotee of Jesus of Nazareth and be a Vedantist at the same time, just as it's entirely possible to be a Quaker and not be a Christian, because this belief that the Quakers have about the "inner life" is really nondescriptive. The enormous majority will say, "Yes, it's something to do with Jesus," but, if you really get down to it, it isn't, necessarily. So this is a situation where it's not necessary to make these kinds of choices, and there's no question of being a missionary if you don't have to "save" people from something. That was what always upset the Christian missionaries in India so much, because they would come to India and they would preach, and they were listened to by Hindus who said, "Yes, we see that Jesus of Nazareth was a divine incarnation, an avatar, and we shall worship him." But what upset the missionaries so much was that the Hindus went right on worshipping other divine incarnations as well. The missionaries said you can only do it through Jesus. They replied that that's perfectly all right, that Krishna in the Baghavad Gita said, "Nobody comes to the truth except through me." But of course, when an avatar says "I" he really means that he's a part of the eternal—it's quite a non-personal statement. And so you go back and forth and sideways and upside down, and some people find this a terrible sticking place, and that's why you find people who feel that the Hindu thing is unacceptable. But the Hindus are more than ready to accept the Christians, if by Christianity you mean the special cult of Jesus of Nazareth rather than of somebody else. Because for the people who are inclined toward devotion, a cult is of course necessary. I mean, this is in itself a way of knowledge. The word "Yoga" is also used without any reference to physical exercises to mean different approaches to religion. This devotional approach is what's called Bhakti Yoga. Then again, there's what they call Karma Yoga, which is what we call "social service"— it's what the Quakers are doing all the time. This is to say you see the eternal in your fellow men, and therefore you serve them, not because you're helping your fellow man—that's a terrible egotism: if anybody is being helped it's yourself, for having the privilege of serving God in these people. Then again there's another path, which is much more rarified, called Jhana Yoga. This is a path of intellectual discrimination where you don't actually worship anything, but maintain a state of rigorous discrimination always asking yourself, "What is the reality? What is unreal? What is real?" to arrive at a state of enlightenment. I suppose this is true, for instance, of people like Krishnamurti, if you're familiar with his lectures, because he's always analyzing. All these different attitudes you can find in Christianity, in a way; you have the three yogas represented: the intensely devotional attitude of somebody like St. John of the Cross, and the intensely intellectual attitude of the Jesuits, and the "serving" orders such as the Franciscans . . .

NOR: It's a question of choosing what's right for you?

Isherwood: Exactly. As a matter of fact, Vivekananda, who is one of Ramakrishna's chief disciples, always said he wished there was a different religion for every single being on this earth. In other words, he felt that you shouldn't try to force yourself into joining something; you should evolve your own attitude toward the unseen. And he said that everyone's attitude should be just a tiny degree different from everybody else's.

NOR: How are you supposed to work this out? Do you have to have somebody who helps you—somebody to follow?

Isherwood: Well, of course I'm very much in favor of a guru, that's to say somebody to help you along the line. I personally can't imagine I could get involved in anything without meeting somebody because I'm that sort of person—I understand things through people. I used to infuriate my intellectual friends by saying, "I should have understood Marxism if I'd met Marx." Or Hegel, or anybody you'd like to name. The British philosopher Freddy Ayer was telling me that he'd been down to lecture at Washington. And I said, "What on earth did you say to them?" And he said, "You come around for lunch tomorrow and I'll tell you." And before lunch he sat me down in a chair and he gave me a lecture. For almost the whole lunch afterwards I understood his philosophy *perfectly*. . . . But then gradually it all faded away. I even had a friend once who met Einstein and that happened. He was mad with excitement—he rushed to the phone, called his wife and said, "I understand relativity!" Einstein did it very simply: he took out some matches and laid them end on end, smoked his pipe and explained—and it was almost within my friend's grasp.

NOR: In your lecture last night you were discussing *Cabaret* and said you were unhappy with the bisexual play that Michael York involved himself in. You didn't like that. You seemed to be saying that there are certain absolute categories: one is either heterosexual or homosexual and there should be no casual crossing over.

Isherwood: When I was discussing *Cabaret* I was criticizing much more the way that something was done, not what it was that was done. I'll tell you what I do dislike, and this of course is admittedly a slanted thing. I dislike people who find it cute to make little sallies from the well-guarded fortress of heterosexual respectability and who then come back and say, "What are the homosexual tribesmen out there fussing about? What are they complaining about? Sure I've had my little flings, and I've done this or that. Why are they so serious about it?" What these people don't understand is that they are being sheltered by the public heterosexual side of their lives, they are protected from anything horrid ever happening to them, from ever coming under any kind of stigma, and by insisting to everybody else, to other heterosexuals, that that's of course the important thing and the other is just a kind of game. They even get a certain approval. People think, "Well he's really a devil, he goes in for anything, he's marvelous, he's a swinger." But what they mean is a swinger swinging very heavily to one side rather than both. Now all of this will be absolutely, utterly unimportant in the Kingdom of Heaven, or even in a genuine democracy, but it's just a little bit distasteful to those of us who are actually suffering from this persecution, which is very real.

NOR: The young boy in *A Single Man* is to some extent playing that game.

Isherwood: Yes, and I deplore this too very often because it's an attempt to pass. Of course, when I say "deplore" and all these angry, superior words, I have the greatest sympathy for anybody who tries to wriggle out from under an intolerable situation, if he finds it intolerable. I have the greatest sympathy for a black who tries to pass. Passing exists in one way or another in every minority. It is not confined to the homosexual by any means. And of course with Jews, too, you'll find it again and again—they assume those Scots names. All right, good luck to them. You see, when there was a question of making the film *Cabaret,* first of all there was another company doing it, and they asked me and my friend Don Bachardy to do a treatment. And after great deliberation we made Chris a heterosexual, for that very reason. We thought, let's not have any "chi-chi" about this. There are only two tolerable positions: either Chris is one thing or the other. If Chris is a homosexual, this of course alters the whole story, and is indeed an absolute fountain of dramatic situations which don't occur in the book because I was sort of fudging. I was fudging for a rather different reason; I wasn't trying to conceal the facts. I just didn't want Chris to be an important character, I wanted him simply to be the narrator. And a character who is a homosexual becomes from a fictional point of view too interesting, too important, too way-out. Especially at the time when I was writing. What I wanted to say to the audience was, "Don't mind me, I'm just telling you the story." What I don't like is teasing the audience—equivocating and trying to make something a little bit naughty. People always say about Berlin in the 1920s, "Oh, it must have been so decadent!" All they mean is homosexual.

NOR: Do you regard your fiction as outstanding from the point of view of the technical evolution of fiction? Do you think that you tried to push forward the form of the novel?

Isherwood: It never occurred to me. Anything that I might have done in that way, if I did indeed do anything, was purely a side effect. What I was concerned with was just trying to say what I thought was interesting about my life. A fan letter that I like almost better than any I've ever received was oddly enough from a war hero who had become some kind of big wheel in British aviation in later life. He said, "You try to describe what it's like to be alive." Of course that was a thing that Hemingway was constantly doing—it was his whole stock in trade.

NOR: But didn't Hemingway always get his sense of being alive by juxtaposing something that was dead, or in the act of killing?

Isherwood: Well, because he was intensely interested in danger and courage. I enormously admire some books by Jack Kerouac. In a sense I find Kerouac more interesting than Hemingway, because Kerouac tells you about the physical thing but also goes into fantasies and philosophical speculations, mysticism and everything. I very much like *The Dharma Bums* and *The Desolation Angels* and *Big Sur.* Fiction or non-fiction is not a very important distinction to me, and Kerouac could have said the same. Kerouac was practically non-fiction, and Hemingway was frequently very close to non-fiction.

NOR: What about your own work? Has there been a shift toward or away from non-fiction?

Isherwood: I find the difference between my fiction and non-fiction slighter and slighter. The difference is diminishing. Because what I'm really interested in is commenting on experience.

NOR: Would this hold for, say, a novel like *A Single Man?*

Isherwood: Well, it's almost entirely a comment on my own experience. But I've hardly ever in my life written about anything that I hadn't done.

NOR: And yet at the end you try to go beyond your own experience—even into the mystery of death.

Isherwood: Yes, well I mean, since it's a mystery, everyone has the right to have an attitude to mystery. That's all it amounts to. The actual scene of the coronary occlusion is lifted out of a splendid book called *Man's Presumptuous Brain* by Dr. A. T. W. Simeons.

NOR: Isn't there also an echo of Auden's poem on Yeats? You talk about the various parts of the body deserting. . . .

Isherwood: Oh yes, "the provinces of his body revolted." Well, you see, not only were we very close friends, but Auden as you know was the son of a doctor and I was a medical student for a short time. One of the many, many connections we had was that we were both very interested in medicine, and therefore rather looked at things in the same way. As a matter of fact you'll find similar images in a passage in *Man's Presumptuous Brain*. So I just rewrote that and I asked some heart specialists about it. In fact one was so pleased with the result that he always reads the ending of *A Single Man* aloud to his students when he's lecturing on coronary occlusions.

NOR: But you go beyond a heart attack and have George's soul or spirit or his unconscious that's gone out to sea come back and find the dead body, his own dead body there, and presumably then have to confront eternity.

Isherwood: Well, that's my guess at it. But what I was going to say was that after all, what does it all amount to? If you write about your own experiences, you turn them into fiction I guess for two or three reasons: one is that experience is so messy; there are far too many people around; things don't fit together very well; and you very often tidy things up by simplifying them in order to tell a narrative. And this involves eliminating characters, and you gradually pass at least in a negative way into fiction. So that's one way, which is the only difference as far as I'm concerned. Secondly of course there's the question of discretion. It's only recently, for instance, that I could write with the extreme frankness that I do now on the subject of homosexuality.

NOR: Why is that? Is that a personal decision, or is it because of changes in society that allow you to be frank in that respect?

Isherwood: I suppose in a way I was sort of moving toward it, and I'm very much a child of my time in that way, I mean I go at the same pace as other people. But quite aside from that, what I have to say now wouldn't be nearly as good if I'd said it in fiction. Because what I'm interested in is not revelations either about physical acts or about specific lovers, but really studying the psychology of my whole outlook on life, which I realize is far more influenced by my homosexuality than I'd ever supposed. And I begin to see that every word, in a way, that I wrote about Berlin and everything, is all very slightly off. It's not absolutely focused.

NOR: Because of its accommodation?

Isherwood: Yes. To give you just one very simple example. It immediately branches out into sociology and politics much more than anything else. You take the whole of my relationship with the working class movement, or let us say, Communism. Now, on the one hand, you get a situation where for socio-logical/sexual reasons—that's to say because I was a kind of upper class boy brought up in a nicey-nice home—I was drawn to another class. And in order to be drawn to another class of course you tend to accept the politics which represent the cause of this class. So you tend towards socialistic or Commu-nistic attitudes. But when you look toward actual Communist states, or toward the labor movement in many countries, you find the deplorable fact that they are exceedingly puritanical, and that they want to impose a hetero-sexual dictatorship just like the capitalist dictatorship. And so you see this is a very intricate pattern, and it causes a lot of bounce back and forth between two attitudes. The question is, are you going to say "my dictatorship right or wrong," or are you going to say "my tribe before anything else"? Also of course it's acutely embarrassing to recognize the dimensions of your tribe, because some of the people in it you'll find deplorable, just as Jews suffer embarrassment over some Jews, and as I'm sure is the case with blacks, and, well, with any minority one could name. But, to return to the question of fiction and non-fiction, nothing is more fascinating than the enormous com-plexity, the subtlety, of certain kinds of fiction. You couldn't have a non-fiction Henry James, it wouldn't be the same thing at all. His sensibility, of course, when he's writing the book about coming back to America, *The American Scene,* is terrific, but there's an element in James that you couldn't possibly have except as fiction, because it's necessary to have a lot of inven-tion and a sort of crystalization of the situation. And that applies to a great many writers.

NOR: You're working, I understand, on a new autobiography?

Isherwood: Yes, you see, *Lions and Shadows* ends when I went for the first time to Berlin in 1929. And this new book starts on that day, and goes through a period of about ten years, to when I embarked for the United States in 1939.

NOR: Do you have a title?

Isherwood: No, I haven't got a title yet. I don't know what to call it. My working title is "Wanderings," but that's just simply because you have to call a book something when you're thinking about it yourself. Either this will be a complete volume in itself, or it will be connected up with a second volume which is about my first three or four years in the United States. Now that's much easier for me to write because I have extensive diaries which I kept at the time. This first section is very difficult because I've forgotten an enormous amount, and I'm reconstructing it out of letters, and bits of my diaries, of other people's memories, which are wildly unreliable—I'm always checking up. Auden didn't even know the year he married Erika Mann—he got it quite wrong! But of course there are always people who love to check these things out, and by degrees I'm zeroing in on most of it.

NOR: Is there anything you'd care to say in conclusion?

Isherwood: Did I tell you my exit line? I was speaking a few days ago, and I was trying to figure out how to leave the podium. I suddenly paused, and I said, "I had this great friend, the actress Gladys Cooper, whom I loved dearly (she's dead now), and she was being asked about acting, because they were talking about method acting and she was very scornful. And she said, 'It's ridiculous, there's nothing to it. You just know your lines, and speak up, and then get off the stage as quickly as possible.'" As I said this I walked off!

Christopher Isherwood: An Interview
Carolyn G. Heilbrun / 1976

From *Twentieth Century Literature* Volume 22 (October 1976): 253–
63. Copyright © Carolyn G. Heilbrun. Reprinted by permission.

My interview with Isherwood is really one conversation in two parts separated by ten months and three thousand miles. Our first talk was in Isherwood's study in his home in Santa Monica, and covered two afternoons
divided by an evening in which my husband and I had dinner with Isherwood
and Don Bachardy.

In May, 1976, just before he flew to England, Isherwood came to New
York, and the conversation was continued in my study. I tried both times to
ask him questions he had not been asked before at interviews: I had studied
them all. Christopher is, of course, a marvelous narrator and story teller; if
you ask him a question to which he has already worked out the answer,
perhaps in the book he is writing, he will present that answer with perfect
aplomb as though he had just thought of it on the spot. Not that he pretends
to have thought of it on the spot—but he is so stimulated by your question
and his answer, that you suppose his response to have been created for this
particular occasion. I think my desire for new questions and answers was
occasionally inconsiderate. Still, I did manage *not* to ask him when he met
Auden, or why he came to the United States.

Let me admit (on the chance that other Isherwood admirers may share my
impression) that I went to California in search of the Isherwood who appears
in all his works, including *An Approach to Vedanta* and *Exhumations,* as well
as in the novels. What I met was the Isherwood who had reached that point
in his life when he wished above all to be absolutely open and honest about
his life as a homosexual. I think that he wrote his forthcoming book, *Christopher and His Kind,* precisely to counter the rather saintlike and unwillful
image of him which his readers had understandably formed from his earlier
works.

Santa Monica, July, 1975.

Heilbrun: Ramakrishna, the Indian avatar whose biography you wrote,
was very yin-yang. A good American might suspect him of being homosexual.

141

Isherwood: Well yes, and there was in fact some man who went around at the time accusing him of this and saying "What's he doing with all these boys around the place?" Actually, Ramakrishna was completely simple and guileless. He told people whatever came into his mind, like a child. If he had ever been troubled by homosexual desires, if that had ever been a problem, he'd have told everybody about them. He said in the most completely calm, uninhibited way of Naren (one of his chief disciples), "when I'm with him, I feel as though he were my husband and I was his wife," and then again he said (taking another disciple), "I see him entirely as a woman." He was completely without any hang-ups, talking about sex-roles, because his thoughts transcended physical love-making. He saw even the mating of two dogs on the street as an expression of the eternal male-female principle in the universe. I think that is always a sign of great spiritual enlightenment. Another thing, related to this, which the Hindus feel, and indeed you find this in the Christian tradition too, is that God can be worshipped in all sorts of different ways; you can look at him as though you were his mother or father, you can look at him as a friend and as a lover—the whole Krishna thing came into that, you see. And you can also look at him as your father or your mother or your master.

H: It is interesting that he worships God in a feminine form, in Kali.

I: Again, he was trying to enter into all the possible spiritual relationships, and one of them was to worship God as a woman, and he found it simpler to do this if he dressed up as one.

H: And yet he would always speak of women and gold as the great threats to the spiritual life. They had to put a footnote in the gospels explaining that he liked women.

I: That's the most deplorable error, because he actually said—you know, his language was very simple—he said "woman" when he was talking to men, but whenever he was talking to women, he said "man and gold." What he meant was sexual lust and greed for possessions.

H: It's never put that way.

I: That's very unfortunate, and I think the phrase "woman and gold" puts people off terribly.

H: You say of yourself in *Kathleen and Frank:* "Heterosexuality wouldn't have suited him, it would have fatally cramped his style." You go on to explain that being homosexual allowed you to see things from an oblique angle, which is important for a writer. But one has the sense that you meant something more than that?

I: What I meant was that I have always had a strong tendency to get involved in domestic relationships. If I had been heterosexual, I would have been married by now about four times, with lots of children and paying every cent I earned in alimony.

H: That brings us to the whole idea of marriage. You've always mentioned conventional marriage with a shudder.

I: For myself, yes. I see it as a social trap. I find it indecent to try to protect a relationship by swearing an oath. What's so sacred about permanence, as such? Why shouldn't you be completely promiscuous? If you could only appreciate the sacredness of one-night stands—and realize that these are all God's creatures, you know, they're all my brothers or sisters.

H: You don't really feel a distinction between love for another person, sexually expressed, and the one-night stands you mention?

I: I don't see, theoretically, why there shouldn't be the most powerful sort of love, like St. Francis's, applied to one-night stands, where you really love a different person each night. But that's very advanced.

H: And a relationship that can go on for twenty years or more is not better, it's just different?

I: I think it's different. It's probably much easier, in one way. Really, to have that feeling, that you are overwhelmed with empathy and with love, not to mention lust, for a person that you just meet for a few hours, that's surely a *very* advanced state to be in. I can imagine that it'd be very near a kind of enlightenment.

H: In *Kathleen and Frank,* Frank said that he was not manly, that he would make a much better husband than lover. Vita Sackville-West said that all men could be divided into lovers and husbands. I take it you believe more in lovers than husbands?

I: It's not that one can't be both, it's more that you're limiting the experience if you put walls around it. I mean, to put it in a much simpler, cruder way, shouldn't it really be that at the end of it all, the central pair always come back to each other and say "Yes, it was absolutely marvelous, but really it only confirms my feeling that I would rather be with you than with anyone else in the world"? And I think that if you really have something going with somebody, one can hope that that will happen, and that applies equally to heterosexual relationships.

H: As long as, you say, you don't have any children. But now homosexual couples speak of marrying and adopting children.

I: Oh I know. I mean, goodness, I don't knock it and I think they should do exactly what they want, but it wouldn't do for me. Of course, I've had several relationships where there was an age difference, I don't feel myself at all far from being a father. In fact, a woman psychologist who's known me for many years, said to me "What a father you are!" I certainly never feel that I've missed anything by not having children of my own.

H: You've said that you had slept with one or two women, but that you didn't really like it.

I: Oh, but it worked all right. There again of course—it's so difficult to say, whether under other circumstances one might be able to feel romantically about a woman. And then, you see, getting right down to the core of myself, I begin to feel the old obstinacy coming up. I've tried to write about that in this book I've just finished. Then I think, "Well, fuck them all, why should I? Why?" As long as there's this pressure, as long as there's this majority saying "that's the way, that's what you ought to do," as long as nearly all the poets, and nearly everybody are going to harp on heterosexuality, I think "No, I won't, I absolutely won't." And I do see that there's a certain streak of perversity in me, of refusal to go along with the others. Somebody was telling me that I said in some interview that I felt that I would certainly have become heterosexual, if everybody else was homosexual— there's a streak of that in my make-up.

Of course, when I was younger, all sorts of other emotions came into the picture. There was a thing about the class structure; like a lot of upper-middle-class homosexuals, I was very much for working-class boys and all that. Into that entered an element of what I call "sexual colonialism." There was a time when, I realize now, I saw my sex partners as belonging to a sort of tribe which I was approaching in the spirit of a colonial exploiter. There was also, I suppose, a shyness involved; I preferred having them not only another class, but another race, so they could speak a different language. Talking English to them embarrassed me. But all of this disappeared. In that sense, America did not disappoint me; as soon as I got here, I got into a much more Whitmanesque sort of attitude, and in the essential democracy of life here I never again had any of these problems. And most of the people I've really cared deeply about have been Americans who I met since I lived in this country—I came when I was thirty-four.

H: I wonder if it's your having spent so much of your life in America that accounts for your attitude toward Jews. A student of mine, when we read *Goodbye to Berlin* in class, was very moved by the section on the Landauers. He had got so used to anti-Semitism in English literature, that your feelings about the Landauers came as rather a shock to him—a good shock.

I: You know, in this book that I've just written, I have a great deal about the Landauers, and particularly about Bernhard Landauer, because, as a matter of fact, I don't altogether like the attitude toward him that's displayed in the story and I try to go more and more into that. As I point out in this new book, he led a life which became incredibly heroic toward the end.

I was enormously involved with Jews at this period, I felt far too involved with them to feel guilty about criticizing them. I really feel that, in a sense, I couldn't be anti-Semitic if I tried, because we're too much in the same apple-cart, you know. On the other hand, with some individuals, on both sides, there's undoubtedly been hostility. We called each other dirty names. But that meant very little.

My real involvement with Jews was after I left Germany, and found myself, wherever I went, in the midst of the emigration. I don't know who it was, some writer, who said jokingly "Christopher is an honorary Jew—*ein Ehrenjude.*" Coming out to California, I was absolutely surrounded with all the refugee writers who'd come to Hollywood, who were almost 97 percent Jewish, of course, and not to mention all the American Jews in the entertainment business. One was always in the middle of this sort of Central European atmosphere.

H: Erika Mann was half-Jewish, and Auden married her to give her British citizenship. Since you knew her through the cabaret where she sang, why didn't you marry her?

I: Well, as a matter of fact, she asked me, first of all. She didn't know him, but I had various reasons for not doing it, one of which, the most valid reason, was that I didn't want to involve my German friend with those extremely prominent anti-Nazis, in this spectacular way. As things turned out, it might well have made terrible trouble for him later, when he got arrested by the Gestapo. Also I did really have the feeling that there was something inherently disgraceful in getting married. I had an absolute horror of the suggestion that I was in any way trying to pass as a heterosexual, even for the noblest motives.

H: You only would have done it if there was no one else?

I: Yes. As a matter of fact, Auden was the first person I suggested, he agreed instantly and Teresa Geihso, the other great artist in the cabaret, a much greater actress than Erika, a really wonderful actress (who only died the other day), she got married to an Englishman too, another arranged marriage, not very long afterwards, with one of our friends, a man named John Simson, who is a writer. Erika was absolutely saved by the gong; it was the very day that Goebbels took away her nationality that she became a British subject; it just happened that the actual order came out that day.

H: I've become impressed, as many have, with the books of J. R. Ackerley. I gather, from *The Ackerley Letters,* that you knew him.

I: Oh, very well, yes, he was very much part of the Forster group, an intimate friend of Forster's. I was with him, actually, about a week before he died, we were all together, very festive; he died quite painlessly in his sleep, there was some idea he had a bad heart, but he was in perfect health, apparently. I must have met him around 1936, but I'm unclear whether I started working for him before I met him or the other way around. He was then the literary editor of the *Listener,* the literary magazine of the BBC, and I started reviewing for him. This was a great financial support for me, at that time, I lived largely on it, and I reviewed about thirty-five books for him in all, in the course of about three years. Then I got to know him, of course, and I saw him again a great deal after the War, with Forster. Ackerley was extraordinarily handsome. He had tremendous style, you know, he was really very, very intelligent and had great charm, but there was a certain kind of dreary sadness about him. Sometimes it was actually irritating, he was so negative; it's very British, a lot of us are like that, gloomy and grumbly. It is a sort of Jewish gloom, but without the Jewish wit which always goes with it, the gallows humour—it's just gloom. Those refugees were masters of it, you know, there was nothing, nothing, nothing you could do to cheer them up, but on the other hand, suddenly they said something piercingly funny, they were just having a ball, that was their way. But you felt that Ackerley wasn't enjoying it very much, and that wasn't so sympathetic.

[Isherwood showed Heilbrun, as she was leaving, a piece of carved wood which was the work of D. H. Lawrence. Isherwood said he had once visited the place where Lawrence had stayed in New Mexico.]

I: We went there, made a pilgrimage; I went up with some friends and we spent the night under the trees, sleeping in bags outside the High Ranch. To my mind, that's one of the greatest passages in English literature, his description in *Saint Mawr,* of the ranch house and the New England woman who hated the wilderness, because it was so frightening. There's a wonderful description of that.

H: You admire him very much?

I: Tremendously, yes. Not his philosophical point of view, but I admire tremendously his approach to writing. It's something very, very basic, and something one can learn from all kinds of different writers, but for me, it came from Lawrence: the revelation that you could write about nature in a purely subjective way. In other words, there wasn't an absolute *truth* about nature; it was all in the eye of the beholder—if you are in a bad temper, the valley is obscene, ugly, and bad, and if you aren't, it's beautiful. Well, *Saint Mawr* is really one of my favorite works, because I find the kind of farcicalness of it so marvelous. This girl marries this artist named Rico who's a rotter, and this horse, which of course is Lawrence, takes one look at him and sees he hasn't got a dark center so it just stomps on him.

New York City, May, 1976.

Heilbrun: In Santa Monica you mentioned a "woman psychologist who's known me for years." Would you tell me something about her?

Isherwood: Evelyn Hooker. Our relationship really started because she was making a study of various types of homosexual. And she was working toward her great thesis which in those days was quite revolutionary: that we homosexuals are not necessarily sick. This she finally demonstrated and got gradually accepted. She was also—and that interested me far more, because whether I was sick or not, I was me and that's all I cared about—she was a social psychologist. She was one of the few people I know who was interested at that time in the structure of the gay world from a purely social point of view. And I used to spend a great deal of time trying to answer her questions. Also she was an exceptionally bold field psychologist and would go to the gay bars at a time when all that was much less usual than it is now. She was therefore widely trusted and loved. She is a very remarkable woman, deeply emotional in her own way and yet as regards the scientific part of her life, I think admirably objective.

She married twice and the second time she married a professor of literature, named Edward Hooker, who was editing an edition of Dryden when he died of a heart attack. And that was a terrible blow to her. They were very devoted. It was a late life romance and they were married for several years. And that's when I knew her. And it was in their garden that I had this little house for a while and lived there. Then when I met Don, it was obviously much too small for two people to live in. It was really just a studio in the garden. I've kept in touch with her and so has Don.

H: I'm also interested in your friendship with Maria Huxley, Aldous's wife. You said that you were very intimate with her.

I: Maria was a person who invited the deepest confidences. What I had going there was a brother-sister relationship, but she was such a devoted wife that she could never have become a possessive sister. I have had some experiences with pseudo-sisters who started to boss me and then there was trouble. Theoretically I was in the market for a sister or two, you know. But in practice, it seldom worked.

During the thirties, one of my strong sister relationships was with John Lehmann's sister, Beatrix, the actress. We've always been very close. And that was a completely successful sister relationship, even though politically we didn't entirely see eye to eye. She was rather more radically Left than I was. And then, as I describe in my book, my Leftism came into a clash with the fact that the Communists were starting to persecute the gays, after declaring earlier that they respected individual freedom in sexual matters. Very much as Jews must have felt who were Communists but then found that Soviet Russia wasn't the best place to be Jewish in. *Goodbye to Berlin* is dedicated to Beatrix as well as to John. There was a whole period when we saw each other daily in Berlin. And then she got to know this man who was the model for the director in my novel *Prater Violet,* Berthold Viertel. I introduced her to him because I wanted to get him to take her on in the film we did together, *Little Friend.* She wasn't right for that but she did play for him in the next picture that he made which was *The Passing of the Third Floor Back.*

H: Will you say something about your new book?

I: What I shall be very curious to know is if you feel that this book, although non-fiction and although autobiographical, is a kind of novel. There are themes that run through it. And there's a sort of payoff. In a curious way, it arranged itself like that. And I don't think that I have bent the facts. It is a description of the inner drives and external forces which took me away from

England. And I wonder to what extent all this will seem to form an artistic whole. I'm always conscious of the psychosomatic aspect of life. I mean, in other words, that there is a part of one's will over which one has no conscious control. It is moving you in certain directions, and makes you do the darndest things. It has its own plans for you, but not necessarily plans which you would think of as being nice or good or benevolent.

H: Are you going to go on to write about your life after you came to the United States?

I: Well, you see Carolyn, that's a very different thing because I have this gigantic manuscript already, at least for the first few years—from the beginning of 1939, when I arrived here, right through 1944, by which time I'd had some experience of the film world and Quakerdom and the Hindus.

H: A lot of which is in "Paul" in *Down There on a Visit.*

I: The material is used in various places. But nevertheless there's a lot more of it. And anyway it has a different significance when it's directly applied to me. It would be easy for me to reprint that with comments, as in *Kathleen and Frank.* I could easily make a book out of that.

H: But you're not sure if you will?

I: Well, you see, in this book I've just finished, the book about the thirties, so many of the characters are now dead or they have become such old friends that I'm sure they won't mind. But if I get into this later stuff, I shall be dealing increasingly with people who aren't dead. So perhaps rather than be overly discreet and be a bore, I shall leave it to be published after my death. But I don't know. It is there anyway.

H: So it isn't what you look forward to doing next?

I: Oh, I would love to do some tiny little thing. One-page stories or sort of exquisite little *pensées.* Everybody always imagines they can do that. It's harder than the longest book in the world.

H: Oh, it's much harder. How much do you feel when you write a book like this and it's about to be published, that part of your obligation to being an author and publicizing it—as opposed to having a sense that it has to make its own way?

I: I do find publicizing a bit embarrassing. First of all I feel embarrassed because you're presumably talking to people chiefly who haven't read the book. And now what are you doing, running an ad for it you know. And then

I feel, particularly in the case of the book, that a lot of people are just going to find it exceedingly distasteful.

H: Why?

I: Because of its aggressiveness. It's not pornographic, not by standards of nowadays. It would never be banned, at least not in any sort of semi-civilized place. But that's not the point. I think a lot of people would say: "What's all the fuss about?" The most effective form of annihilation is to say "Yes, so he's a fag, what else is new? Some of our best friends are fags and we don't mind."

H: Much of what you have to say about the situation in Berlin is important; many people don't really know about Berlin in the thirties, and need to learn.

I: Well of course there is a great deal about Berlin in this book. And I go through the whole thing and take all the major characters in the Berlin story and tell the real facts which were always a bit different. But all that only takes up about a quarter of the book. I mean there is what happened after that, wanderings about in different countries and meeting all sorts of people.

H: When you first came to California and talked to the swami, did the question of homosexuality come up?

I: Instantly.

H: Instantly?

I: I mean I never had any religion before except what I was raised with and had rejected. And I was determined that at least we should get off on the right foot.

H: And what did he say?

I: Well you see, he's a monk. And his view is that all attachment is attachment, that life exists only for God within one's self and that everything which hinders that is to be kept to a minimum, or sublimated. In a word, he said homosexuality is merely another form of attachment, neither worse nor better. And that was all I wanted to hear. I said all right, good. Now we can understand each other. The friend I was with at the time when I met Swami also became a devotee. So that made it immediately in itself much easier because then we had the status of householder disciples, as the Hindus would say. But you know, I've really come to the conclusion, in the wisdom of my seventy-one years, that there are even more beautiful and terrible obstacles to enlightenment than sex. And one of them is writing.

H: Why writing?

I: Well I just found, for instance, while I was working on this book, that as Katherine Mansfield said, "I look at the mountains, I try to pray and then I think of something clever." I really couldn't meditate at all until it was finished. The moment the mind became the least little bit calm, it simply said to me, do you realize that in Chapter 3, you completely forgot to refer to Anna, or something. And I thought, Oh Jesus, I forgot, I must remember that. I was afraid I wouldn't even remember it until I'd finished my meditation and could note it down.

H: Do you think this could in any way be a comment on meditation? After all, what could be better than to calm one's mind and get on with one's own work?

I: Perhaps I should have done what I believe Gide used to do. It seems he actually had periods of literary meditation. Every day he spent an hour just pacing up and down and sort of letting the whole book (*The Counterfeiters*) go through his head. Now of course it's arguable that then you might have two periods of meditation. During the meditation on *The Counterfeiters,* you think of nothing but God and you would be absolutely unable to think about *The Counterfeiters.* And during the period of meditation on God, you would have all your literary ideas. I don't know why I've never tried playing this trick on myself.

Christopher Isherwood Interview

Roger Austen / 1976

From *Gay Sunshine Interviews* Volume 1 (San Francisco: Gay Sunshine Press, 1978): 191–99. Reprinted by permission.

Two separate interviews are printed here: Interview I was taped in summer 1973 by Winston Leyland, editor of *Gay Sunshine,* and originally appeared in *Gay Sunshine* 19 (September–October 1973). This interview is copyright © 1978, 1984 by Gay Sunshine Press Inc. Winston Leyland (San Francisco) is the publisher of Gay Sunshine books, information on which can be accessed at www.gaysunshine.com. Interview II was taped in San Francisco in December 1976 while Isherwood was touring with his book *Christopher and His Kind.* It was conducted under the auspices of Fruit Punch, gay men's radio, which broadcast an edited version over KPFA (Berkeley) in February 1977. The late Roger Austen, who conducted the second interview, authored the book *Playing the Game: The Homosexual Novel in America* (1977) and wrote the introductions to the two books of writings by turn-of-the-century California writer, Charles Warren Stoddard: *Cruising the South Seas* (Gay Sunshine Press, 1987); and the novel *For the Pleasure of His Company: An Affair of the Misty City* (Gay Sunshine Press, 1987). Both interviews are reprinted with permission from the book *Gay Sunshine Interviews Volume 1,* edited by Winston Leyland, Gay Sunshine Press, 1978, 1984.

Austen: In your latest book *Christopher and His Kind,* you have given an autobiographical look back into the years 1929–1939, which provides a real-life commentary to the fiction that you wrote at that time, with particular emphasis on the gay realities which were occasionally muted in such novels as *Goodbye to Berlin, The Last of Mr. Norris,* and, later on, *Down There on a Visit.* Did you ever sense in the thirties that there would come a day in your lifetime when such a frank book as this could be published?

Isherwood: I suppose so, yes. I suppose I took it for granted that things would get better rather than worse. But that wasn't really the reason that I didn't write more frankly, although it was one reason at the time. There was also the reason that I was just trying to narrate this whole thing in the most unobtrusive manner possible. If the narrator were something as unusual as a homosexual, this would have made him too interesting, and then we would have got drawn aside into his affairs, his way of looking at things, his prejudices, his view of the world, and taken the interest away from Mr. Norris and Sally Bowles and all these characters. It's a different kind of writing.

Austen: I suppose that because of your living at the Hirschfeld institute and seeing things that were being done thirty and forty years ago that your perspective on gay liberation is much broader than it is for those who believe everything began with Stonewall. Things were really happening in Berlin in the twenties and thirties?

Isherwood: Oh, my goodness, yes. Hirschfeld was certainly one of the great heroes of gay liberation, one of the earliest people. He several times actually risked his life by going to Munich, where there were already an awful lot of Nazis around, and did get beat up on one occasion. He was almost killed—they left him for dead. And he went right back! He was fantastic in that way, because he was very much the sort of funny German professor, with glasses and everything, and one didn't see him as a fiery, daring person. But, in fact, he was.

Austen: Was there anyone comparable to Hirschfeld in England at the time?

Isherwood: The great figure, of course, was Edward Carpenter, who was one of the greatest figures anywhere in the liberation movement and was not only writing about it and speaking about it but living a life of domestic bliss with his lover. And that was quite something—people were horrified. There's that wonderful story about when he was visited by some sort of religious person who started this spiel about hell and "Don't you care about your soul?" and "Don't you want to go to heaven?" Carpenter's lover said, "Listen. We're in heaven right here."

Austen: But in those day there were a lot of people who were much more pessimistic, too. In 1906 Lytton Strachey wrote a letter to Keynes saying that he felt it was impossible to make the dowagers understand that feelings were good and that very often the best of feelings were sodomitical. He felt that only a hundred years hence could this ever be done.

Isherwood: Yes, well, that's very understandable. It must have seemed incredible before the War, but World War I was, psychologically and philosophically speaking, much more of a disturber than World War II. There was a different world at the end of World War I.

Austen: In choosing the title "and his kind," was that the phrase that was used fifty years ago? Weren't homosexuals supposed to go away and live with their own "kind"?

Isherwood: As a matter of fact, it was Don Bachardy, my friend, who found the title. As you know, we write together. In the book I'd been using the word "tribe" to describe gay people, but "kind" was deliberately chosen as being more ambiguous, and it also suggested "my kind of person." Because after all I do have quite a lot of intimate heterosexual friends of both sexes, and they had to be included. It's not just about my gay friends.

Austen: Have you read Martin Green's *Children of the Sun,* the overview of what it meant to be a "dandy" in England in the twenties and thirties?
Isherwood: Yes, I looked into it.

Austen: He's not very sympathetic towards people like Brian Howard, for instance.
Isherwood: Well, of course, Brian was a bird of another feather altogether. And yet he had a great deal of courage—admittedly a rather destructive kind—but courage is always remarkable.

Austen: Did you think of Brian as a dandy, and did he think of himself as a dandy, and was there any correlation between being a dandy and being gay in the thirties?
Isherwood: Well, he was the sort of person who got into tuxedos and tails, all of which were absolutely taboo to me. The reason I'm dressed up like this is because of our quaint idea down south that when one gets to San Francisco one must put a tie on. [*Laughter.*]

Austen: All you need to do is to go to Eighteenth and Castro to see how little we wear.
Isherwood: Well, I think it would be very amusing to go to Eighteenth and Castro and have a tie on—it would be like appearing in evening tails.

Austen: To get back to Martin Green: although I realize he started out in his book not to be particularly kind to you all, he ends up with a sort of grudging admiration. He pegged you as a *naif*—there were rogues and dandies and *naifs*—and he says "*naifs* were men who offered their minds and hearts as being all limpid sensitiveness—always about to join the Communist Party, to become comrades, fighters, members, but most of them didn't." Would you quarrel with Green's pigeonholing you this way?
Isherwood: I think pigeonholing is a foredoomed operation. It's much beloved by certain types of minds, but really, people won't go into pigeonholes. You have to start chopping bits of them off in order to get them in. Of

course, the basic thing about Russia was that when the revolution took place in '17, the Communists had come out with a big platform which included the idea that private life was not the concern of the state. That it was bourgeois to have all these laws regulating behavior between consenting adults. Hirschfeld took this very seriously and welcomed them as allies—and, therefore, added to his crimes (of being gay and a Jew) the crime—according to the point of view of the Nazis—of being a Communist fellow-traveler. Of course, if Hirschfeld had lived and witnessed the turnaround when the Soviets began arresting gays and deporting them to Siberia and so forth, he would obviously have denounced them. There was a feeling, as you've quoted just now, about "brotherhood" and so forth, and that was sort of nice, and had something to do with comrades and thus had something to do with Communists. But if we were woolly-minded, we had good cause. Somewhere we probably smelled rats that we didn't like to refer to. All was not well, because there was always the suspicion that the Party felt we were decadent and bourgeois.

Austen: Did you think of your generation (i.e., you and Auden and Spender) as more enlightened because of your politics than the preceding Bloomsbury group of Strachey, Woolf?

Isherwood: You know, just speaking for myself, I really wasn't all that political. I was very much concerned with getting on with the job, which for me was just writing books, having decided that I was a writer. Everything else was rather secondary. Among my friends were some perfectly serious Communists, who were Communists in the way that Quakers are Quakers, and you can't criticize that. They were so totally different from us—we weren't serious in that sense. Auden, too—his eye was on something quite different. Although he was prepared to risk his life to go to Spain and all that, his fundamental thing was to write poetry.

Austen: In literary history, though, it seems to me that Auden particularly has been pegged as a poet whose political views have colored his works. The left claimed him as their own—in those days, at least.

Isherwood: In those days. Later he moved much more across the center and in some positions toward the right. He was very individualistic.

Austen: Let me ask you a little about Americans whom you may have met during the thirties but did not mention in this book. Did you ever bump into Parker Tyler, Charles Henry Ford, Robert McAlmon, Frederick Prokosch, Hart Crane?

Isherwood: Prokosch, but I couldn't swear when I met him, exactly.

Austen: Were you reading any of his books?

Isherwood: Well, I certainly read the first one. I met Paul Bowles very briefly—that's why Sally Bowles is called Sally Bowles—but in fact I had no idea that he was an extremely talented composer or writer. He was nineteen at the time, and there was no reason I should have known. He said I had a very "superior" manner, and I don't doubt it because I was in my late twenties, which, of course, *was* superior.

Austen: One of the Americans, McAlmon, wrote some stories during the twenties about Berlin gay bars in which his main characters were usually just slumming, going to watch the "decadent" people. There seems to have always been this sort of remove for Americans—they could not admit in print to being gay themselves. Did you sense there was a difference between the British point of view and this American nervousness?

Isherwood: No, not necessarily. There were an awful lot of slummers who came by, and I was meanwhile being very salty and dressed like a hustler myself most of the time. I wore one of those sweaters with a great big turnover neck and bell-bottom pants. But in retrospect none of those bars seems to have been very rough and tough—nowadays it seems much more violent—but I think they committed murder and stole, of course, and other things people do when they don't have very much money.

Austen: Most of the German boys in the Cozy Corner bar were just hustling because they were poor? And then they would go on to get married?

Isherwood: Oh, yes. One of them said, "I'm homosexual for economic reasons."

Austen: And everyone else there was homosexual for other reasons?

Isherwood: Oh, of course, one wouldn't go there, otherwise. No, heavens, what for?

Austen: When you were describing these bars in your earlier novels, you referred to them obliquely as "amusing," but the gay reader could sense that when you wrote "amusing" that you meant "gay," right?

Isherwood: Yes. People like my uncle, who belonged to an earlier generation, talked about "frightfully amusing" places.

Austen: So that there were these code words that gay readers could pick up on—

Isherwood: Oh, yes.

Austen: And what you're saying in *Christopher and His Kind* is merely confirmation, or sort of a key to the code.
Isherwood: Yes.

Austen: One reviewer in the thirties called your narrator Christopher "this sexless nitwit"—
Isherwood: Wasn't that beautiful? Yes, I've always treasured that.

Austen: Do you discount the validity of this criticism?
Isherwood: No, I don't discount it. I think it was one of the disadvantages of my method.

Austen: Or all gay men's methods in those days when they had to be obscure and oblique.
Isherwood: Yes, I was in a dilemma, and the dilemma was not solved by just avoiding the subject of the narrator's sexuality, which is in fact what I did. It's a valid criticism. "Nitwit," I don't know. I don't see him as a nitwit.

Austen: No, I don't either. Going from the specific to the general, though, do you think that gay writers of the thirties and the forties who had to "pass" through one ruse or another wrote things that, as a result, suffered aesthetically? They could not be as forthright about their minority status as, for instance, Jews who were writing "Jewish novels" or blacks who were writing "black novels."
Isherwood: Yes, I do feel a sort of lameness in some books that are otherwise quite remarkable. There's an excellent novel by William Plomer that I was rereading the other day. It's called *The Invaders* [1934] and it has to do with someone from the upper class and someone from the lower class. But the whole thing is blunted by the fact that Plomer can't really quite come out and say it. It's really a moving love story without any lovemaking of any kind, but something in the reader nowadays calls for something more—at least one explicit scene.

Austen: Let's go into the concept of the upper class and lower and into what the parallel was here in America. My idea of the average gay man in the thirties here—and I was born in 1935 so I don't really remember this—is that he must have aspired to a certain Clifton Webb elegance, and they all considered themselves a mystical brotherhood just a little lower than the angels. Was this part of the gay mystique in England as well, this sense of elitism?

Isherwood: Well, certainly we fortified ourselves with that to some extent, as all minorities do. Everybody is the Chosen People. You have to have something to give you gumption, a quiet superiority—at which the British are very good, anyway. There's nothing like our "superiority" anywhere to be found, and the less there is to be superior about, the more valuable it is, of course.

Austen: But I think American gay men were pretty good at that—they wore all the right scarves and subscribed to the *New Yorker* and had very smart apartments. However, to get to the parallel with the lower class, I'd say the American counterpart to going to Berlin to look for a lower-class German boy would have been to go out and look for what used to be called "rough trade." Can you explain why the members of the upper classes felt a certain virility did not seem to be obtainable among wealthy young men, and why gay men everywhere used to place such a great premium on seducing someone who was supposed to be straight?

Isherwood: It probably has something to do with the awareness of difference and likeness in other people, and how this awareness leads to loving or merely liking someone. When you suddenly feel you can bridge the frightful gap between the Montagues and the Capulets, that's the awareness of difference, which love leaps over. When you realize that you and the person you just got into conversation with are both crazy about stamp collecting, that's awareness of likeness, but that usually leads to friendship rather than love.

Austen: Were you in Germany at this time, had they started to round up the gay men and send them to concentration camps?

Isherwood: You see, I left Germany only a few months after Hitler got into power, so they really hadn't got under way.

Austen: Did you know of anyone who was impounded, or who died wearing the pink triangle?

Isherwood: No, no I didn't.

Austen: Apparently there were hundreds of thousands.

Isherwood: Oh, yes, undoubtedly. There's no question about that.

Austen: We haven't heard very much about them, though, have we?

Isherwood: No, they never had a spokesman, really.

Austen: And the rationale was that the Nazis didn't want any men who were not virile for the Third Reich, that all gay men were effete?

Isherwood: Yes, that was the excuse, I suppose.

Austen: And yet there's quite a mystique today here in San Francisco revolving around neo-Nazi menace and so forth. Are you troubled that some gay men are flirting with all of this Nazi memorabilia and storm-trooper trappings?

Isherwood: I must confess to a terrible ignorance of S & M, and I really don't know what goes on in their heads quite, but as I have tried to find traces of it in my own libido, it seems to me that one might quite as easily just pretend to be a Jew being tortured or something and get a kick out of that without necessarily subscribing to the Nazi philosophy. Is it a political question under those circumstances? You could just as soon say, "Today I'm going to be a homosexual being beaten up in the Lubianka Prison by the Soviets." Now does that mean you've changed your political orientation? I think it's better to get all that junk out in the open. In a word, I'm not so terribly frightened by it.

Austen: Let me ask you about George Orwell. Did you see eye to eye with him during the thirties and later?

Isherwood: I saw eye to eye with him much more later. We were tremendously shocked at first by his monumental book *Homage to Catalonia,* in which he said that the Russian Communist were destroying the cause of the Spanish revolution.

Austen: By the time he wrote *Animal Farm,* you tended to agree with him more?

Isherwood: Oh, yes.

Austen: There's a contemporary of yours—maybe a little older—Joe Ackerley, and in his letters you get the idea that his gay life was not quite as happy and breezy and successful as yours. He just had his dog. He did not seem to love life quite as much as you have. Was there some difference in his not accepting his gayness?

Isherwood: Oh, he was one of the greatest pessimists who has ever lived! But it was constitutional, I think. He was constitutionally melancholy. He was an extraordinary man, blessed with amazing good looks, great literary talent, a very intelligent person, a hero in World War I at the front. And this man, who might have had everything, had that sort of fatal flaw of melancholy.

Austen: Was there a good deal of that in gay men you remember thirty, forty years ago as compared with the younger gay men today?

Isherwood: No, I can't feel that. It's just as varied. Temperaments vary just the same in both categories.

Austen: You have never been of the melancholy temperament yourself, I would gather, for any great length of time?

Isherwood: I played with it when I was young, then when I began to see what life was like, I realized that it's dangerous and intolerable.

Austen: To be consistently melancholy?

Isherwood: Yes, I mean, you're just destroying yourself.

Austen: Your reaction to coming to New York and America at the end of *Christopher and His Kind* is the sense that New York City is saying to you, "Do things our way or take the next boat back." Do your feel that America in the late thirties was not particularly congenial to one of the British temperament?

Isherwood: Well, it enormously attracted me as a challenge, but I did feel it was very rough and tough.

Austen: Has Santa Monica been less rough than New York City?

Isherwood: Oh, I feel perfectly at home in Santa Monica. I've lived longer in this country now than I did in England.

Austen: At the end of your book, you suggest that with Don Bachardy there may be a sequel to this. Are you now writing "Christopher and His Kind, Part Two," that will pick up in 1939?

Isherwood: Oh, much more so than that, you see. What I have—and it's all finished and typed—is massive diaries covering the years from '39 through 1944. I was going to publish them. I said to myself, "The moment has come that I'm going to edit them and publish them." And I thought, well, before I do that I'll have to have just a chapter which explains how I came to the States in the first place. That book's the first chapter. In other words, it got longer and longer. I went further and further back in time and finally I decided that in the sense that one's life is a chess game, the moment that I made the move to go to Berlin all the other moves were inevitable.

Austen: Is this diary going to be published shortly?

Isherwood: I don't know, because there are grave difficulties. First, the embarrassment of material—far too much. And secondly, the question of people who are still alive who might be hurt. Certain indiscretions of one kind or another. But all that is secondary. I could produce it with some amputation in about six months, and there's a lot of interesting material—all about Huxley, the Hindus, the Quakers, Garbo, Ingrid Bergman, the stars.

Austen: So one way or another we may well be able to look forward to reading a continuation of this book?

Isherwood: Oh, yes, sure, one way or another.

Interview with Christopher Isherwood

Tony Russo / 1977

From *Christopher Street* March 1977: 6–10. Reprinted by permission.

Christopher Isherwood's new autobiography, *Christopher and His Kind,* is fast becoming one of the most popular new books among gay people this year. The chief characters in his book are indeed Mr. Isherwood's "kind," the people he regarded as his friends and natural allies—among them, W. H. Auden and E. M. Forster.

Tony Russo recently spoke with Mr. Isherwood. For the gay literary world, the following is a fireside chat.

Russo: The first time I met you was at the Modern Language Association conference—the famous one where you apparently "came out." It was at that meeting that a friend of mine had said, "I don't know what all the fuss is about. All you had to do was to read *Berlin Stories* and you would have known."

Isherwood: Oh yes, I see what you mean. Well, as a matter of fact it wasn't like that at all. I didn't sort of come out. I came out imperceptibly. What I mean is, in the first place, every soul who knew me knew about it because my lifestyle came out when I was twenty-five, or even earlier, and never changed. In other words, there was never a kind of back street in my life. If I had a friend, we went everywhere together and there was never any shit about it. Nor was the MLA by any means the first place where I had spoken in that way. It was more that the MLA "came out." What I mean by that is—and I'm not saying this arrogantly—it was a question of *their* introducing this subject and facing it for the first time ever, and they just brought me in as one of the people to make it happen. So, really, the big deal was not that I announced it, but that they sat still for it.

Russo: Did you feel that in your early works, there is a certain gay sensibility? For example, *Berlin Stories.*

Isherwood: Oh, yes. I think that anybody who really had any sensibility of that kind could tell at a single glance. Even in earlier books. For instance, there was quite a bit about it in *The Memorial,* my second novel. And before

162

that, my first novel. I remember very well when I showed it to the publisher—
and that was in 1928—a woman in the office said that it seemed homosexual
to her. But, as a matter of fact, it wasn't meant to be. So, my work has always
been full of it. In *The Memorial,* which was published in 1932, there is very
definitely a gay character, and no nonsense made of it. He's gay, and that's
that. In fact, the book ends with a conversation between him and a hustler in
Berlin.

Russo: Do you feel that "coming out" has changed the way people view
your work?

Isherwood: You mean the opposition?

Russo: Yes.

Isherwood: Yes, I dare say so. It is almost impossible to tell. Those kinds
of things you never get to hear directly.

Russo: Do you feel that gay writers should come out?

Isherwood: I think everybody has a different duty. It's all a question of
who you are, what obligations you have, whom you would hurt by doing so,
etc., etc. In my case it would be absolutely inexcusable not to "come out"
and, indeed, impossible. I mean, what is there "in" anymore? One thing you
can bet on, you can hide, you can be seen around with the straightest of
people, you can do this, you can do that, but the little birds in the trees know.

Russo: Have you had to pay a toll? Do you feel that people who review
your work have displayed a certain homophobia?

Isherwood: Yes, it's been known.

Russo: Do you feel that your books should be reviewed by gay reviewers?

Isherwood: Well, you see, Tony, there is another difficulty there. We're
now solidifying a bit and forming our ranks and confronting the world. It's a
very awkward situation. If you're a gay writer, or anyone who has any art
products on the market, what do your brothers and sisters do? It becomes
sort of a duty to praise it and that's bad in itself. You see, until our subculture
is more established we can hardly afford to criticize each other very strongly.
We don't like to. And it's a very natural and a decent human feeling. We
think, well, after all, considering that he is one of us or she is one of us, we
want to say it is a great book or great film or great play. And so, I would
really rather be reviewed, in a way, by heterosexuals. Because I don't want
the reviewer to feel obliged to say, well this is an absolute masterpiece, when
they really mean, gosh how nice of him to join us.

Russo: But can't it also be that gay people identify so much with the book, and rarely does that happen, that the effect is more overwhelming.

Isherwood: Well, I confess. I am strongly prejudiced in favor of a gay book, for openers. And if I like it, I mean, if it seems to have literary merit, then of course I go overboard. I begin to think, this is a darling book. I'm the first to admit I have prejudices of this kind.

Russo: Now that you are in your seventies, have you given much thought to growing old and being gay?

Isherwood: Well, I've led a very lucky life in almost every respect. It's not a thing which has presented itself as a great problem. I don't mourn my youth or anything of that kind in the slightest bit. As a matter of fact, while it was a lot of fun, I'm really in some ways as happy, and maybe even happier, now. It just hasn't ever been a problem.

Russo: Do you have any regrets?

Isherwood: No, I really don't think so. I see that there were all kinds of different paths I might have taken, but to say that one might have been better than another, if you really analyze it, it's very hard to decide.

Russo: Did you ever envision that you would be where you are today?

Isherwood: Yes, I always wanted to be a writer. I really took it for granted. I did make an awful fuss, despaired, carried on, but underneath I always felt that that was what I was born to be. When I was very young, I toyed with the idea of being an actor or a film director. But, after all, that's very much the same thing.

Russo: Recently, I saw one of the last performances of Harold Pinter's play, *No Man's Land.* After having seen it a second time, I wondered if Spooner was not meant to be Auden.

Isherwood: Evidently John Gielgud thought so, and, in fact, Gielgud did several mannerisms which were Auden's. One thing he certainly did which Auden used to do was to hold the cigarette so that the burning point is out, pointing it between the finger and the thumb. And, of course, very characteristic was the tie not being fixed properly, and sort of turned inside out. Some of the other movements were like Auden's.

Russo: Do you think the character represented him?

Isherwood: Well, certainly it was very amusing, but I have great difficulty with things that I can't understand. After I saw the play, I had dinner with Gielgud—he is a good friend of mine—and he was saying that the more you play in it the more you understand it.

I'm a great admirer of Pinter. I've seen a great number of his plays. Of course, as Gielgud once said, the great thing about Pinter is that he has been an actor. He has a wonderful instinct for what is good on the stage, what sounds right, what words to put into the actors' mouths, what effects certain words create. Sometimes his words *are* simple, but they are like a pistol being fired—they are just right. They really hit, on the funny bone. He does it over and over again. And all the stage effects are thought out in the same kind of way.

I must say that a bit of the audience enthusiasm for *No Man's Land* was that they loved the British accents. They thought that was very funny, and of course the actors played it up a lot.

Russo: Having lived in England for a while, I found it difficult to understand how, on a cultural level, an American audience could fully grasp the play.

Isherwood: Well, you know that business about the Anglo-American accent. Years and years ago, when I was quite young, Pauline Laud, an American actress, came over and played in *Anna Christie*. I swear to you, we sat there in raptures saying this is supreme, and I don't think we understood one word in twelve. It was like going to a French play. Considerably later, toward the end of the nineteen-thirties, I talked with the cast who came over for *Golden Boy*—the Odets play—and they told me that after the first night they had to modify their accents. They might as well have been playing in French. No one could understand a single word. That's a real dialect play! But there it didn't quite work—the audience preferred to know what was happening. In *Anna Christie* it is even more evident what is happening.

What makes *No Man's Land* work is the comic despair. The English are great masters of comic despair. When things are so awful, all you can do is roar with laughter. That's what makes Brian Bedford's performance in *Equus* so marvelous. I've seen several people in his role, but he alone has that grin-and-bear-it English style. As a consequence, he is much more realistic. *Equus* is a very heavy-handed, slow, grinding play, and he completely takes the curse off of it by the way he plays it. Yet, you feel all the compassion, all the everything, just the same. He is a real English provincial doctor who has seen everything, and who has sort of weary fun. It makes *Equus* seem ten times better.

Russo: Apparently you must do a lot of travelling. In *Christopher and His Kind* you talk at great length about your travels. Do you enjoy travelling?

Isherwood: Well, I really am a stay-at-home. It's true that I've travelled a great deal. I've always liked it, *after* it happened.

Christopher Isherwood

Studs Terkel / 1977

Reprinted by permission of the Chicago Historical Society.

ST: Our guest today is Christopher Isherwood, memoirist and novelist, best known for his *Berlin Stories,* which became the play *I Am a Camera* as well as the musical—film and theater—*Cabaret.* Mr. Isherwood has revised his autobiography. It's a new look at himself, one of those fresh third-person approaches, so he's outside, looking inside. *Christopher and His Kind,* it's called, which details further his experience in Berlin, 1929 to 1939. [Terkel plays a recording of Lotte Lenya singing a song from *The Rise and Fall of the City of Mahagonny.*] Christopher Isherwood, in hearing Lotte Lenya doing this Kurt Weil–Bertolt Brecht song, about a man making his bed and therefore he must lie in it, what is your first thought?

CI: Well, of course I think of Lenya, whom we know. I first saw her on film in Germany before I knew her, and then I met her the first time I came to this country in 1938. We came to New York, and there she was. We were introduced to her by George Davis, who subsequently married her after Weil died.

ST: I was thinking of the idea of that song and you being in Berlin at that time. *Christopher and His Kind* opens about a previous work you'd done, *Lions and Shadows,* and you say that now you are going to tell the truth about yourself: "The book I am now going to write will be as frank and factual as I can make it, especially as far as I myself am concerned. It will therefore be a different kind of book from *Lions and Shadows* and not, strictly speaking, a sequel to it." So, there you are in Berlin in 1929. So the question is, what led you to Berlin in 1929?

CI: Well, the immediate reason was that my friend W. H. Auden was there and wanted me to come over and visit him. I was also very drawn to the idea that I was going to meet a lot of German boys there. Being homosexual, that idea appealed to me very much. I went over there and spent ten days or so with Auden, and then I began to think I really would like to go back, to see more. I quite fell under the spell of Berlin. Later in the year, I came back on my own, having made arrangements so that I could live there at least for a while. I just found out how I liked it.

ST: You were looking for a home. There's a feeling here of a restless youth wanting to write so bad, so much you could taste it. You were looking for not-quite-England.

CI: I really wanted to be on my own; I wanted to be in another world where I could speak another language. I wanted my own language, so to speak, for myself, while I was writing, but I wanted to have a sort of different persona, as they say nowadays. I wanted to be "German Christopher" instead of "English Christopher."

ST: Is this true too: being in a different land, a different culture, you as a writer could know more about your home there than in England, which is why so many writers went to Paris in the 1920s and realized so much about America.

CI: Oh, that's very true. Yes, and also, I was strongly persuaded at that time—indeed I still believe it—that you are a different person in different places. You see, you go to Berlin, and suddenly you're a "German Studs," and it's very interesting to find out what the German Studs is like. For instance, I was being asked just now about England and America, and I said that while I'm in England, my American half—after all, I have lived here more than half my life—comes out; but while I'm here, my English half comes out. Here, I always think of myself as English. So, I suppose the answer is that I think of myself as a foreigner.

ST: So, wherever you may be, you're a foreigner, a foreigner and yet at home.

CI: Yes, I don't mind. I like being a foreigner. I don't understand this thing very well about roots to tell you the truth. I mean, I have roots, very strong roots—I'm very, very British in many ways—but I can replant them anywhere in a moment. It's no problem.

ST: You took a trip to pre-revolutionary China with Auden. And then you went to New York. You never felt alien in all these places?

CI: Well, we felt a bit alien in China. We didn't speak Chinese, and we were on the move the whole time, often on foot or on trains going someplace and wandering through little villages where of course we were the object of tremendous curiosity, everybody staring at us.

ST: Have you been back to China since Mao?

CI: No, unfortunately. I would like to.

ST: It would be interesting to contrast the two. Coming back to you and traveling . . . in your previous works, especially *Goodbye to Berlin,* the narrator, Christopher, he's there, but barely. His sexual preferences and all. What does Sally Bowles say to him—"It's just as well we never went to bed. It wouldn't have mattered"—Sally seemed to have a feeling . . .

CI: Yes, yes. Well, it was a terrible problem, that. If I'd said all about my sexual preferences, it would have meant dragging a whole lot more characters into the thing. I wanted to tell about these people. I wanted to be as anonymous as possible, as anonymous as Flaubert is in his novels, that kind of attitude to the material. I wanted just to tell. Now I'm trying to do something quite different: I'm telling about myself.

ST: No longer the camera. Your friend Stephen Spender was more the camera than you.

CI: Well, he certainly took all the pictures.

ST: What's moving to me about *Christopher and His Kind,* which you call a revisionist autobiography because—in a way you are a camera—you are looking at yourself now and saying here is the real Christopher Isherwood, not the one you've read about earlier. In a sense you are still outside looking at yourself.

CI: There are actually three, aren't there? There's the author, now, seventy-two; there's the character who appears in *The Berlin Stories,* in his thirties, and there's also the real Christopher—not as he's presented in *The Berlin Stories*—in his thirties. Those are three quite different people.

ST: And in a way you use the second person and the third person—and the first. You use all three, which makes it very exciting. But what's very moving to me is the candor and the good humor. There's a joy to it. You're free; you've always been a free man, but within limitations, haven't you? Certain things you always had to hide.

CI: Oh, yes, that's true.

ST: I'm thinking now about the people. We see *I Am a Camera* or, later on, *Cabaret,* and the people in it, you have certain feelings, you've painted them a certain way. The landlady, Frl. Schroeder, whose real name was Thurau, and yet she was not quite—that's a real person.

CI: Oh, yes. As a matter of fact, she is very realistically described. There's very little made up about her. She isn't changed in any way; she's exactly the way she was.

ST: There's an interesting picture of her later on. She is, I suppose, just like any person in any society who is non-heroic, just trying to get along—she became whatever the politics was at the time.

CI: She just endured, yes. She went right through with it.

ST: So we come to Jean Ross/Sally Bowles. Who is Jean Ross? You describe her in *Christopher and His Kind.*

CI: She had respectable, upper-middle class parents, and she was revolting from them to the extent of going to Berlin and being on her own. And she was very determined to lead a very free life, which meant all these lovers. To this day, I've never been sure how many there really were. She really talked such a "loving mouth"—I don't think she can possibly have known all these people. Of course, I met some of them; they really existed, but nothing in comparison to the number there really were, according to her.

ST: By the way, as we're talking, it's just accidental, you are missing Julie Harris who soon will be in town. She was "Sally Bowles," she created Sally in *I Am a Camera.*

CI: She was quite amazing in the part, but there again, she became somebody else. She became herself.

ST: You met the director Berthold Viertel through Jean Ross/Sally Bowles, and that's how you became a screenwriter. She had this flow, didn't she?

CI: Oh yes, she went tearing off.

ST: But, it was through her, Jean Ross, the real Sally Bowles, that you became a screenwriter in a way.

CI: Yes, I owed her. That was tremendous because it wasn't just any old director. This was a most remarkable man, Berthold Viertel. We were friends for the rest of his life. I actually came to live in the place where I live in America because it was near his home.

ST: This is a marvelous description the way you describe it here. He liked one of your books, *Prater Violet.*

CI: No, which one was it . . . *The Memorial.*

ST: And then you became a screenwriter. Here, talking about yourself: "Christopher wasn't an innocent, but he could be infantile, which is the next best thing. He could take the pressure off crises in their film work by displaying such baby-like dismay that he made Viertel laugh at him and cheer up and get a new idea." How did you come to look at yourself this way? This is one of those mysteries. How did you come to recognize your foibles, because it's hard for a person to recognize his own foibles.

CI: Well, you know I was taught by masters. Auden told me from morn' till eve what all my peculiarities were. He was very outspoken and very candid about them, and he was always telling me that I was this or that or the other. He decided that I was infantile, and we both agreed basically that people who are incapable of being silly are really not intelligent. I mean, people who take themselves too seriously—who reach something called "maturity" or the wisdom of senior citizens or something—that's terrible, a kind of death, I think. The idea that you grow wise in some way and then can't be silly anymore or can't do anything funny any more and you find out something called "the truth about life." But the truth about life is of course just the same when you're young and when you're old. It's a double-sided affair, life, and to say that it has to be taken seriously is just as silly as to say that it has to be taken frivolously.

ST: You know, that's beautiful. Not to be afraid to look like a fool, to take risks, and never to lose that childlike—not childish—childlike sense of wonder, I suppose.

CI: Well, I wish I could say that I could maintain it. This is only a kind of aim rather than something I've succeeded at. I have noticed with people that I thought were really the most marvelous people, like Forster for instance, who had this kind of gaiety all through his life, which is extraordinary.

ST: There's a marvelous description of Forster here, about his writing. You listened to him; he was talking about simplicity almost as though it were Zen (though I don't know what Zen is), that came from him without any pretence or pomposity.

CI: Well, of course, that image of the child actually runs through Zen and Hindu philosophy. For instance, they say, a thief comes into a room and steals something and there's a baby in the room. The baby doesn't know that the thief is a thief; it doesn't know what theft is. It just knows a man came into the room and took something and went out again. All of our concepts are broken up if we can constantly return and look at the thing in another way. The rigidity of not ever being childish or childlike is what is so dangerous.

ST: That's why this book is so beautiful: it is anti-rigid and anti-pomposity. The rigidity and the pomposity: I guess when a person is really serious, pomposity must be one of the attributes.

CI: Yes, you can be in earnest. That's different from being serious.

ST: Yes, you describe Viertel, who was serious but not pompous: "Christopher saw Viertel as the kind of intellectual who takes his intellectualism too seriously and thus becomes the captive of his own opinions. He could be dazzlingly witty, grotesquely comic, but never silly, never frivolous." And of course you needed that silliness and frivolity, which is what you get from Auden and from Forster and from Spender.

CI: Oh yes, well he never stops. He's always bubbling with laughter.

ST: Here you compare Viertel with Forster and Auden and a friend of yours, Edward Upward, who was a serious guy. Upward for a time was a sort of political mentor of yours for a while.

CI: Yes, but even he had a great capacity for being silly and funny.

ST: "Seeing the vast difference between Viertel and them, Christopher said to himself that only those who are capable of silliness can be called truly intelligent."

CI: As a matter of fact, in *Lions and Shadows,* there's a story about Stephen Spender from when I'd first met him. I went into the park and there was a new carillon, bells were playing. All the people were sitting around looking with terrible, serious, sacred, church-going faces listening to these bells, and I suddenly saw this tall, tall figure roaring with laughter. And this was Stephen—he just found the whole thing so funny, the bells and the people. . . .

ST: We have come to something that is so much a part of that time, 1929–39. Just to touch on it. These ten years were traumatic, overwhelming, cataclysmic years for the world, and there you were in Germany. Were you ever as politically committed to anti-fascism, say, as Spender at that time and Auden were at the time the Spanish Civil War broke out?

CI: Oh, very much so, yes, absolutely. Also, you see, I did have a sort of special kind of indoctrination as regards the homosexual aspect because, by pure accident, I became a boarder at this house which involved our going to have lunch everyday at the institute of Dr. Magnus Hirschfeld, who was the great expert on sexology and so on. He was himself homosexual and Jewish and also leftist-inclined, and he was very well aware of the fact that the Nazis, even long before they came to power, said that Germany lost the First World War because of the leftists, the Jews, and the homosexuals. These three groups undermined her morale and caused her to be defeated. They were passionately on the warpath against Hirschfeld—they tried to kill him a couple of times, and once they almost succeeded—long before Hitler came to power. Because Hirschfeld was so daring; he went and made speeches in Munich, which was their headquarters and breeding ground at that time. So I did get at least through my head very early, one thing: that the Nazis were bad news for me and my kind.

ST: It's interesting, the association of all three in Hitler's mind. Of course, later on, there was the attempt to kill Hitler by Captain Roehm; within Nazism itself, there was an erasing of what they felt was homosexuality.

CI: Of course, the absolute truth is that Hitler was well aware of Roehm's homosexuality from long before and was quite cynical about it as long as he was his ally. But he was afraid of Roehm for political reasons.

ST: Coming back to Magnus Hirschfeld's Institute for Sexual Science, which you describe here vividly and with remarkable insight. Hirschfeld was all three outsiders in one. . . . You were meeting the German boys at these places where boys gathered to be picked up. Were these mostly working class kids?

CI: Yes, that was really because I had a sort of preference for them. There were lots and lots of middle class German boys who were homosexual, but I always thought they were a bit prissy and too dainty. What I liked about the German working class was, as they say in that song of Brecht's, that "even his Sunday collar wasn't white as snow."

ST: You imply attraction of opposites here. The blond Teutonic and you were a dark-haired young, small Englishman.

CI: Yes, there was that, and I was upper class. I felt the lower class was forthright and less tricky somehow.

ST: This was a semi-romantic version too, to some extent. But you were socially conscious in that respect.

CI: Yes, these feelings I would have had every bit as much if I were heterosexual. That wouldn't have made any difference. I think in this period I would have been drawn to working class girls for exactly the same reasons.

ST: Now there's your mother, Kathleen. She was almost an Edwardian figure. When did your mother recognize your preference that you were homosexual? Did she ever accept it?

CI: Well, she did and she didn't. My mother was the sort of person who was very good at kind of glossing things over. Yes, she accepted it, but she said to me once, in a moment of candor, that it didn't seem real to her because she really couldn't imagine any kind of sexual act in which a woman wasn't involved. I suppose lesbianism would have been perfectly natural to her. [*Laughs*]

ST: There is one part when she met a German working class kid, your young friend Heinz I think it was, and she wasn't too crazy about him. She accepted it, but when a couple of English boys came along, upper class ones, that was different.

CI: That was much nicer, yes. She liked that.

ST: Let's come back to *The Berlin Stories.* The two characters, the Jewish girl, Natalia Landauer and Gise Soloweitschik.

CI: Yes, she's called Natalia Landauer in the book. I don't think anyone would call a character in a novel Gise Soloweitschik.

ST: Was there a difference between the real girl and Natalia?

CI: Oh, there was a great difference. I feel that this character more than any other does wrong to its original because Gise was an altogether warmer and emotionally more responsive kind of person than Natalia, and I was rather driven into the position, for purely technical reasons, of making Natalia an opposite of Sally Bowles. Therefore, to some extent, the more Sally Bowles was outrageous, the more Natalia had to be sort of conservative, prudish, capable of being shocked. This was very hard on the original.

ST: Did any of the originals read *The Berlin Stories?*

CI: Yes, the original of Bernhard Landauer, Wilfrid Israel, did.

ST: Israel is a different figure too.

CI: Yes, indeed. There again, it was partly because I didn't know what was going to happen when I started to write his part of the book. Also, for technical reasons, I didn't bring out how extremely remarkable the original Wilfrid Israel was. He was the Anglo-German Jewish proprietor—one of the owners—of a very large department store, maybe the largest in Berlin. This young man could at any time have left Berlin after Hitler came into power, because he had a British passport as well as a German passport. He nevertheless stayed on because he wanted to defend and protect his Jewish employees as much as possible. The Nazis were always a little bit prudent when it came to tampering with big business. Goering's great exclamation dealing with another Jewish family was, "I decide who's a Jew in this country." In other words, he sometimes chose to ignore it if it was necessary to get something out of it.

Anyway, the point was that Wilfrid was consistently very heroic and very firm with them. He wouldn't even allow them to fly the Nazi flag over his department store when the whole of Germany was flapping with Nazi flags at that time. He wouldn't have it. He always said that if they did anything like that, he would close the store, and that they didn't want, you see. Finally, as it so happened, shortly before the outbreak of the war, another firm, a non-Jewish firm, or the government (I don't know the technical arrangements) took over the store, and so Wilfrid had no further reason to remain in Germany. He went to England, and he did his best to help Jews who were stranded in Europe, and that's how he met his death. He went to Portugal because he had heard there were a whole lot of Jews in Spain, and he could make arrangements to help these Jews to emigrate to what was then called Palestine. He did all of this successfully and got on a plane to fly back to England. Leslie Howard, the famous actor, was on the same plane. And these planes used to fly regularly between Portugal and England, and they were a way in which a whole lot of people, some of them very famous, did travel to England at that period during the war. They were unarmed and unescorted, and they were usually not intercepted by the Nazis, although they had to fly very close to the coast of occupied France. But on this occasion they ran into a whole lot of Nazi fighter planes which had been out on some other mission. The fighter planes, as long as they saw this plane there, swooped down on it and opened fire. The Nazis later said that they had no particular reason for doing this; other people said they thought Churchill might have been on board—he'd been at a conference in Algiers—anyhow, everybody was killed, and that was the end of Wilfrid.

ST: And that is how Leslie Howard died.

CI: Yes, Leslie Howard too.

ST: You mentioned Spain, and so we come to another aspect, very important in your life and certainly in Auden and Spender's lives, the Spanish Civil War.

CI: Yes, indeed. That was a tremendous event in everybody's life. Auden went originally prepared to fight, but the government wanted him to make propaganda, and he did make some propaganda there, but then he found out that, due to the fact that the Franco forces were blocking the radio, it wasn't getting outside of the country properly and he didn't feel he was doing any

good, so he returned. Stephen went on several missions and went as an observer and wrote about it and so on. I at that time wasn't able to go for
personal reasons, but I was all set to go later when Auden was going to return
to Spain on a delegation of writers from England and America—Paul Robe-
son was on it, and Jacob Epstein, the sculptor, Rose Macaulay, the
novelist. . . . But at the same time we were invited to go to China, where war
had just broken out. We thought that it would be much more interesting to go
to China; everybody goes to the Spanish Civil War. So, the Spanish people
kept delaying the visas for us to go over, so we gave up and went to China
instead. In fact, I never did go to Spain during war, but I intended to. . . .

ST: Back to German refugees. There is a very funny story about the marriage of convenience with Auden and Erika Mann, Thomas Mann's daughter;
it is a very funny scene. She wanted to marry you. Suppose you set the scene
on that.

CI: Erika was traveling around various countries bordering on Germany—
she couldn't come back to Germany—she had an anti-Nazi cabaret, and they
used to perform in such places as Holland and Belgium, in Austria, which
then was not occupied by the Nazis yet, and in Switzerland and Denmark. At
the time, I was in Holland, and she said to me one day, "Christopher, I have
something rather personal to ask you—will you marry me?" The reason was
that she'd just heard that the Nazis were going to take away her citizenship,
and she realized that, while she could probably stay with her folks, who had
taken refuge in Switzerland, quite safely, it would be very awkward for her
not to have a proper passport. She wanted to travel as much as possible
because she was very, very active against the Nazis and was always traveling
and speaking everywhere, so she needed to become British. At that time, the
law was that if you married a British subject, you became British instantly,
without any further formalities whatever. I had a couple of reasons why I
didn't want to get married; one sounds really, truly childish, but it was curiously strong. I was terribly embarrassed at the idea that anyone would think
I was trying to pass as a heterosexual by getting married. So, I thought, well,
at least I'll see if I can't get somebody else, and I immediately thought of
Auden, who was always very adventurous in anything of this sort. And he
wired back delighted. Well, they got married and that was all right. A little
while later, we went to the United States, we went to stay with the Manns. I
was already a good friend with Erika and with Klaus, one of the sons. A *Time*
magazine photographer came, the picture was shown again not very long ago

in *Time* magazine—of us all sitting together, and the photographer said, "I can understand why Mr. Auden is sitting in this family group because after all he's your son-in-law, but what is Mr. Isherwood doing there?" And Thomas Mann answered in German, which everybody understood except the photographer. He said, "He's the family pimp."

ST: Throughout this book, we have this aspect of it, in which you are so open. I suppose you might call this a liberating book.

CI: Well, it's liberating for those who need to be liberated. Do you mean liberating for me? Yes, yes to some extent. It does make a difference; that's the funny thing. I mean, one can feel things and talk about them to one's friends and be perfectly open about them, but actually to print them and see them going out to book shops and all sorts of people reading them—it does make a slight difference; there's a slight sense of extra relief. There's a sort of feeling now that it doesn't matter a bit, I don't have to be the least bit cautious with anybody.

ST: I suppose it's an obvious question: could you have done this book ten or fifteen years ago, assuming you had the time and energy at that time to do it?

CI: Fifteen years ago, maybe not, no; ten years, maybe so. I should explain to you also that there's another thing involved. You see, very soon after my first arrival in America, I got to know this Hindu monk who had a tremendous influence on me. . . . This Hindu monk had a center in Los Angeles and knew Aldous Huxley and Gerald Heard. That's how I knew about him at all. I became, by degrees, his disciple and remain so ever since. As far as he was concerned—he knew all about me, including my homosexuality—the Hindus take a very different view, they are not moralistic in the same sense. Everything was perfectly understood, but like everybody else, he had a congregation, and many of the members of the congregation brought with them their Western prejudices. They were always a little bit worried about me because from time to time rumors about me would come around and reach their ears since I was living right there in the city, so I had a certain hesitation in really embarrassing him beyond a certain point. But then, as time went on, this became less and less of a problem, which is why I say that fifteen years ago, quite aside from anything else, I might have hesitated.

ST: There is a tender passage here of your love and affection and the risks you took for your friends, Heinz for one. I'm thinking about a marvelous description of a certain event and Conrad Veidt the actor.

CI: Oh, yes, yes. He's a wonderful man.

ST: But more than that, the description of acting. . . . Were you working on a film with Viertel?

CI: No, he was working at the same studio on a different film, *Jew Suss,* which was a famous historical film of the period.

ST: This was the film by Feuchtwanger. You should describe this, set the scene, and tell us who Conrad Veidt was, this quite remarkable German actor.

CI: He was a very famous German actor and probably one of the greatest of the early film actors. Everybody agreed that he was extraordinary as a film actor. This is just a description of the kind of actor he was. The character he was playing was a Jew who had been very wealthy in a medieval town; now, suddenly he's brought to ruin and he's going to be executed and he is in the cart on the way to the execution. Now they are going to shoot this scene in the studio and there sits Veidt in the cart. This is what I write about it: "However, just as the filming was about to begin, something went wrong with the lights. There was to be a delay of five minutes. Veidt stayed in the cart, and now a stenographer came up to him and offered him a piece of candy. The gesture was perhaps deliberately saucy. Some stars would have been annoyed by it because they were trying to concentrate on their role and remain in character; they'd have ignored the stenographer. Others would have chatted and joked with her, welcoming this moment of relaxation. But Veidt did neither. He remained Suss, and through the eyes of Suss, he looked down from the cart upon this sweet Christian girl, the only human being in this cruel city who had the heart and the courage to show kindness to a con- demned Jew. And his eyes filled with tears. With his manacled hands, he took the candy from her and tried to eat it for her sake, to show his gratitude to her, but he couldn't. He was beyond hunger, too near death, and his emo- tion was too great. He began to sob. He turned his face away."

ST: It's a remarkable picture of an actor's concentration, isn't it?

CI: He was fantastic. Of course, some people said he was such a ham. . . .

ST: The book deals of course with many of the people you meet and work with aside from Auden and Spender and Forster. There's Virginia Woolf and John Lehmann, who was an editor of Hogarth Press and got one of your works published by them.

CI: Yes, my second book, and then they of course published both the books about Berlin and an autobiographical book called *Lions and Shadows*. They published in fact everything until I moved to this country.

ST: But there's a picture of Virginia Woolf; she was more ivory tower, wasn't she, in her view?

CI: Oh, yes. She was a very strange, interesting, extraordinary person. She was very beautiful. She was one of the most beautiful people I think I've ever seen, but not in a conventional way. She was like a great princess; the face had a kind of fineness which is sometimes associated with the aristocracy at its best. Whatever it was, she looked very striking, sort of tragic, and yet of course actually above the tragedy, she had a great deal of humor. Like great depressives, which of course she was (she had actual mental breakdowns from time to time), she also had a manic side in which she was gay and full of gossip and made jokes and was very entertaining and a great hostess.

ST: On the subject of being a hostess. . . . you and Auden on the boat to China, you met a businessman and a young planter, and you and Auden said this man was right out of a Maugham short story.

CI: Yes, well, there were several short stories on the boat that were sort of potentially Maugham stories. There was another one that I remember too of a girl that was a terribly tragic little moment. She was coming out to join her husband in Saigon. It was a French boat, so we steamed up the river. And as we were approaching Saigon, the pilot came out on the launch and said confidentially to the captain that the girl's husband had just been killed in an automobile accident. This was whispered around on board, and before you knew it, almost everybody on the boat knew about this husband being dead, and nobody of course would say it to the girl. And the girl began to be aware, because she had been very popular on board—she was very attractive and all the young men were seeing a lot of her and laughing with her and talking and so on—and she began to feel that they were drawing away from her, avoiding her, and she began to look at the shore and she became more alarmed and desperate. Then of course we docked, and somebody came on board and said, "Madam, I have to speak to you. Your husband . . ." and took her away somewhere. That was a terrible scene. There was another story which I tell in this book which is much more involved. I don't think I can tell it on the air; it's so long.

ST: Tell that story about the planter—he's the Maugham figure.

CI: Well, there was a young man who was a rubber planter, and he got very confidential with us, as people do on ships because after all you'll never see them again. He said, "You know, I'm having a tremendous affair with the wife of my best friend and I feel terrible, but I can't help it. We love each other." We said, "Why don't you run off with her?" He said, "I can't because if you're a rubber planter, there are only two or three places you can go, and the planters are very clannish, and if anybody steps out of line or does anything like that, I would be blackballed completely. I couldn't stay on there, in Malaya. I would have to leave because it would be made impossible for me to do business." Now on the same boat, by pure happenstance we met this very, very rich man, a millionaire, a tycoon. He was traveling first class, and he was a great admirer of Auden's poetry, so he made much of us and entertained us and was very amusing and loved talking, and he got us better cabins for the same price. He started telling us how he was going to open up an entirely new area of rubber planting in what was then called Siam— Thailand—which of course would be miles away from all the other plantations; it would be a whole different planet as far as they were concerned. And he said, "You know, I'm looking for somebody to manage these plantations, an experienced planter." And Auden and I looked at each other, and we both thought the same thought: we could have the power to interfere in the lives of all these people.

ST: You did it again. Arrangers.

CI: And so, we just brought the two of them together. To this day, I don't know what happened.

ST: You told that to Maugham, that these two people were characters out of one of his stories. I notice here that you have a piece of the diary of Woolf. She said about you, "Isherwood I met on the doorstep. He was a slip of a wild boy." How many years ago was that?

CI: What year was that? It was 1938: I was thirty-four.

ST: "With quicksilver eyes, nipped; jockeylike. That young man, said W. Maugham, 'holds the future of the English novel in his hands.' "

CI: Well, I don't know where he got that opinion. He really hadn't read enough to have such an opinion, even if it had been true. What had he read? Two books, I guess.

ST: But, there you go putting yourself down, as you do in this book. At the same time, the insights are there; I find this a delightful experience, filled with insights. Before we say goodbye for now, we touched in a cursory fashion on the book *Christopher and His Kind* by my guest Christopher Isherwood. Not that you were less committed, but you are now fully committed to the idea of, in a sense, liberation of the homosexual.

CI: Yes, and in more general way, if you asked me what my politics were, I should really say I'm a member of the ACLU. That is to say, I'm a regular kind of liberal. I'm much more interested in local causes, by and large. I mean I'm more interested in California politics than in national politics.

ST: Well, perhaps you may have the answer to a great deal of what is the dilemma today of people looking for some little triumphs, little victories, some little effect of what they do since they are overwhelmed by other events. Maybe community victories and community matters might in a sense extend to the city, to the country, and to the world. Little victories.

CI: Oh, yes, I know many people whose lives are absolutely enriched by doing these things.

ST: Perhaps you can read this last part. You speak in third person. This part, in a sense, might be close to your credo.

CI: "He must never again give way to embarrassment, never deny the rights of his tribe, never apologize for its existence, never think of sacrificing himself masochistically on the altar of that false god of the totalitarians—the greatest good of the greatest number—whose priests are alone empowered to decide what good is."

ST: That probably is what it's about, isn't it, as far as Christopher Isherwood is concerned. Thank you for all of your works and specifically for *Christopher and His Kind,* a marvelous book. Mr. Isherwood, what a delight.

The Youth that Was "I": A Conversation in Santa Monica with Christopher Isherwood

W. I. Scobie / 1977

From *London Magazine* NS 17 (April/May 1977): 23–32. Reprinted by permission.

WS: Like *Lions and Shadows,* your new autobiographical book *Christopher and His Kind* reads very much like a novel, although this time everyone gets his or her rightful name. Did you plan that deliberately?

CI: I may have done it subconsciously. I cut down enormously on the number of characters, friends who just didn't fit into the story. This is the first sign of passing from truth into fiction. Basically this is the story of my relations with my friend Heinz, his arrest and its aftermath, and the attitudes I developed as a result of that.

WS: "His Kind" refers to what?

CI: I first thought of calling it "Christopher and His Tribe," since I sometimes use the word tribe in referring to my fellow-homosexuals. But "His Kind" means more than that—it means all the people one feels a rapport with. My kind of person, as they say.

WS: In the past you have been quite harshly criticized on moral grounds. Celebrating the Munich reprieve by fucking in front of a mirror was, for instance, considered inappropriate. Your whole attitude towards the war, and towards the party line for leftist intellectuals was seen as improper, if not a betrayal. You have been accused of frivolity, of not really caring about serious issues, of "dandyism," etc., etc. This new book, which is so extremely frank, perhaps disarms that kind of charge . . . but what's your response?

CI: Well, I didn't write to apologize for my behaviour forty years ago. Rather, I wanted the book to be, in a way, a moral parable for others. Right or wrong, this was how Christopher behaved, and I hoped people would turn round when they'd finished it and admit to a large extent, it was like that for them, too. So often we pretend to care more than we do, when mostly we don't really give a shit. Certainly I have a tone of voice that some find distasteful: it's apparently frivolous, but in fact I hate real frivolity in the sense of trifling in a silly way with serious matters. It is simply that sometimes a light touch, a little irony, is needed in regard to things you believe in deeply. This church face one is supposed to put on for serious scenes is entirely for civilians, for nonparticipants in whatever struggle may be going on. These outsiders believe you can't possibly make jokes in dreadful situations, though they're constantly reminded that people do. They feel that there is an appropriate behaviour for every occasion, and any other reaction is taken to be in bad taste.

WS: What is the major problem for a writer in an autobiographical book?

CI: For me, narration always is the problem. Writing in itself is just know-how; but to tell a story chronologically and yet build it into something dramatic, that carries you along—that's tricky. What do you cut out? What do you leave in? If *Christopher and His Kind* does in fact read like a novel, perhaps it's because I've always felt very little difference between fiction and non-fiction. What matters is what you say about a given situation. Maybe you can explain its reality better by heightening its drama, by way of a comment on it. Fiction enters the garden in a serpentine way. What lies we tell to our friends, after all, when we're telling "true" stories!

WS: You refer to yourself in the book always in the third person as "Christopher." Sometimes you have the "I" of today talking about the "Christopher" of yesterday in the same sentence. Isn't this going to be very disturbing to the uninitiated?

CI: Well, we shall see. In many of my early books the "I" character is completely withdrawn. He's in the background, describing other people. But this book is about how that "I" reacted: it's entirely about me, my feelings and reactions in those years between 1929 and 1939. I feel a great distance between the I of today and the character Wystan describes in his poem

> That funny-looking young man, so squat with a top-heavy head,
> A cross between a cavalry major and a rather prim landlady . . .

There's an American physicist, Erwin Schrödinger, who says something I found very interesting in this respect in a book called *What Is Life?* I can find the exact passage if you wish. (CI finds the book.) He won the Nobel prize for his work. This book is mostly technical stuff about genetics and the quantum theory, but at the end he has an epilogue giving his personal subjective thoughts, and he says:

> The youth that was "I": you may come to speak of him in the third person; indeed the protagonist of the novel you are reading is probably nearer to your heart, certainly more intensively alive and better known to you. Yet there has been no intermediate break, no death. And even if a skilled hypnotist succeeded in blotting out entirely all your earlier reminiscences, you would not find that he had killed *you*. In no case is there a loss of personal existence to deplore.

And then he adds, "Nor will there ever be," but that's nothing to do with us. It's simply that he brings up this question of "the youth that was I," and how you may come to speak of him in the third person, and how remote he seems.

WS: I liked very much the Auden poem addressed to you which is quoted in *Christopher and His Kind*. Is there more of it?

CI: Oh, the landlady poem. Yes, there are three pages. He wrote it in the blank pages at the beginning of a copy of D. H. Lawrence's *Birds, Beasts and Flowers* which he gave me in 1937.

I've never quite understood about that line in French [*Il y a des complaisances que je detéste.*] It comes from a French film called *La Bataille* in which Charles Boyer played a Japanese naval officer. We adored it—we saw these things again and again. Boyer trying to look Japanese was alone worth the price of admission. His wife is having an affair with the British naval attaché, but the Japanese need this officer's expertise in gunnery because they're at war with the Russians. So Boyer goes to some important Buddhist sage and asks what he should do, his honour is destroyed, but the honour of the nation demands, etc., etc. And the sage tells him, "There are some complacencies that I detest." Which as far as I can see has absolutely nothing to do with anything in Auden's poem. The film is so gloriously ridiculous. It has such utter contempt for history, engineering, naval strategy, Japan, Buddhism, adultery, artillery. . . .

WS: Did Auden write many such things in people's books?

CI: Oh yes, a lot. Most were short, and many are lost forever now. Edward Mendelson is bringing a book out which will include these oddments, possibly the thing I quoted among them. Then there's a ballad which I put together from pieces I had, about a girl called Sue.

WS: I notice in *Christopher and His Kind* that you performed minor surgery not only on Auden's but on Spender's early poems. You changed the word order, for instance, in the crucial last line of "I think continually. . . ." Did you often do that? Did you do it with other poets?

CI: Yes, I used to make suggestions. But you know it made very little difference. Wystan used to sneak the lines I objected to back into other poems: he knew what he was about. It's simply that any kind of critic who will be quite honest in his opinion is of value. It's a matter of having somebody say *something*: it helps you make up your own mind.

WS: You've never written any other poems besides the one that appears in Larkin's *Oxford Book of Modern Verse?* You must be the only one-poem poet ever anthologized.

CI: I wrote a very little more beyond what appears in *Exhumations.*

WS: But poetry obviously is very important to you as a writer. You've translated Brecht, and I've been surprised at the slabs you know by heart of unlikely poets. Once I heard you quote from memory a long stretch of Swinburne, for instance. And some obscure piece by Hardy. And that entire Auden poem "The Voyage," which you said was one of your favourites.

CI: Yes, but writing it isn't really my thing. There's only one other poem that might be publishable, but I don't believe it's good enough.

WS: In the new book you make Auden out to be rather a pill-fiend. Did he really rely on uppers and downers to such a degree?

CI: That he began long before such things became popular. He called it "the chemical life." He did literally what I said, started the day with Benzedrine and took Seconal at night for at least twenty years. Perhaps all his life: I'm not sure about the last years. I know a doctor told him that he'd gone on so long, neither drug was having any effect.

WS: And he drank heavily on top of that? Didn't it harm his work?

CI: I must say it doesn't seem to have done, does it? His output was fantastic and went on being so to the end. He didn't drink heavily in the days I describe in the book. He got straight down to work every day after breakfast, whatever it was—a lecture, a poem. He was the most disciplined writer I ever knew. He never groaned or complained. He just went on doing it until it was done.

WS: In *Christopher and His Kind* you portray Brian Howard very sympathetically, but he's been hauled over the coals in several books recently, notably Martin Green's *Children of the Sun* where he's the archetypical "decadent leftist" of the thirties. You admired him and his poetry?

CI: I don't think the *Sonnenkind* book showed much understanding of what it was all about. Why write it, if he disapproved of them all? I must show you Brian's poems. Three or four are quite beautiful—Auden admired them too. . . .

WS: I read one, in the old *Golden Horizon*. I think it was called "Mr Pleasure.". . .

CI: Yes? . . . You know, good old Brian, "decadent" as he was, had a tremendous amount of courage. And "decadence" so often seems to me just a codeword for homosexuality. We were fond of Brian, but he was impossible in large doses because of his way of life. The dope, the drink and so on.

WS: Auden said he wanted all his personal correspondence destroyed and no biography written. What is your feeling about that?

CI: I think we belong to something more than ourselves in that respect. The results of guessing can be so tedious. Look at what's happened in the case of Byron. His friends burnt his journals, and what is the result? Simply that scholar after scholar is guessing what is in them. I think the idea is deplorable, and in a funny way I don't believe Auden meant it to be taken quite literally. I don't believe he *really* wanted everything burned. I don't feel it. He was very fond of attacking our modern indiscretion in writing absolutely everything about everybody. I was of course quite the other way about, although obviously I believe in some discretion while people are alive.

WS: Your new book begins in 1929, the year we leave you in *Lions and Shadows*. Did you deliberately set out to write a sequel that would be more sexually frank?

CI: Not really. At first I simply planned to publish some quite extensive diaries about How I Came To America, and my early years here. But then it seemed to me that I had to explain *why* I came here, and explaining that took me farther and farther back into my past, and what started out as an introduction became a book of nearly 100,000 words. I felt that I should set the record straight about the Berlin situation, in what way the Berlin books were fictitious and why, about the whole gay thing, my relationship with Auden, and so forth. You see, "Christopher Isherwood" in the early books wasn't *me* at all. He was a device used to tell the story in the first person. If he had been a person, and he had announced that he was homosexual, he would have upstaged everyone else. The reader would be constantly wondering what he would do next. So he had to shut up, push the other characters into dialogue, and so on.

WS: Do you still ask Edward Upward's advice on your work in progress?

CI: Oh, yes. I changed a number of things in *Christopher and His Kind* that he didn't like or said were factually wrong. Edward is my polar opposite in most ways, yet we've always remained very close. We've been corresponding recently about what he should call his trilogy, which I admire enormously.

WS: Do you agree with the received opinion that Auden's later work, after his conversation, say, was inferior to the earlier?

CI: You say conversion: but I believe Auden was always deeply religious, and that out of solidarity with the whole leftist, anti-fascist thing in the thirties he rather put it aside. I thought that his mother, in other circumstances, might have become a nun, even a saint; she was an extraordinary woman and he was deeply influenced by her. As for his work, I think he produced wonderful things at all stages of his life. It's very possible that if he had lived longer, he would have had another great period, like Yeats. His work didn't become inferior: scaled down, perhaps, and he grew more interested in this private, jokey writing. But he never faked it, as some do. He was always intensely himself, full of attitudes and opinions about everything.

WS: I'm curious about Denham Fouts, who appears not only as Paul in your *Down There on a Visit,* but also in Vidal's *Three Strategems* and now Capote's *Answered Prayers,* along with yourself of course. . . .

CI: Yes, did you see, I'm in the masterpiece. Truman and Gore knew Denny much later than I did, shortly before he died. I met him in London in 1938, and again out here in the early forties. It's "Fowts," by the way, not "Foots": it's a Dutch name.

WS: Was he so remarkable? Have you all romanticized him?

CI: I can't speak for Capote and Vidal. I *liked* Denny. He was witty, he could make me laugh, and he could instruct me how to live in this country. He was an American from the South, but he knew Europe well, and with his very sharp eye he could appreciate what Europeans found absurd in America and vice-versa. And for all his reservations and sneerings about religion, he did take Vedanta seriously. He resisted it, he attacked it, he hated it: but he knew it wasn't merely silly, a freaky game. He knew, in a very basic way, which end is up—no pun intended. He was a curiously serious person, despite his air of frivolity.

WS: So he wasn't the world's most expensive male whore, the sort of universal male hetaera-cum-saint all three of you have painted?

CI: No. But he was fond of pretending to be. In that way he was very much like Sally, they both tended to play-act their lives. He laid the whore act on rather thickly, although he did have affairs with several famous people.

WS: You don't seem to be greatly afflicted by this famous conflict between writing for the screen and writing your own fiction.

CI: I have an enormous passion for film. I don't rank one, as an art, above the other. What draws me to film writing is the great fun of constructing stories. I love being told that there are these elements, and those: how do you relate this to that? How can you build a little house out of it? It appeals almost as a kind of parlour game. Had I been more deeply involved in film-making, I would have wanted to be the writer-director, the creator.

WS: So in fact, far from being "destroyed" by working for Hollywood you've rather enjoyed it?

CI: Yes, and also I met people who were totally different from those I was used to, people I wouldn't, before, have chosen to go along with. I became very fond of Oscar Levant, for instance, who appeared in all those forties films and had his own TV show, a highly eccentric one—once he brought the entire mad ward from Mt. Sinai Hospital on. My favourite recollection of Oscar was when I was dining with him in a Beverly Hills restaurant, and a man came up to him and said, Mr. Levant, I want to tell you that in our home, we just worship you, we watch your show religiously, my wife loves you, I love you, my daughter loves you, you can do no wrong. Oscar looked at him and said, "I don't like your attitude."

WS: Among the many famous people you've met, are there some you cherish especially?

CI: Perhaps the three most remarkable people I've met were E. M. Forster, Stravinsky and Swami Prabhavananda, and oddly enough each made me think of the others. They were all rather cuddly, you felt protective towards them. They had some of the appeal of the baby—absolute vulnerability which is at the same time a kind of invulnerability, because few people have the nerve to massacre the innocent. Auden once wrote to me that Forster, who described himself as agnostic, "was a person who is so accustomed to the presence of God that he is unaware of it; he has never known what it feels like when that Presence is withdrawn." If he'd said that to me in the thirties, of course, he would have heard a yell of fury.

WS: What about your American diaries? Will you now publish them?

CI: Well, there's a hell of a lot. About 300,000 words for the years 1939–44 alone. After that there's much more. At the moment I'm rereading these diaries from start to finish to note what is interesting in them. They are less self-engrossed than my earlier diaries, which were often used as therapy and can be boring beyond belief—all the I-can't-go-on, what-will-happen-to-me-next stuff. The later diaries will be published, but in what form I haven't yet decided. Another thing I'm thinking of writing is a portrait of Prabhava-nanda, based on my personal memories and the diaries. It would describe my whole relationship with him. It is fascinating material because it's so unusual. The solidarity of his presence meant a great deal to me: one went sashaying off after some other interest and then came back rather rumpled and battered, and there he was. He had a quality of being *there.*

WS: A last question: why is it so tricky to write an overtly homosexual novel? Either people fall into the propaganda trap, or they make the whole thing sound so obsessional and psychopathic, like Genet. Are there any novels you especially admire in this field?

CI: I don't see why one shouldn't be able to do it successfully. It's true that books like *The Charioteer* and *The Front Runner* present their homosexual characters as insufferably noble and too good to be true. But in both cases the structure is there for a very good novel, had the writing itself been a bit better. It's certainly difficult to write a novel of that sort, today, without making it to some degree political. A love affair given the sanction of society is quite different from one that takes place under the conditions homosexuals face. Even though you may not stub your toe against the prohibitions, they are there. And they make the homosexual act of love into an act of protest, a political act. When you come to write about it, you cannot escape the political climate. One book that impressed me was the school novel by Michael Campbell, *Lord Dismiss Us*—very much school of Forster. It was very moving—that was the great thing. It contained real emotion. One always comes back to that in the end. The question is: can you convey the intensity of the emotion?

Without that you have nothing.

The First Couple: Don Bachardy and Christopher Isherwood

Armistead Maupin / 1985

The *Village Voice* Volume 30, Number 16 (2 July 1985): 16, 18. Reprinted by permission.

Just as much as his literary fame, Christopher Isherwood's personal candor qualifies him splendidly for his unsolicited role as Hero Emeritus of the modern gay movement. The eighty-year-old author of *The Berlin Stories,* which became the basis for *Cabaret,* writes of his homosexuality with remarkable matter-of-factness in his 1976 autobiography, *Christopher and His Kind.* His 1964 novel, *A Single Man,* more pertinent now than ever, chronicles a day in the life of a gay man whose lover has unexpectedly died.

Isherwood's lover of thirty-two years is Don Bachardy, a Los Angeles native who met the English-born author when he was eighteen and Isherwood was forty-eight. Long respected as an artist, Bachardy was thrust into the spotlight two years ago when his state-commissioned portrait of former Governor Jerry Brown was vilified by members of the California General Assembly.

I have known Chris and Don since 1978, when we met at an Oscar Night party in Hollywood. For this interview I talked to them at their hillside home overlooking Santa Monica Canyon and the Pacific.

So you first met Don on the beach?

Christopher Isherwood: Yes, right down the cliff here. A whole bunch of people used to go down there. Naturally, we put our towels where the nice-looking boys were and one thing led to another. Don was young and full of life and he was a perfect darling. It was just as simple as that. You know, when you feel that the right person has come along, then all that's required is a certain sassiness.

You told me once that you felt you had entered the gay rights fray too late, that you wished you'd gotten involved earlier. In what way?

CI: Well, I never really felt, myself, that I was leading the charge, or taking the role of some kind of leader. Never for one moment. On the other hand, I never denied that I was queer. During all those years in Hollywood I just took it for granted that they knew what I was doing. I suppose it was a kind of arrogance.

When were you first aware you were gay? What are your earliest memories of feeling homosexual?
   CI: Very early. I suppose those boys in Germany.

What about you, Don? Your first sexual experience?
   Don Bachardy: I really hadn't had very much experience before I met Chris, nothing romantic or of very much interest. I never really identified with people my own age. The great liberation for me was finding somebody old enough, I suppose.

How did you feel when you first met Chris? What was your first reaction?
   DB: He was just fun. I'd never met anybody like him, and he was so easy to be with. I was delighted. In fact, wasn't it I who proposed to you?
   CI: That's not the kind of thing you ask a gentleman. You *remember.*

Chris, your long-term friendship with Wystan Auden is a matter of record. Did you begin that as lovers?
   CI: We had lots of sex, but there wasn't a romance at all.

What we call a fuck buddy these days.
   CI: A fuck buddy, yes, that's what we were. It would have been unthinkable under the circumstances if we hadn't at least *tried.* It was an enormous convenience because, quite aside from everything else, it was somebody to screw. We both lived very imprudent lives in the sense that we were always fussing around with rough trade and so on. But with Auden there was a very deep friendship, as we had gotten to know each other so early. And then I discovered that he was one of our major poets, which he proceeded to start being at quite an early age.

And you went on to California while he stayed in New York. Do you observe any differences in the way the two coasts handle homosexuality?
   DB: I do think New York is an interesting place to be because I feel it's much more a battlefield than here. You're confronted with the really violent forces of opposition. I do think the queers who live there are more conscious of the enemy, and in a way that makes it more exciting. There are more people dying of AIDS, too. And there's more disapproval; it gets into print and people take stands much more openly than they do here.

Do you personally know anybody who has AIDS?

DB: Certain of our friends have died of it. That black nude in the studio—he died about a month ago, a beautiful, charming, funny, nice man. His friend is a brilliant journalist who lives in Venice, and they were having sex just last November. He must be very worried.

CI: What one should be, of course, is very well informed on the subject, which I don't feel I am. I don't feel I know nearly enough about the AIDS situation. But these younger men who find they have it—some absolutely awful pressures begin to assert themselves. They're told by their relatives that it's a sort of punishment, that it's dreadful and it's God's will and all that kind of thing. And I think they have to get very tough with themselves and really decide which side they're on. You know, fuck God's will. God's will must be circumvented, if that's what it is.

Do you still encounter the closet mentality? It seems that we have a situation today where gay people who are famous and in the closet are forced to coexist openly with those who are open about it.

DB: And they feel awkward and it makes them almost resentful of their queer friends who have been identified. We're in that situation. Two very good friends of ours really don't like gay liberation—they don't want to be liberated; they liked it better before. Their attitude toward the two of us coming out in print was one of total dismay. When one of them was told that I'd given an interview to the *Advocate*—in fact they put my picture on the cover—he said, "Oh, no." He thought I'd made a disastrous career move. And who knows, he may be proved right. (Laughs)

CI: Well, we have to look at the example of David Hockney. He never made any bones about it.

DB: I must say he was outspoken at a time when I thought it precarious. Ten or twelve years ago he was taking some boy magazines back to England from here, and their customs seized the magazines. Now all David was out was maybe twenty or thirty dollars that he spent on the magazines, but he went to court and challenged them. He said he used the magazines for his work, and of course it got top billing in the newspapers. And David won the case.

There must have been some serious tongue-clucking, Don, when you and Chris became a couple in Hollywood.

DB: Well, I felt sufficiently protected because I was always in the company of Chris. I think it was much more difficult for him. I mean, I was just regarded as a sort of child prostitute.

CI: You were never snubbed in public.

DB: Joseph Cotten once said within earshot that he deplored the company of these "half-men," referring to me. And I always felt the injustice was that, by that definition, Chris was every bit as much a half-man as I, and yet, because of his age and literary distinction, all the disapproval was leveled at me. But even on that occasion with Joseph Cotten, for instance, Louis Jourdan's wife came to my defense. She made it clear that she disapproved of that kind of baiting.

Chris involved you in his religious studies with Swami Prabhavananda about that time, didn't he?

DB: Yes, and at the time, I wasn't aware of what was at stake. I'm stunned, really, by the frankness of his behavior. Taking me up to Vedanta Place was much more daring than taking me to David Selznick's. And it wasn't Prabhavananda; it was the congregation, wondering why he didn't take a "moral" stand.

I've seen the pictures; you looked fourteen when you were eighteen.

DB: This was in the early '50s; that was a time of maximum discretion. It was a sort of demonstration of your innate arrogance.

Chris, did you and Tennessee Williams go to bed with each other?

CI: Yes, but that was actually neither here nor there.

I'm sorry to hear that. (Laughs)

CI: It was not a big deal; we just found each other very sympathetic, and we went to bed together two or three times, I imagine. In his autobiography, you know, he wrote very handsomely about me and in fact said flat out that it almost came to a romance.

DB: And Chris looked—I mean, I think it was the time of your greatest beauty.

CI: (Laughs)

DB: Chris at forty was just a knockout.

Did you ever feel the pressure to get married, Chris?

CI: No, not really.

DB: Only from Erika Mann.

(General laughter)

DB: I always felt it was so ingenious of Chris to wiggle out of that and to get poor Wystan to do it instead.

CI: Well, she wanted to get another nationality, and the Nazis had her on their top list; they were out to get her. She needed to marry somebody who was above suspicion.

Did you talk Auden into it, or did she?

DB: I think Wystan accepted immediately.

CI: Oh, yes. It was very characteristic of him; he liked taking bold attitudes, and there were a few by-products, of course. They got the unceasing gratitude of Thomas Mann and the entire family. It was considered a great, liberal stroke, a sort of anti-Hitler gesture. The Manns themselves were very remarkable liberal preachers, and they would never have objected to the fact that Auden was homosexual or anything of the kind.

DB: Well, they could hardly object since Erika was a lesbian.

Do either of you ever receive any anti-gay taunts?

DB: Oh, sure, . . . and the beach is a battleground between the fags and the surfers. It's been a fag beach since I can remember, and long before that—certainly since the mid-'40s. The surfers were a very late development, and they started claiming the beach as their own. So quite often when I'm just running by myself on the beach, a group of young kids will yell out "faggot" or something. I always wonder how they know. (Laughs)

Chris, where did you come up with the idea for the man who lost his lover in A Single Man? *Was that simply your own creation, or was it based on someone you knew?*

CI: It was an obvious idea, you know, the widower who doesn't present himself as one—that's what it amounted to. No, I was never in that situation myself.

DB: I always suspected he was imagining what it would be like if we split up because I remember that period was a very rough time for us, and I was making a lot of waves. I was being very difficult and very tiresome.

How were you being tiresome?

DB: Just by being very dissatisfied. I was approaching thirty, and thirty for me was the toughest age of all. I started suffering from it around twenty-eight, and I didn't really get over it until about thirty-two. And since then, every birthday has been a breeze. My forties were the best time of my life.

*I feel a little audacious asking this one, but when you met, and you put your
relationship together, was there an understanding that you could have affairs
on the side? It's what every gay couple has to deal with.*

DB: We didn't discuss it very much, but my attitude was that I had a
certain priority to have experience because Chris had had all of his before I
knew him, and he owed me that freedom. However unfair it may have seemed
to Chris, that was my attitude.

Did it seem unfair, Chris? Did you balk at that?

CI: I don't think so. Did I balk?

DB: No, you behaved very well. You didn't encourage me to see people
on the side, but you behaved fairly well about it. But if he thought there was
any danger of my getting involved with anybody, he made it clear that he
didn't like the idea, which is really what I wanted. It was a way of testing his
love.

CI: It's terrible, though; it's so French, that thing of not being jealous.

DB: Well, if one isn't jealous, one is indifferent, I think. Chris occasionally
had his own feelings, and I was tolerant, but just up to a point.

You hadn't, after all, had Berlin.

CI: Those goddamned boys, all stealing.

DB: But whatever it was, it was certainly experience with a capital E, and
that's what I wanted. And that's why I went off to London for a year and
went to school. Chris came over and stayed with me for the summer, but I
had to do it; I had to have some sort of independence.

Chris, why do you lie in the back seat when Don is driving?

CI: Because I believe I'm the only person who's fit to be on the road at
all; therefore, I prefer to just miss it when other people drive.

DB: For years, it was one of the real bones between us, Chris's objection
to my driving. Years ago we used to have to drive our own cars to the same
destination to avoid the fights. I can't even remember now whose idea it was,
but one of us decided that Chris should not only sit in the back seat, but that
he should lie down so he couldn't see what I was doing. And once we discovered that, it was bliss.

*Today I was trying to think who there is of Chris's generation who has never
made any bones about being gay, and there simply is no one. With the loss
of Williams and Truman Capote, that's it. For years, Chris, Capote, and
Williams were sort of the three graces of the older generation.*

DB: What about Gore Vidal? It's funny, he's never really declared himself, has he?

No, he hasn't. He's deliberately fuzzy about it.
   CI: I think that's partly because of his political aspirations. As a matter of fact, his friend Howard Austin is a model mate. Howard is absolutely devoted to Gore. And he to Howard.
   DB: They've been together longer than we have.

Have they really?
   CI: Oh, yes, at least a year or two longer. At one period, you know, when Howard was having some health problems, Gore was really concerned. They really care for each other.

He dedicated his best book to you, or at least what a lot of people consider to be his best book, Myra Breckinridge.
   DB: And Chris dedicated his best book to him, *A Single Man.*
   CI: Yes, that's right.
   DB: Which was a tough mouthful for Truman to swallow.

Do you mean that Capote felt that it should have been dedicated to him?
   DB: I remember he referred to it in a sort of joking way.

Don, your success in the last three or four years must be very satisfying, since you had a period where you were the cute boy who lived with the great man.
   DB: Yes, and I've always said that if I had choices, I would much rather have my success later in life than early. When you're young you can put up with all sorts of rebuffs and failure because you still have your youth and vitality. A little success is very encouraging in middle age.

Do you and Chris sleep in the same bed?
   DB: We always have. And not only in the same bed, but really, you know, intertwined.

Index